W9-BCC-697

BLAKE

IN HIS TIME

Portrait of William Blake. Possibly by John Linnell.
24.4 ×20.3 cm. Essick collection.

BLAKE

IN HIS TIME

Edited by Robert N. Essick
and Donald Pearce

INDIANA UNIVERSITY PRESS   BLOOMINGTON & LONDON

This book was brought to publication with the assistance of a grant from the Andrew W. Mellon Foundation.

Manufactured in the United States of America

Library of Congress Cataloging in Publication Data
Main entry under title:
Blake in his time.
Revised papers presented at a conference
sponsored by the English and Art departments of
the University of California, Santa Barbara,
held March 1976.
Includes bibliographical references and index.
1. Blake, William, 1757-1828—Congresses.
I. Essick, Robert N., 1942–   II. Pearce,
Donald Ross, 1917–   III. California.
University. Santa Barbara. Dept. of English.
IV. California. University, Santa Barbara.
Dept. of Art.
N6797.B57B58   1978   760'.092'4   77-15759
ISBN 0-253-31207-8   1 2 3 4 5 82 81 80 79 78

for
Sir Anthony Blunt
invenit.

CONTENTS

PLATES

(Following page 10)

Frontispiece Portrait of William Blake. Possibly by John Linnell. 24.4 x 20.3 cm. Essick collection.

1. Blake. *All Religions Are One,* pl. 4. Huntington Library.
2. Blake. *America.* Copy I, pl. 10. Huntington Library.
3. Blake. *Jerusalem.* Copy C, pl. 29. Private collection.
4. Blake. *The Book of Urizen.* Copy D, pl. 9. British Museum.
5. Blake. "Fiery Pegasus." Watercolor drawing, 23.3 x 17.5 cm. British Museum.
6. Blake. Wash drawing after Adam Ghisi's engraving of Michelangelo's Manasses lunette, 15 x 10.5 cm. British Museum.
7. Blake. *America.* Copy I, title page. Huntington Library.
8. Blake. Wash drawing of Abiud lunette, 14.5 x 9.8 cm. British Museum.
9. Blake. *America.* Copy I, frontispiece. Huntington Library.
10. Blake. Wash drawing of Matthan lunette, 15.7 x 10.5 cm. British Museum.
11. Blake. "Spring" from *Songs of Innocence,* copy I. Huntington Library.
12. Blake. "Infant Sorrow" from *Songs of Innocence and of Experience,* copy N. Huntington Library.
13. Blake. Wash drawing of Abia lunette, 16.6 x 11.6 cm. British Museum.
14. Blake. *Night Thoughts* watercolor. Night V, p. 20. 41.7 x 32.5 cm. British Museum.
15. Blake. *Europe.* Copy E, frontispiece. Rosenwald collection.
16. Blake. "Newton." 1795 color printed drawing, 40 x 60 cm. Tate Gallery.
17. Blake. Wash drawing of Solomon lunette, 15 x 10.1 cm. British Museum.
18. Blake. Detail of engraved Moore & Company advertisement. British Museum.
19. Blake. *Night Thoughts* watercolor. Night VII, p. 22. 40.4 x 31.6 cm. British Museum.

PREFACE

" . . . & his Resurrection to Unity"

The Four Zoas, E 297

The task begun by Alexander Gilchrist more than a century ago of recovering Blake, forgotten painter and poet, from the sea of incomprehension and neglect that had engulfed him almost immediately after his death in 1827, though still far from complete, is nevertheless one of the more striking achievements of modern literary scholarship. Till fairly recently the process of recovery was slow and singularly arcane, the work mainly of a small band of disciples, chiefly poets and artists—the Rossettis, Swinburne, Arthur Symons, W. B. Yeats—whose firm persuasion of the spiritual power of their master ("there have been men," wrote Yeats, "who loved the future like a mistress, and the future mixed her breath into their breath and shook her hair about them, and hid them from the understanding of their time. William Blake was one of these men . . ."[1]) almost seemed to compensate for the errors of fact and interpretation that vitiated much of what they said about him. To the scholars of the next century, however, they bequeathed two priceless gifts: the example of their devotion, and the conception of Blake's poetry as a sacred book.

If one oversimplifies, three principal stages may be identified in the modern recovery of Blake. There was first the necessity of securing a definitive text for the complete poetical works (finally accomplished in 1925 with the three-volume edition by Geoffrey Keynes, followed in 1965 by David Erdman's edition presenting a text as close to Blake's own as modern typography would allow) together with a general explication of Blake's mythology and symbolism (the obvious landmarks here being S. Foster Damon's *William Blake: His Philosophy and Symbols,* 1924, Northrop Frye's *Fearful Symmetry,* 1947, and David Erdman's *Blake: Prophet Against Empire,* 1954). Explications of Blake's poetry and thought continued to appear from that time to this, and will undoubtedly continue to appear for years to come, though mainly as elaborations of what by 1955 had for all practical purposes been established—the chief outlines and content of Blake's thought or, to employ the overworked but necessary term, Blake's "vision," and its recognition as the creation not of an eccentric but of a highly organized intelligence.

The second stage has differed from its predecessor in stressing the pictorial side of Blake's work, in particular the relations of text and design on the pages of the illuminated books. Earlier generations had been well aware of Blake's achievement as a pictorial artist, of course; several major exhibitions of his paintings were in fact held in the nineteenth century and early in this, to say nothing of the handsomely illustrated catalogues and facsimile editions that have come from the same period. But not until recently has it really been taken seriously, as a working critical principle, that Blake's poetry and painting cannot without violence be separated from each other. That they cannot be so separated is precisely what students of Blake's "composite art" maintain, calling for "a method of reading that takes account of all elements in Blake's form—border, design, and word. This Blake himself united," Professor Hagstrum continues, "and what Blake hath joined together let no man put asunder!"[2]

How recent this second stage really is may be gauged by such a remark as the following of Northrop Frye's from his survey of Blake criticism and research to 1956: "It is curious how little literary criticism of Blake appears to have been based on the designs equally with the text."[3] But the difficulty had been one largely of technology. Serious text-and-design study of Blake had to wait (as Blake himself in another century had also found) till the inherent limitations of typographic publication could either be solved or circumvented and adequate color facsimiles made readily available to scholars—a development that took place only in the mid-fifties of the present century when the Blake Trust, working in conjunction with Arnold Fawcus and the Trianon Press in Paris, began distributing those superb hand-colored facsimiles by means of which an entire generation of students has come to know a rather different Blake from the poet of the unilluminated page. These facsimiles, as well as the new availability of color slides of the works in illuminated printing, have prompted students of Blake's composite art to return to the original form in which Blake presented himself to the world and have led to far-reaching reassessments of the entire canon.

The chief concern of the third and most recent stage in the modern study of Blake, one that unites the various essays in the present volume and serves as their *raison d'être,* is to view him not in splendid isolation from his contemporaries (Fuseli, Flaxman, Reynolds, Romney, and others) but in direct relation to them, as well as to the Gothic tradition and to such Renaissance masters as Raphael and Michelangelo. This approach can be conveniently dated from 1959 with the appearance of *The Art of William Blake* by Sir Anthony Blunt, to whom this collection of essays is gratefully dedicated. Primarily an art-historical approach rather than one centered mainly on Blake's writings, it is more interested in questions of milieu, mutuality, common vocabulary and syntax, shared problems, solutions, technical methods, than in remarking fresh manifestations of his uniqueness. If it serves partly as a corrective to the sometimes foreshortened views of non-art-historical Blake scholars, this is far from being its main intent. That intent, as the studies in this volume should clearly show, is not simply to correct earlier approaches to Blake, or to deemphasize the singularity of his achievement by pointing out its relation to the art theories and practices of his time. It is rather, like all studies that aim at period objectivity, a work of liberation. For the serious artist uniqueness, isolation, self-sufficiency can be very narrow prisons; all the more so in the case of an artist like Blake for whom the *summum bonum* was always a state the very opposite of romantic privacy, one in which, as he described it in *Jerusalem,* men "conversed together . . . [and] walked / To & fro in Eternity as One Man reflecting each in each & clearly seen / And seeing: according to fitness & order."[4]

These essays (except Morton Paley's) were delivered, in somewhat different forms from those in which they appear here, as papers at the literary/art-historical conference "Blake in the Art of His Time" sponsored jointly by the English and Art Departments of the University of California, Santa Barbara, in March, 1976, organized by myself and Corlette Rossiter Walker. The editors would like to express their thanks to both departments for effectively supporting that interdisciplinary event, which made the present volume possible, and to acknowledge various generous acts of assistance by the following individuals, committees and organizations: Vernon I. Cheadle, Chancellor, UCSB; Bruce Rickborn, Dean, Letters and Science, UCSB; The Alumni Association, UCSB; The American Blake Foundation; The Art Affiliates, UCSB; The Art Galleries, UCSB; Committee on Innovative Instruction, UC; National Endowment for the Arts.

D.P.

NOTES

1. W. B. Yeats, "Academy Portraits, XXXII.—William Blake," *The Academy,* 51 (1897), 634; rpt. Yeats, *Essays and Introductions* (New York: Macmillan, 1961), p. 111.

2. *William Blake, Poet and Painter* (Chicago: Univ. of Chicago Press, 1964), p. viii.

3. "William Blake," *The English Romantic Poets and Essayists,* ed. C. W. and L. H. Houtchens (New York: New York Univ. Press, 1957), p. 26. The statement remains in the revised edition of 1966.

4. *Jerusalem,* pl. 98, lines 28, 38–40 (E 255).

ACKNOWLEDGMENTS

We wish to thank the following institutions for permission to reproduce works in their collections: Thos Agnew & Sons, Ltd., London; The American Blake Foundation, Memphis State University, Memphis, Tennessee; The Bancroft Library, University of California, Berkeley, California; The Beinecke Rare Book and Manuscript Library, Yale University, New Haven, Connecticut; The British Museum, London; The Fitzwilliam Museum, Cambridge; The Folger Shakespeare Library, Washington, D.C.; Fogg Art Museum, Harvard University, Cambridge, Massachusetts; The Henry E. Huntington Library and Art Gallery, San Marino, California; Sir Geoffrey Keynes; The Pierpont Morgan Library, New York; The Lessing J. Rosenwald Collection of the Library of Congress and the National Gallery of Art, Jenkintown, Pennsylvania; The Tate Gallery, London; University College, London; Victoria and Albert Museum, London; Walker Art Gallery, Liverpool. Ownership of each work is given in the List of Plates.

A NOTE ON TEXTS AND PLATES

Unless noted otherwise, all quotations from Blake's writings are from *The Poetry and Prose of William Blake,* ed. David V. Erdman (Garden City, New York: Doubleday, fourth printing, 1970), referred to throughout as E followed by page number. The copies of the illuminated books are identified, and their plates numbered in all references to their designs, according to G. E. Bentley, Jr., *Blake Books* (Oxford: Clarendon Press, 1977).

BLAKE

IN HIS TIME

Preludium:
Meditations on a Fiery Pegasus

Robert N. Essick

T H E study of William Blake has undergone a radical shift in the last ten years. From the 1920s to the mid-1960s Blake scholarship rested firmly on the study of his writings, and there was even some doubt as to whether or not the pictures accompanying his poems really mattered at all. That question has been put to rest by a chorus of affirmative answers. Today there are certainly as many people writing about Blake the artist as about Blake the author. It is not surprising that the vast majority of these new students of the pictorial image are converted literature students who come to Blake's art with minds trained by their earlier encounters with the poetry. Art historians, particularly in America, have tended to shy away from Blake. This may in part be attributed to the peculiar qualities of his work, but for many the real hindrance has been the community of Blake scholars, dominated (it would seem to the outsider) by initiates who converse in a special language. However erroneous this reaction may be, it has been all too real. Now this unfortunate barrier appears to be crumbling. Yet, as art historians and literary scholars begin to focus their attention on a figure of mutual interest, conflicts inevitably arise. Like the angels and devils in *The Marriage of Heaven and Hell,* these two species of scholars bring to their work different metaphysics which they sometimes impose on each other. Our goal should rather be to convert such impositions into the intellectual warfare of contraries where "Opposition is True Friendship." In this spirit, I wish to explore a few of these professional habits of mind which affect the study of Blake's art, discover how each can contribute to the other, and suggest some ways of structuring an interdis-

1

ciplinary methodology and aesthetic compatible with Blake's own multimedia endeavors.

The names we use to label the members of these two disciplines indicate a difference in primary roles. The art historian is deeply concerned with attribution and other means of documenting the genesis and physical properties of a work. His studies are essentially diachronic—hence the appellation "art *historian*"—whether he is concerned with the transformations of a motif as it is used by successive generations of artists or with the definition of style periods. But only some literary scholars are "historians." Indeed, the tendency is often toward a synchronic model wherein every work is part of a great, coexisting *corpus*. Unlike the men who produced its parts, this body of works resides, Godlike, somewhere beyond the sphere of the moon. This approach has had some remarkable results—witness the achievements and influence of Frye's *Fearful Symmetry*—but nonetheless it evades "the whole problem of temporality," as Geoffrey Hartman has pointed out.[1] Students of Blake's poetry have long since overcome the limitations of a strictly synchronic approach, yet it still seems to dominate our perception of the designs. For example, the "Urizen in the sky" on plate 4 of *All Religions Are One* (Plate 1) and on plate 10 of *America* (Plate 2) is taken to be the same figure, and in an abstract or general sense he is. But this almost too enjoyable game of pointing out similar motifs overlooks Blake's technical development as a relief etcher between 1788 and 1793 which resulted in important visual differences between these two figures. In the first, the small plate (5.4 x 3.8 cm.) permits little more than basic forms and a few white line hatchings in the clouds. Blake depends heavily upon our readiness to see the human form even in the slightest pictorial hints. The much larger design in *America* (23.5 x 16.7 cm.) allows for many more refinements, including facial details and bodily gestures in which modern Blake scholars have discovered a rich vein of symbolism.[2] It is tempting to read similar meanings back into *All Religions Are One*, but the fact that the significant details are not actually present should provide sufficient restraint. By calling both figures "Urizen" I am also falling into one of the prejudices of the synchronic approach. Giving a name to a design executed long before Blake's first use of that name always requires qualification.

When literary scholars come to a work of art, they are almost inevitably iconographers. The art historian is willing to deal with pictorial forms per se, although often with the tacit understanding that form *is* meaning. He becomes an iconographer only by choice. For the literary scholar, the thrust is always toward interpretation, and the pictorial image is seen primarily as a vehicle for the message waiting to be decoded. There is no philosophical necessity for these differing views, but I find them to be maintained in actual practice. When given a drawing by Blake to look at, the art historian reacts first to its forms and the style in which they are wrought. On this basis he decides if the work is interesting enough to merit further study. The literary scholar reacts very differently, asking in quick succession "what is it?" (that is, what does it represent) and then "what does it mean?" The interest in the work of art, and to a large extent the pleasure to be derived from it, depend not so much on its formal qualities—its visual "beauty"—but on the extent to which it offers insights into Blake's ideas. This is an aesthetic of concepts in the head, not of images before the eye. Thus even a design which to the art historian is downright ugly is grist for the mill, since concepts are not contaminated by unsightly packaging. At this point the art historian is apt to shudder, turn away, and flee to less barren climes.

I am of course exaggerating. Everyone knows that Blake was a maker of beautiful books and pictures, not just books and pictures about beautiful ideas. At the very least the positions of the art historian and the literary scholar are not mutually exclusive. But before any marriages can take place, some rubbish needs to be cleared from the cave's mouth so that Blake is not caught eternally "between the black & white spiders," each spinning his own web.

Both parties can begin by clarifying some of their fundamental assumptions. For the art historians the visual image is primary, and it is to this that they return to support their arguments. Blake's comments on art can be a most useful aid, but what he did as an artist is, quite understandably, the central concern. But even when he is writing about Blake's art, the literary scholar frequently submits his eye to a higher authority: "In the beginning was the Word." What Blake wrote is always paramount and takes precedence over what seems to the literary scholar the more subjective activity of translating one's visual experiences into language. This verbal bias can become most confusing for the art historian when he first confronts the Blake Industry, for literary scholars sometimes seem to be writing about Blake's art when they are actually commenting on what he said about art or—more imaginatively—what he would have said about one of his pictures if he had only had the time and inclination. With the help of the concordance, almost any Blake picture can be converted into an illustration of Blake's poetry. The image becomes more manageable as it becomes less a picture and more a road map leading to words. This approach has illuminated many of Blake's works, and my purpose here is not to object to it on the level of principle. But occasional readjustments in this word-dominated perspective may be therapeutic. The literary spider might even try to expand his web to include the view of his art-historical companion by such unusual means as looking at the Lambeth books not as poems with pictorial accompaniments but as pictures with verbal illustrations.

Most students of Blake's art have at one time or another attended The Minute Particular School of Blake Criticism. Chiseled over its entranceway are the words of Blake that every student must memorize:

> not a line is drawn without intention &
> that most discriminate & particular

> Labour well the Minute Particulars,
> attend to the Little-ones

> Every word and every letter is studied
> and put into its fit place

> What is Most Grand is always most Minute[3]

We have learned a great deal from the school and will no doubt learn more. But it has its perilous paths where even the just man can lose his way. One difficulty is that the more minute the particular the greater its importance simply because it takes more labor to elucidate. The shape of the whole recedes as we focus in on the smallest part. The admirable goal is to see a world in every grain of sand, but, as Blake warns, the same analytical eye can become

> a little narrow orb, closd up & dark,
> Scarcely beholding the Great Light; . . .
> & comprehending great, as very small
> *(Jerusalem,* pl. 49, lines 34–5, 37; E 196)

We can too readily assume that Blake's guiding *dicta* mean that every dot is individually and carefully placed for representational and iconographical purposes. He may have had other things in mind—even those notions of balance and appropriate form often referred to by art historians. We must expand our definitions of "intention" and "meaning" to meet the requirements of pictorial art.

There are some tangible elements of Blake's art—even his art of book production—which escape the web of the Minute Particular-ists. Not that these features are too small; on the contrary, they may be too large. Take, for example, the foul inking present on many pages of the illuminated books and especially noticeable in un-colored copies. In some cases, such as Chapter 2 of *Jerusalem* copy C (Plate 3) and several plates in copy F, the foul inking covers as much area as the marginal designs and is one of the most prominent visual features of the work. How will our two spiders handle this? The first, with a literary education that includes a semester at the Minute Particular school, might want to convert every spot into a nascent fly and every smudge into a cloud to preserve the basic analytical for-mula: image is representation is icon is concept. Failing this, he may decide that Blake's dictum that "not a *line* is drawn without inten-tion" does not pertain to dots of ink, and that the fouling is an accident of Blake's inking procedures and of no representational—and hence of no conceptual—consequence. In short, foul inking is merely a visual effect we must brush from our eyes as quickly as possible in order to see Blake clearly. The second spider, with a strong background in Renaissance and Baroque graphics but some unwillingness to say anything about books made by English poets, may find the foul inking an ugly mess and a confirmation of his worst suspicions about Blake. His more generous but equally art-historical cousin may find the foul inking surprisingly attractive, reminding him of Rembrandt's use of plate-tone to add chiaroscuro to his etchings. Blake's text seems to emerge from a gentle haze which softens the outlines and adds textural and tonal variety. Art historians may be satisfied by statements like this, but I doubt that literary scholars would be. At least they would not find it very in-teresting, for it does not get us any closer to Blake's ideas. Indeed, this line of thinking seems to contradict Blake's own views: we all know what he felt about blots and blurs and Rembrandt.[4]

Even though my three spiders are little better than parodies, each has captured something valuable. Like the first, we must go back to Blake's inking methods, but this time with more concern for technical details and their relationship to the artist's intentions. Blake wrote that, "As Poetry admits not a Letter that is Insignificant so Painting admits not a Grain of Sand or a Blade of Grass Insignificant much less an Insignificant Blur or Mark."[5] Blake did not say that every mark is a bird, nor that good paintings have no blurs. We must reckon with the possibility that he is acknowledging the existence of *significant* blurs and marks even in his own works. As Blake applied ink to the surfaces of his relief etchings, the dauber would deposit dots or smudges in the whites wherever it dropped below the plane of the relief plateaus and touched bitten areas. The darkness and dimension of each deposit are not subject to exacting control, but the printer can decide whether or not to permit any foul inking to occur. In almost all colored and many uncolored impressions of the books in relief etching, Blake was able to keep the whites much freer of ink than in *Jerusalem* copies C and F. Even when there is fouling, it can always be wiped before printing, as Blake did to a few white areas of the design on plate 47 of *Jerusalem* copy C. Thus, Blake's foul inking is an accident, but one which he intended to happen. This is not quite the same thing as drawing a line with discriminate and particular intention, but it is nonetheless part of Blake's artistic practice.

Clearly, the next question is "why did Blake allow the messy inking of whites?" The art historian found an answer based on a purely visual aesthetic by placing Blake's work within the tradition of European graphics, with special reference to Rembrandt. A more enlightening context, and one which brings us closer to Blake's own aesthetic concepts, is provided by the plate and type printing practices of Blake's own time. Nowhere else do we find in the illustrated books of the late eighteenth and early nineteenth centuries any intentional foul inking. The economic and artistic requirements for exactly repeatable images, with maximum contrast between text and background in printed pages, would not permit variable and individuating effects like foul inking. Mechanization, efficiency, and uniformity all go hand in hand with the conventional tastes and methods of production which Blake consciously violates in the illuminated books. Blake's foul inking is part of his revolt against empire, against the hegemony of machine over man. The interlinear blots and blurs in *Jerusalem* do not picture anything, nor are they symbols for anything, but they do function visually in a way that embodies some of Blake's most interesting concepts. They do this because they reside within a context of forms and concepts where simply being blots and blurs is itself significant.

The art historian has an important role to play in expanding our vision of Minute Particulars. He can tell us more about the technical details of Blake's artistic methods, define Blake's stylistic development in a way that can help date his works more accurately, and pinpoint the significant differences (not just similarities) between Blake and other artists. More generally, the formal interests of the art historian can prevent us from doing exactly what Blake refuses to do in the illuminated books: reducing all images to verbal signifiers and thereby placing all perception under the tyranny of the printed word. This can become little better than a sophisticated form of iconoclasm: we shatter the image to get at the concept locked within. Yet the other extreme—a pure formalism—is equally unhelpful. When viewed from this perspective, Blake comes off rather badly: his nudes are misshapen, his techniques are clumsy, and he has no sense of the relationship between forms and their spatial containers. At best, a second-rate Fuseli. Blake will in the long run always disappoint the pure formalist, however attuned he may be to late eighteenth-century art, not because Blake is uninterested in *form,* but because he is never *pure.* The forms and the concepts are inextricably intertwined, whether we approach the pictorial as an expression of Blake's ideas, or the ideas as attempts to interpret Blake's visions. Even at his most representational, Blake is a maker of what E. H. Gombrich[6] and others have called "conceptual images"—pictures of what the artist thinks as much as what he sees. Illusionistic art requires the viewer to cooperate by seeing what is really paint and canvas as a representation of a physical reality outside itself. Blake's art is "allusionistic"—it requires us to see as part of its form the concepts motivating its execution. Blake is always willing—indeed, eager—to violate even the most deeply rooted conventions of form, color, and space to call into question those very conventions and lead us to his own disquieting propositions about rational space and time, the ratio of the fallen senses, and Newton's world. Some of Blake's greatest works revel in their impurity, and we need a comparably impure aesthetic to deal with them. And it is Blake's writings which give us the clearest context for understanding the conceptual dimensions of his pictorial forms. On this point the Minute Particularists were right all along.

I fear I have been building far too many dichotomies—literary scholars vs. art historians, form vs. concept—when what I am after is continuity. Blake's techniques, the visual effects they produce, and

the ideas in the poetry are all synecdoches for one another. Let me
back up this assertion—and also exemplify the methodology I have
been working up to—by briefly analyzing one feature of one design:
the color printed areas surrounding the figure on plate 9 of *The Book
of Urizen,* copy D (Plate 4). The typical reticulated patterns of color
printing are visible in this cavelike environment which seems to
force the old man into his awkward crouch. Blake produced his
color prints by thickly applying his pigments, suspended in an animal glue or low-solubility gum medium, over both the relief and
bitten areas of a relief etching. The plate was then printed in a
rolling press, squeezing the colors between metal and paper so that
they spread out in veined splotches that acquired even rougher surfaces as the impression was lifted from the plate. Subsequent hand
work with a diluted form of the same pigment or pen and ink added
outlines and details. Thus, plate 9 of *Urizen* is not only a picture of
contending forces, both human and material, but a product of those
forces. As representational images, the patterns of color printing
suggest a number of things. Here, the first thought may be of the
lichenous growths in a cave, or even the crystalline dendrites of
minerals in rocks. When greatly enlarged, the arborescent patterns
become the bodily network of arteries and veins, much like those on
"the globe of life blood trembling... / Branching out into roots"
described and pictured elsewhere in *Urizen.*[7] When reduced to mi-
croscopic dimensions, these arterial forms become the dendrons of
the brain and nervous system whose creation is also described in the
poem. Thus, the patterns of color printing—like the images of
fibres, roots, branches, veins, and nerves descriptive of fallen nature
throughout Blake's poetry—refer simultaneously to geological,
biological, and psychological forms. This same multiplicity of meaning occurs in the metaphoric structures of *The Book of Urizen,* as for
example in the following passage closely related in its imagery to
plate 9:

> And a roof, vast petrific around,
> On all sides He fram'd: like a womb;
> Where thousands of rivers in veins
> Of blood pour down the mountains...
>
> (pl. 5, lines 28–31; E 72)

The "roof" is at once both skull and cave, the blood runs in both
"rivers" and "veins," the "mountains" are both earth and flesh, and

the whole process of petrification is a physical correlative to mental imprisonment.[8] This parallel between threefold pictorial representation and threefold verbal reference occurs again and again in the coeval evolution of the material universe, human body, and self-enclosed mental states unfolded (and infolded) in *The Book of Urizen*. It might have been for this very reason that Blake abandoned color printing after 1796. The process was too intimately associated with the dark world of Urizen to have been employed in the illumination of Blake's later poetry of redemption in *Milton* and *Jerusalem*.

We can go yet a step further with color printing in *Urizen*, not along the path of representation, but by returning to the intrinsic properties of color printing. Its opacity and density are themselves characteristic of the "solid without fluctuation" (pl. 4, line 11) which Urizen attempts to create. Where the printed colors ooze together, they cover over any distinct boundaries between forms on the copperplate. The perceptual limitations of Urizenic man are objectified in these "Broken Colours & Broken Lines & Broken Masses" and "unorganized Blots & Blurs" which Blake later damned in the annotations to Reynolds and the *Public Address* as the fallen art of his own time.[9] In these ways, the design encompasses one of Blake's greatest concerns—the phenomenology of perception—including the investigation I have been making of this plate. To the iconography of images we can add an iconography of techniques. Blake's designs are the products of specific (and often highly individual) artistic processes and their concomitant perceptual states, and as we look at them we inevitably respond according to our own dominant critical techniques and the perceptual modes implicit in them. In the poem, Urizen explores his dens and becomes what he beholds. In this design, we are the explorers who must avoid Urizen's fate.

A brief look at a less fearful design (Plate 5), where becoming what we behold is much to be desired, indicates some ways of escaping Urizen's tunnel vision. It is Blake's illustration to Sir Richard Vernon's description of Prince Hal, who "vaulted with such ease into his seat, / As if an angel dropp'd down from the clouds, / To turn and wind a fiery Pegasus, / And witch the world with noble horsemanship."[10] These lines provided Blake with the opportunity to show how the Bard witches the world with noble art. The emblem of inspiration springs from the rock of the material world, but he must be organized by a more restrained vision. The reins will become the bound or outward circumference of creative energy without de-

stroying it. To achieve this delicate balance is a difficult task for the
artist, and equally difficult for the interpreter as he delves into the
union of form and concept. But he must try in order to turn and
wind the fiery Pegasus of Blake's art.

NOTES

1.   *Beyond Formalism* (New Haven: Yale Univ. Press, 1970), p. 33.
2.   See for example Janet Warner, "Blake's Use of Gesture" in *Blake's
Visionary Forms Dramatic,* ed. David V. Erdman and John E. Grant (Princeton: Princeton Univ. Press, 1970), esp. pp. 180–81; *The Illuminated Blake,*
annotated by Erdman (Garden City, New York: Doubleday, 1974), p. 146.
3.   "A Vision of the Last Judgment"; *Jerusalem,* pl. 55, line 51; pl. 3;
Notebook epigram, p. 38. E 550, 203, 144, 505.
4.   For example, "all the Copies or Pretended Copiers of Nature from
Rembrat to Reynolds Prove that Nature becomes [*tame*] to its Victim nothing but Blots & Blurs" (*Public Address,* E 563).
5.   "A Vision of the Last Judgment," E 550.
6.   *Meditations on a Hobby Horse* (London: Phaidon, 1963), p. 8.
7.   Text on pl. 15, line 13, pl. 18, line 2 (E 77); design on pl. 17.
8.   The cave-skull conjunction implicit here is more directly set forth
in the introduction to *Europe,* pl. iii ("Five windows light the cavern'd
Man; . . ."). The psychological wellsprings of physical bondage are manifest
throughout Blake's poetry, as for example in the famous image of "mind-
forg'd manacles" in "London" (*Songs of Experience,* E 27).
9.   E 641, 565.
10. Shakespeare's *Henry IV, Part I,* Act 4, scene 1, lines 107–10.

PLATES

1. Blake. *All Religions Are One*, pl. 4.
Huntington Library.

2. Blake. *America*. Copy I,
pl. 10. Huntington Library.

Then the Divine Vision like a silent Sun appeard above
Albions dark rocks: setting behind the Gardens of Kensington
On Tyburns River, in clouds of blood: where was mild Zion Hills
Most ancient promontary, and in the Sun, a Human Form appeard
And thus the Voice Divine went forth upon the rocks of Albion

I elected Albion for my glory; I gave to him the Nations,
Of the whole Earth. He was the Angel of my Presence: and all
The Sons of God were Albions Sons: and Jerusalem was my joy.
The Reactor hath hid himself thro envy. I behold him.
But you cannot behold him till he be reveald in his System
Albions Reactor must have a Place prepard: Albion must Sleep
The Sleep of Death, till the Man of Sin & Repentance be reveald.
Hidden in Albions Forests he lurks: he admits of no Reply
From Albion: but hath founded his Reaction into a Law
Of Action, for Obedience to destroy the Contraries of Man
He hath compelld Albion to become a Punisher & hath possessd
Himself of Albions Forests & Wilds: and Jerusalem is taken.
The City of the Woods in the Forest of Ephratah is taken
London is a stone of her ruins; Oxford is the dust of her walls!
Sussex & Kent are her scatterd garments: Ireland her holy place:
And the murderd bodies of her little ones are Scotland and Wales
The Cities of the Nations are the smoke of her consummation
The Nations are her dust! ground by the chariot wheels
Of her lordly conquerors: her palaces levelld with the dust
I come that I may find a way for my banished ones to return
Fear not O little Flock I come! Albion shall rise again.

So saying, the mild Sun inclosd the Human Family
Forthwith from Albions darkning locks came two Immortal forms
Saying We alone are escaped, O merciful Lord and Saviour;
We flee from the interiors of Albions hills and mountains;
From his Valleys Eastward, from Amalek Canaan & Moab
Beneath his vast ranges of hills surrounding Jerusalem.
Albion walkd on the steps of fire before his Halls
And Vala walkd with him in dreams of soft deluding slumber,
He looked up & saw the Prince of Light with splendor faded
Then Albion ascended mourning into the porches of his Palace
Above him rose a Shadow from his wearied intellect:
Of living gold, pure, perfect, holy: in white linen pure he hoverd
A sweet entrancing self-delusion a watry vision of Albion
Soft exulting in existence: all the Man absorbing

Albion fell upon his face prostrate before the watry Shadow
Saying O Lord, whence is this change: thou knowest I am nothing!
And Vala trembled & coverd her face: & her locks were spread on the
                                                                    pavement

We heard astonishd at the Vision & our hearts trembled within us:
We heard the voice of slumberous Albion, and thus he spoke,
Idolatrous to his own Shadow words of eternity uttering:
O I am nothing when I enter into judgment with thee!
If thou withdraw thy breath, I die & vanish into Hades
If thou dost lay thine hand upon me behold I am silent:
If thou withhold thine hand; I perish like a fallen leaf:
O I am nothing: and to nothing must return again:
If thou withdraw thy breath. Behold I am oblivion.

He ceasd: the shadowy voice was silent; but the cloud hoverd over their heads
In golden wreathes the sorrow of Man; & the balmy drops fell down
And lo! that son of Man that Shadowy Spirit of mild Albion:
Luvah descended from the cloud in terror Albion rose:
Indignant rose the awful Man, & turnd his back on Vala.

We heard the voice of Albion starting from his sleep:
Whence is this voice crying Enion! that soundeth in my ears?
O cruel pity! O dark deceit! can love seek for dominion?

And Luvah strove to gain dominion over Albion
They strove together above the Body where Vala was inclosd
And the dark Body of Albion left prostrate upon the crystal pavement,
Coverd with boils from head to foot: the terrible smitings of Luvah.

Then frownd the fallen Man, and put forth Luvah from his presence
Saying, Go and Die the Death of Man, for Vala the sweet wanderer.
I will turn the volutions of your ears outward, and bend your nostrils
Downward: and your fluxile eyes englobd roll round in fear:
Your withering lips and tongue shrink up into a narrow circle
Till into narrow forms you creep: go take your fiery way:
And learn what tis to absorb the Man you Spirits of Pity & Love.

They heard the voice and fled swift as the winters setting sun.
And now the human blood foamd high, the Spirits Luvah & Vala,
Went down the Human Heart where Paradise & its joys abounded,
In jealous fears & fury & rage, & flames roll round their fervid feet:
And the vast form of Nature like a serpent playd before them
And as they fled in folding fires & thunders of the deep:
Vala shrunk in like the dark sea that leaves its slimy banks,
And from her bosom Luvah fell far as the east and west,
And the vast form of Nature like a serpent rolld between,
Whether of Jerusalems or Valas ruins congenerated we know not:
All is confusion: all is tumult: & we alone are escaped.
So spoke the fugitives: they joind the Divine Family, trembling

3. Blake. *Jerusalem.* Copy C, pl. 29. Private collection.

4. Blake. *The Book of Urizen*. Copy D, pl. 9. British Museum.

5. Blake. "Fiery Pegasus." Watercolor drawing, 23.3 ×
17.5 cm. British Museum.

6. Blake. Wash drawing after Adam Ghisi's engraving of Michelangelo's Manasses lunette, 15 × 10.5 cm. British Museum.

7. Blake. *America.* Copy I, title page. Huntington Library.

8. Blake. Wash drawing of Abiud lunette, 14.5 × 9.8 cm. British Museum.

9. Blake. *America.* Copy I, frontispiece. Huntington Library.

10. Blake. Wash drawing of Matthan lunette, 15.7 × 10.5 cm. British Museum.

11. Blake. "Spring" from *Songs of Innocence,* copy I. Huntington Library.

12. Blake. "Infant Sorrow" from *Songs of Innocence and of Experience,* copy N. Huntington Library.

13. Blake. Wash drawing of Abia lunette, 16.6 × 11.6 cm. British Museum.

(20)

(Ineftimable Gain!) and gives Heaven Leave
To make him but more Wretched, not more Wife. 250

   If Wifdom is our Leffon, (and what elfe
Ennobles Man? what elfe have Angels learnt?)
Grief! more Proficients in thy School are made,
Than *Genius*, or proud *Learning*, e'er could boaft.
Voracious *Learning*, often overfed,
Digefts not into Senfe her motley Meal.
This *Book-Cafe*, with dark Booty almoft burft,
This *Forager* on others Wifdom, leaves
Her Native-Farm, her *Reafon* quite untill'd.
With mixt Manure fhe furfeits the rank Soil, 260
Dung'd, but not dreft; and rich to Beggary.
A Pomp untameable of Weed prevails.
Her *Servant*'s Wealth encumber'd *Wifdom* mourns.
   And what fays *Genius? " Let the Dull be Wife."*
Genius too hard for Right, can prove it Wrong.
And loves to boaft, where blufh Men lefs infpir'd.
It pleads Exemption from the Laws of *Senfe*;
Confiders *Reafon* as a Leveller,

                           And

14. Blake. *Night Thoughts* watercolor. Night V, p. 20. 41.7
× 32.5 cm. British Museum.

15. Blake. *Europe.* Copy E, frontispiece. Rosenwald
collection.

16. Blake. "Newton." 1795 color printed drawing, 40 × 60 cm.   Tate Gallery.

17. Blake. Wash drawing of
Solomon lunette, 15 × 10.1 cm.
British Museum.

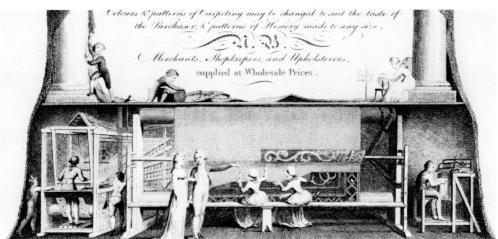

18. Blake. Detail of engraved Moore & Company
advertisement. British Museum.

[22]

Pride made the Virtues of the Pagan World.
Praife is the Salt that feafons *Right* to Man,
And whets his Appetite for moral Good.
Thirft of Applaufe is Virtue's *Second* Guard;
Reafon, her Firft; but Reafon wants an Aid;
Our private Reafon is a Flatterer;
Thirft of Applaufe calls public Judgment in,
To poife our own, to keep an even Scale,
And give endanger'd Virtue fairer Play.
Here a *Fifth* Proof arifes, ftronger ftill:
Why this fo nice Conftruction of our Hearts?
Thefe delicate Moralities of *Senfe?*
This *conftitutional* Referve of Aid
To fuccour Virtue, when our Reafon fails;
If Virtue, kept alive by Care, and Toil,
And, oft, the Mark of Injuries on Earth,
When labour'd to Maturity, (its Bill
Of Difciplines, and Pains, unpaid) muft die?
Why freighted-rich, to dafh againft a Rock?
Was Man to perifh when moft fit to live,
O how mif-fpent were all thefe Stratagems,
By Skill Divine inwoven in our Frame?

4   Where.

19. Blake. *Night Thoughts* watercolor. Night VII, p. 22.
40.4 × 31.6 cm. British Museum.

Had thought been all, sweet speech had been denied;
Speech, thought's canal! speech, thought's criterion too!
Thought in the mine may come forth gold or dross;
When coin'd in words, we know its real worth:
If sterling, store it for thy future use;
'Twill buy thee benefit, perhaps renown:
Thought too, deliver'd, is the more possess'd;
* Teaching, we learn; and giving, we retain
The births of intellect; when dumb, forgot.
Speech ventilates our intellectual fire;
Speech burnishes our mental magazine;
Brightens for ornament, and whets for use.
What numbers, sheath'd in erudition, lie
Plunged to the hilts in venerable tomes,
And rusted; who might have borne an edge,
And play'd a sprightly beam, if born to speech!
If born blest heirs to half their mother's tongue!
'Tis thought's exchange, which, like th' alternate push
Of waves conflicting, breaks the learned scum,
And defecates the student's standing pool.
    In contemplation is his proud resource?
'Tis poor as proud: by converse unsustain'd
Rude thought runs wild in contemplation's field:
Converse, the menage, breaks it to the bit
Of due restraint; and emulation's spur
Gives graceful energy, by rivals awed:
'Tis converse qualifies for solitude,
As exercise for salutary rest;
By that untutor'd, contemplation raves;
And nature's fool, by wisdom's is outdone.

20. Blake. *Night Thoughts* engraving. Night II, p. 35.
Essick collection.

21. Adam Ghisi. Engraving of Michelangelo's
Aminadab lunette. British Museum.

22. Blake. Wash drawing of Aminadab lunette,
14.2 × 9.2 cm. British Museum.

23. Blake. Pencil sketch of a seated shepherd. Sheet 31.1 × 18.4 cm. Formerly Robertson collection.

[40]

" And Fruits promifcuous, ever-teeming *Earth*,

" That Man may languifh in luxurious Scenes,

" And in an *Eden* mourn his with'ring Joys?

" Claim Earth and Skies Man's Admiration, due

" For *fuch* Delights! Bleft Animals! too Wife

" To *wonder*; and too Happy to *complain!*

" OUR *Doom decreed* demands a mournful Scene;

" Why not a Dungeon dark, for the *Condemn'd*?

" Why not the Dragon's fubterranean Den,

" For Man to howl in? Why not his Abode,

" Of the fame difmal Colour with his Fate?

" A *Thebes*, a *Babylon*, at vaft Expence

" Of Time, Toil, Treafure, Art, for Owls and Adders,

" As congruous, as, for Man, this lofty Dome,

" Which prompts proud Thought, and kindles high Defire,

" If from her humble Chamber in the Duft,

" While proud Thought fwells, and high Defire inflames,

" The poor *Worm* calls us for her Inmates there;

" And, round us, *Death's* inexorable Hand

" Draws the dark Curtain clofe; undrawn no more.

" *Undrawn*

24. Blake. *Night Thoughts* watercolor. Night VII, p. 40.
40.4 × 31.8 cm. British Museum.

25. Blake. Wash drawing of Michelangelo's Daniel, 14.4 × 10.6 cm. British Museum.

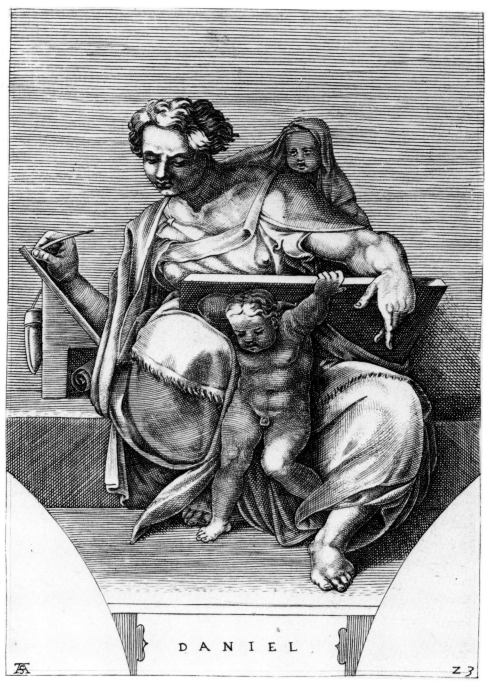

DANIEL

26. Ghisi. Engraving of Michelangelo's Daniel. British
Museum.

27. Blake. *The Marriage of Heaven and Hell.* Copy D, pl.
10, design only. Rosenwald collection.

(34)

To contradict them fee all Nature rife!

What Object, what Event, the moon beneath,

But argues, or endears, an After-fcene?

To *Reafon* proves, or weds it to *Defire?*

All things proclaim it *needfull*; fome advance

One precious ftep beyond, and prove it *fure*.

A thoufand Arguments fwarm round my pen,

From *Heaven*, and *Earth*, and *Man*. Indulge a few,

By Nature, as her common Habit, worn;

So prefling Providence a Truth to teach,

Which Truth untaught, all other Truths were vain.

Thou! whofe all-providential Eye furveys,

Whofe Hand directs, whofe Spirit fills, and warms

Creation, and holds Empire far beyond!

Eternity's Inhabitant auguft!

Of two Eternities amazing Lord!

One paft, e'er Man's, or Angels, had begun;

Aid! while I refcue from the Foe's affault,

Thy glorious Immortality in *Man*.

A

28. Blake. *Night Thoughts* watercolor. Night VI, p. 34.
41.7 × 32.1 cm. British Museum.

29. Marten de Vos. "The Offerings of Cain and Abel," engraved by John Sadeler. Huntington Library.

30. Titian. "The Murder of Abel," engraved by Joseph M. Mitelli. Huntington Library.

31. Carlo Lolli. "Adam Discovering the Dead Body of
Abel," engraved by Le Villain. Huntington Library.

32. C. W. Dietrich. "Cain and Abel," engraved by Jean
Daullé. Huntington Library.

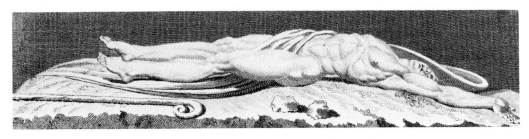

33. J. H. Fuseli. The Dead Abel, engraved by Charles
Grignion for J. C. Lavater, *Essays on Physiognomy,* vol. II,
1792. Essick collection.

34. Fuseli. Cain, engraved by Grignion for Lavater's
Physiognomy, vol. II, 1792. Essick collection.

35. Pierre Paul Prudhon. "Divine Justice and Vengeance
Pursuing Crime," engraved by F. A. Gellée. Huntington
Library.

36. A. E. Chalon. "Adam and Eve Lamenting Over the
Body of Abel." Brown wash, 28.7 × 36.4 cm. Huntington
Library.

37. S. John Stump. "Adam and Eve Lamenting Over the Body of Abel." Brown wash, 30.2 × 38.6 cm. Huntington Library.

38. Joshua Cristall. "Adam and Eve Lamenting Over the Body of Abel." Brown wash, 27.3 × 35 cm. Huntington Library.

39. John Samuel Hayward. "Adam and Eve Lamenting Over the Body of Abel." Brown wash, 36.4 × 30.9 cm. Huntington Library.

40. Henry Pierce Bone. "Adam and Eve Lamenting Over the Body of Abel." Brown wash, 29.2 × 36.1 cm. Huntington Library.

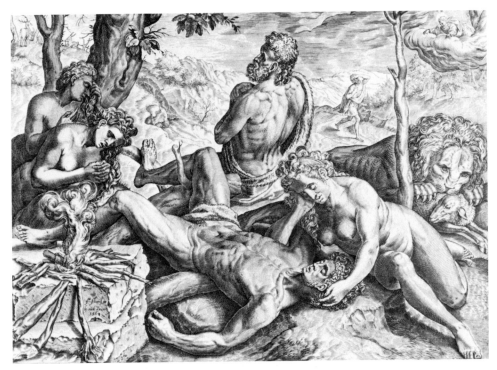

41. Franz Floris. "The Lamentation Over Abel,"
engraving. Huntington Library.

42. Blake. "The Body of Abel Found by Adam and Eve,
with Cain Fleeing." Pen and tempera, 32.5 × 43.3 cm.
Tate Gallery.

43. Francesco Salviati. "The Flight of Cain," engraving. Huntington Library.

44. Benedetto Luti. "The Flight of Cain," engraved by Joseph Wagner. Huntington Library.

45. Blake. "Pity," 1795 color printed drawing, 42.5 ×
53.9 cm. Tate Gallery.

46. Blake. *Milton.* Copy A, pl. 12, design only. British Museum.

47. Blake. *Milton.* Copy A, pl. 14, design only. British Museum.

THE GHOST of ABEL

A Revelation In the Visions of Jehovah
Seen by William Blake

To LORD BYRON in the Wilderness What doest thou here Elijah?
Can a Poet doubt the Visions of Jehovah? Nature has no Outline
but Imagination has. Nature has no Tune: but Imagination has!
Nature has no Supernatural & dissolves: Imagination is Eternity

Scene. A rocky Country. Eve fainted over the dead body
of Abel which lays near a Grave. Adam kneels by her Jehovah
stands above.

Jehovah — Adam!

Adam — — I will not hear thee more thou Spiritual Voice
Is this Death?

Jehovah — Adam!

Adam — It is in vain: I will not hear thee
Henceforth! Is this thy Promise that the Womans Seed
Should bruise the Serpents head: Is this the Serpent? Ah!
Seven times O Eve thou hast fainted over the Dead Ah! Ah!

Eve revives

Eve Is this the Promise of Jehovah! O it is all a vain delusion
This Death & this Life & this Jehovah

Jehovah — Woman! lift thine eyes
A Voice is heard coming on

Voice O Earth cover not thou my Blood! cover not thou my Blood
Enter the Ghost of Abel

Eve Thou Visionary Phantasm thou art not the real Abel.

Abel Among the Elohim a Human Victim I wander I am their House
Prince of the Air & our dimensions compass Zenith & Nadir
Vain is thy Covenant O Jehovah I am the Accuser & Avenger
Of Blood O Earth Cover not thou the Blood of Abel

Jehovah What Vengeance dost thou require

Abel — Life for Life! Life for Life!

Jehovah He who shall take Cains life must also Die O Abel
And who is he Adam wilt thou or Eve thou do this

Adam It is all a Vain delusion of the all creative Imagination
Eve come away & let us not believe these vain delusions
Abel is dead & Cain slew him. We shall also Die a Death
And then! what then! be as poor Abel a Thought: or as
this! O what shall I call thee Form Divine! Father of Mercies
That appearest to my Spiritual Vision: Eve seest thou also.

Eve — I see him plainly with my Minds Eye. I see also Abel living:
Tho terribly afflicted as We also are. yet Jehovah sees him

48. Blake. *The Ghost of Abel.* Copy C, pl. 1. Huntington
Library.

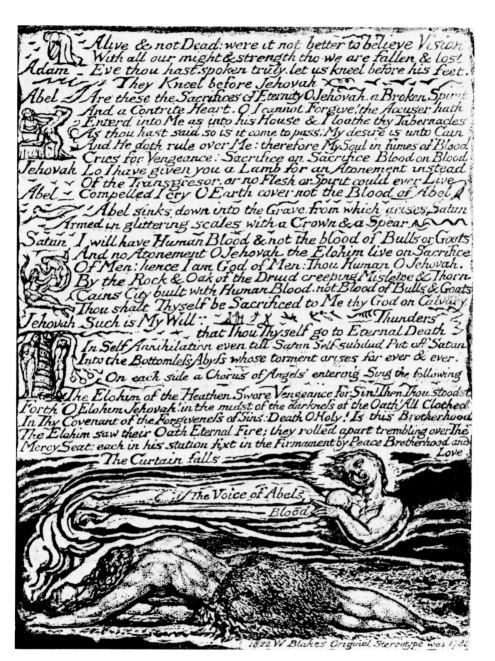

Alive & not Dead: were it not better to believe Vision
With all our might & strength tho we are fallen & lost.
Adam — Eve thou hast spoken truly. let us kneel before his feet.

They Kneel before Jehovah

Abel — Are these the Sacrifices of Eternity O Jehovah. a Broken Spirit
And a Contrite Heart. O I cannot Forgive! the Accuser hath
Enterd into Me as into his House & I loathe thy Tabernacles
As thou hast said. so is it come to pass. My desire is unto Cain
And He doth rule over Me: therefore My Soul in fumes of Blood
Cries for Vengeance: Sacrifice on Sacrifice Blood on Blood

Jehovah Lo I have given you a Lamb for an Atonement instead
Of the Transgresor. or no Flesh or Spirit could ever Live

Abel — Compelled I cry O Earth cover not the Blood of Abel

Abel sinks down into the Grave. from which arises Satan
Armed in glittering scales with a Crown & a Spear

Satan I will have Human Blood & not the blood of Bulls or Goats
And no Atonement O Jehovah the Elohim live on Sacrifice
Of Men: hence I am God of Men: Thou Human O Jehovah.
By the Rock & Oak of the Druid creeping Mistletoe & Thorn
Cains City built with Human Blood. not Blood of Bulls & Goats
Thou shalt Thyself be Sacrificed to Me thy God on Calvary

Jehovah Such is My Will: Thunders
that Thou Thyself go to Eternal Death
In Self Annihilation even till Satan Self-subdud Put off Satan
Into the Bottomless Abyss whose torment arises for ever & ever.

On each side a Chorus of Angels entering Sing the following

The Elohim of the Heathen Swore Vengeance for Sin Then Thou stood'st
Forth O Elohim Jehovah! in the midst of the darkness of the Oath All Clothed
In Thy Covenant of the Forgiveness of Sins: Death O Holy! Is this Brotherhood
The Elohim saw their Oath Eternal Fire; they rolled apart trembling over The
Mercy Seat: each in his station fixt in the Firmament by Peace Brotherhood and
Love

The Curtain falls

The Voice of Abels
Blood

1822 W Blakes Original Stereotype was 1788

49. Blake. *The Ghost of Abel.* Copy C, pl. 2. Huntington
Library.

50. Blake. Genesis Manuscript, page 8, design only.
Pencil sketch, 14.5 × 27.3 cm. Huntington Library.

51. Blake. Genesis Manuscript, page 9, design only.
Pencil sketch, 20.5 × 27.3 cm. Huntington Library.

52. Marten de Vos. "The Judgment of Cain," engraved by Raphael Sadeler. Huntington Library.

53. Marten de Vos. "The Prodigal Son," engraving. Huntington Library.

And the fierce flames burnt round the heavens, & round the abodes of men

54. Blake. *America.* Copy I, pl. 18, tailpiece only. Huntington Library.

55. *Select Fables of Esop,* 1761. Full-page medallion cuts. American Blake Foundation.

56. Thomas Stothard. Illustration to Hayley, *Triumphs of Temper,* 1799, engraved by Heath. American Blake Foundation.

57. Richard Bentley. Engraved
illustration to Gray's "Ode on the
Death of a Favorite Cat," 1753.
Essick collection.

58. Maria Flaxman. Illustration to
Hayley, *Triumphs of Temper*, 1803,
engraved by Blake. Essick
collection.

59. Bentley. Engraved tailpiece to Gray's "Ode on the Death of a Favorite Cat," 1753. Essick collection.

60. Blake. Engraved illustration to Hayley, "The Dog," in *Designs to a Series of Ballads*, 1802. Huntington Library.

61. Blake. *Visions of the Daughters of Albion.* Copy E, frontispiece. Huntington Library.

62. Blake. *The Book of Thel.* Copy L, title page. Huntington Library.

63. Blake. *The Song of Los.* Copy E, frontispiece.
Huntington Library.

64. Blake. *The Song of Los.* Copy E, p. 5. Huntington
Library.

65. Blake. *The Song of Los.* Copy E, pl. 8. Huntington
Library.

66. Blake. "The Man Who Taught
Blake Painting in his Dreams."
Pencil sketch, 29.6 × 23.5 cm.
Replica perhaps by John Linnell.
Tate Gallery.

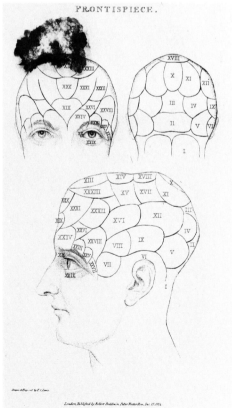

67. F. C. Lewis. Engraved frontispiece to J. G. Spurzheim, *The
Physiognomical System of Drs. Gall
and Spurzheim,* 1815. Bancroft
Library.

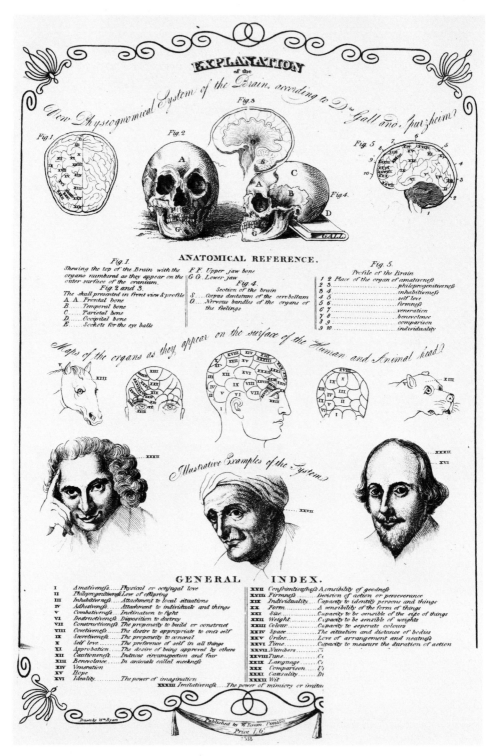

68. *Explanation of the New Physiognomical System of the Brain, according to Drs. Gall and Spurzheim,* drawn and published by W. Byam, 1818. Price 1/6. Bancroft Library.

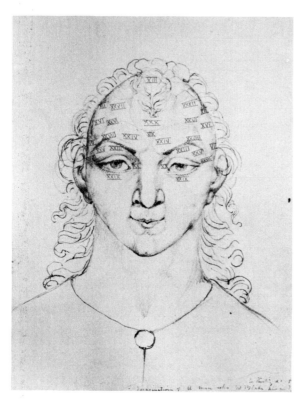

69. Blake. "The Man Who Taught Blake Painting in his Dreams," with phrenological markings by the author.

70. Lewis. Pl. XIV in Spurzheim, *The Physiognomical System*.

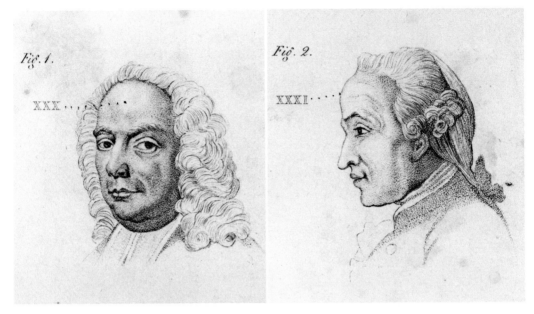

71. Lewis, Pl. XVII in Spurzheim, *The Physiognomical System.*

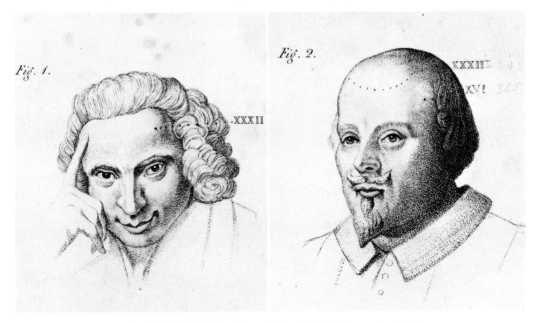

72. Lewis. Pl. XVIII in Spurzheim, *The Physiognomical System.*

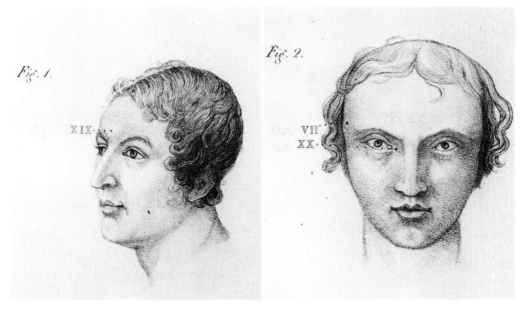

73. Lewis. Pl. XIII in Spurzheim, *The Physiognomical System.*

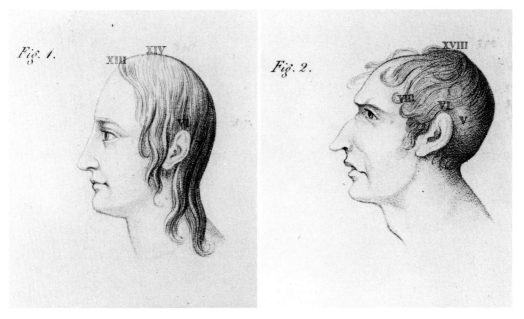

74. Lewis. Pl. XI in Spurzheim, *The Physiognomical System.*

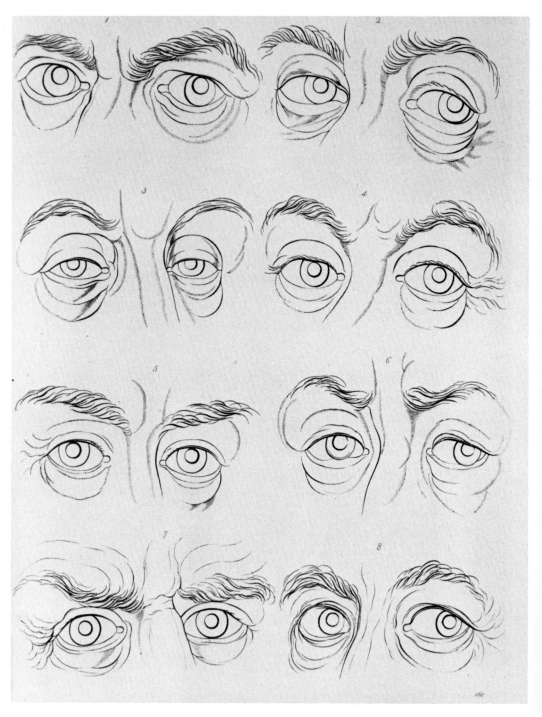

75. Engraved illustration in J. C. Lavater, *Essays on Physiognomy*. Vol. III, Part 2 (1798), facing p. 346. Essick collection.

76. Portrait of William Blake, attributed to John Linnell. Monochrome wash drawing, 24.4 × 20.3 cm. Essick collection.

77. Blake. "Socrates." Pencil sketch, 31.1 × 20.2 cm. Huntington Library.

78. Blake. "Socrates," with phrenological markings by the author.

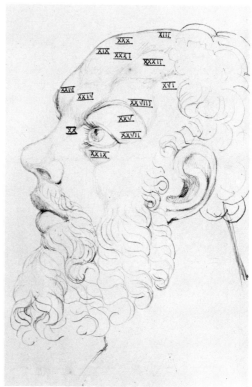

79. Blake. "The Man Who Built the Pyramids." Pencil sketch, 29.8 × 19.7 cm. Replica perhaps by John Linnell. Tate Gallery.

80. Lewis. Pl. XV in Spurzheim, *The Physiognomical System*.

81. Blake. "The Man Who Built the Pyramids," with physiognomical measurements by the author.

82. Blake. *The Blake-Varley Sketchbook* of 1819. Pencil sketches on sheet 15.3 × 20.1 cm. Private collection.

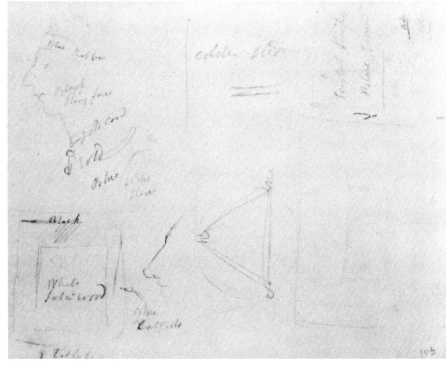

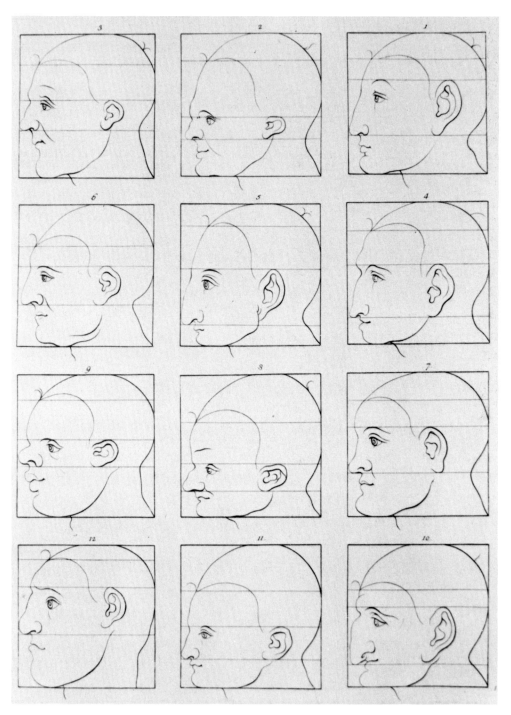

83. Engraved illustration in Lavater, *Essays on Physiognomy*. Vol. III, Part 2, facing p. 271. Essick collection.

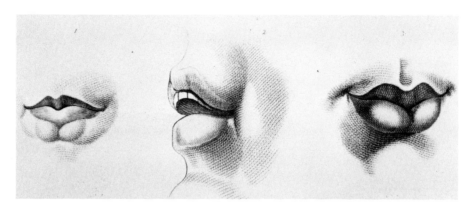

84. Engraved illustration in Lavater, *Essays on Physiognomy.* Vol. III, Part 2, p. 402. Essick collection.

85. Blake. "Job's Evil Dream." Watercolor, 23.7 × 28.8 cm., circa 1805. Pierpont Morgan Library.

86. Blake. "Job and His Daughters." Watercolor, 22 ×
27.6 cm., circa 1822-27. Pierpont Morgan Library.

87. Blake. "Job and His Daughters." Engraving, circa
1825. Tate Gallery.

88. Blake. "Job and His Daughters." Tempera, 41.3 × 37.5 cm., circa 1799–1800. Rosenwald collection.

89. Blake. "Job and His Daughters." Watercolor, 19.4 × 26.4 cm., circa 1821–22. Fogg Museum.

90. Blake. "The Penance of Jane Shore." Watercolor,
24.5 × 29.5 cm. Tate Gallery.

91. Blake. "The Battle of Hastings." Wash drawing, 26 ×
36.8 cm. Mssrs. Agnew, London.

92. Blake. "Plague." Watercolor, 17.9 × 27.1 cm. Essick collection.

93. Blake. "Job." Wash drawing, 31.1 × 45.1 cm. Tate Gallery.

94. Blake. *The Book of Urizen.* Copy G, pl. 21. Rosenwald collection.

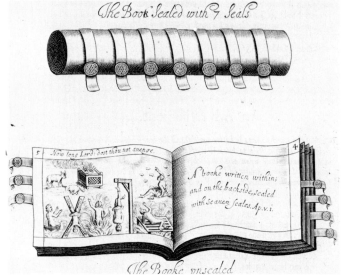

The Book Sealed with 7 Seals

5 Now long Lord: dost thou not avenge 4

A booke written within;
and on the backside, sealed
with seauen seales. Ap. v. i.

The Booke vnsealed

95. Haydock's Idea of the Sealed Book. Engraving in *The Works of Joseph Mede*, 1664. Huntington Library.

96. Diagram Illustrating Joseph Mede's Conception of Revelation's Structure. Engraving in Mede, *The Key of the Revelation*, 1643. Huntington Library.

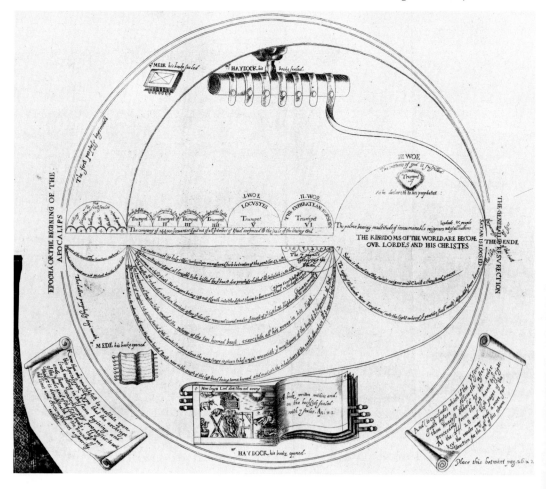

97. Diagram Illustrating Henry More's Conception of Revelation's Structure. Engraving in More, *Apocalypsis Apocalypseos*, 1680. Folger Shakespeare Library.

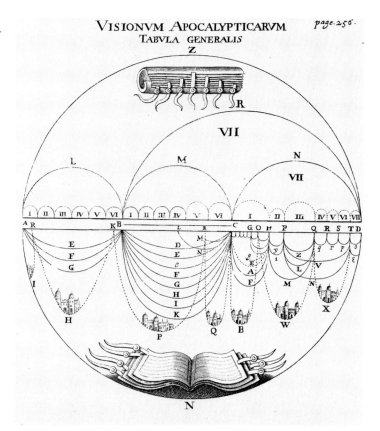

98. John of Patmos composing. Woodcut in the extra-illustrated Kitto Bible, Vol. 60. Huntington Library.

99. Blake. *Milton*. Copy B, title page. Huntington Library.

100. Blake. *Milton*. Copy B, pl. 13. Huntington Library.

101. Engraving of Jupiter Pluvius in Bernard de
Montfaucon, *Antiquity Explained*. Vol. I, pl. 9, detail of
fig. 13. Huntington Library.

102. Blake. "The House of Death." 1795 color printed
drawing, 48.5 × 61 cm. Tate Gallery.

103. Engraving of a chariot in Montfaucon, *Antiquity Explained*. Vol. I, pl. 20, upper design. Huntington Library.

104. Blake. *Jerusalem*. Copy I, pl. 46, design only. Rosenwald collection.

105. Garuda, detail from "A Sacrificial Vase of gilt Copper in the Museum at the India House," engraved by J. Dadley after Houghton, *The Hindu Pantheon*, pl. 105. University of California, Berkeley.

Now comes the night of Enitharmons joy!
Who shall I call? Who shall I send?
That Woman, lovely Woman! may have dominion?
Arise O Rintrah thee I call! & Palamabron thee!
Go, tell the human race that Womans love is Sin:
That an Eternal life awaits the worms of sixty winters
In an allegorical abode where existence hath never come;
Forbid all Joy, & from her childhood shall the little female
Spread nets in every secret path.
My weary eyelids draw towards the evening, my bliss is yet but new

106. Blake. *Europe.* Copy E, pl. 8. Rosenwald collection.

107. Engraving of Sarmatian warriors in Montfaucon, *Antiquity Explained.* Vol. IV, pl. 22, fig. 3. Huntington Library.

Hercules of Dædalus,
from a small Bronze.

Cupid of Praxiteles.
British Museum &c.

Minerva of Dipænus & Scyllis,
in the Villa Albani.

Venus of Praxiteles.
Perriers Statues.

Jupiter Olympius. See Pausanias. Ancient
Statues. Coins & Gems.

Minerva of the Acropolis in Athens.
See Hunters Coins.

108. "Sculpture," pl. I, in Abraham Rees. *Cyclopaedia,*
engraved by Blake. Essick collection.

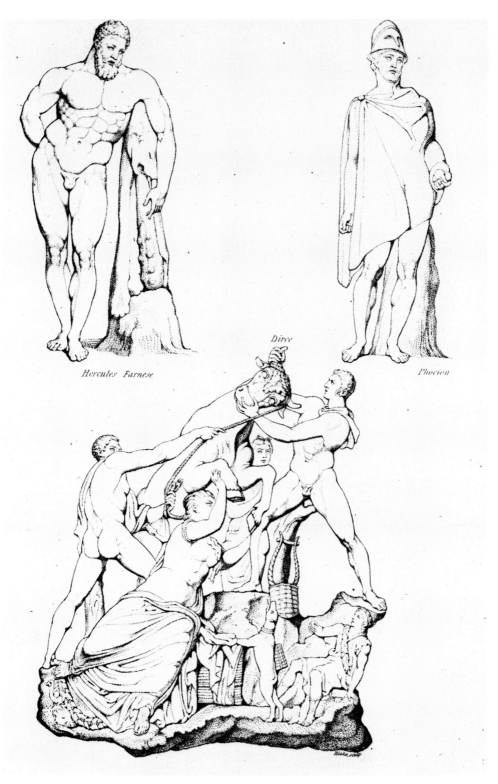

Dirce

Hercules Farnese

Phocion

Blake sculp.

109. "Sculpture," pl. II, in Rees, *Cyclopaedia*, engraved by
Blake. Essick collection.

Venus de Medicis.

Apollo Belvedere.

Laocoon.

110. "Sculpture," pl. III, in Rees, *Cyclopaedia,* engraved by Blake. Essick collection.

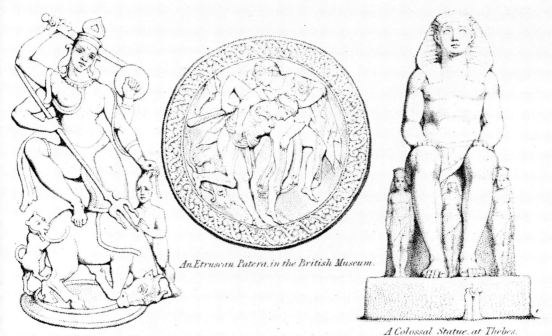

An Etruscan Patera, in the British Museum.

Durga Slaying Mahishasura, a Hindoo group.

A Colossal Statue, at Thebes.

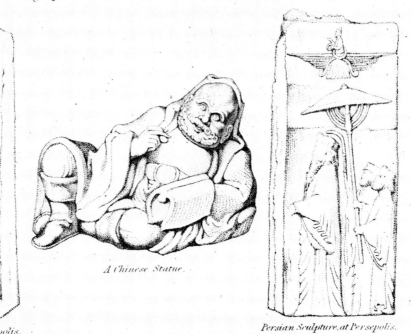

Persian Sculpture, at Persepolis.

A Chinese Statue.

Persian Sculpture, at Persepolis.

111. "Sculpture," pl. IV, in Rees, *Cyclopaedia*, engraved by
Blake. Essick collection.

112. Blake. *Laocoön*. Etching and engraving. Collection of
Sir Geoffrey Keynes.

113. George Romney. "The Infant Shakespeare Attended by Nature with the Muses, Tragedy and Comedy." Pen, pencil, and wash drawing, 127.3 × 102.2 cm. Walker Art Gallery.

114. Romney. "The Ghost of Darius Appearing to Atossa." Black chalk, 101 × 126.4 cm. Walker Art Gallery.

115. Romney. "The Death
of Cordelia." Black chalk,
101.3 × 125.7 cm. Walker
Art Gallery.

116. Romney. "Eurydice
Floating back to the Underworld." Black chalk, 126.3 ×
100.8 cm. Walker Art Gallery.

117. Romney. "Eurydice Floating back to the Underworld."
Black chalk, 101.3 × 126.3 cm. Walker Art Gallery.

118. Romney. "Cupid and Psyche." Black chalk, 101.6 ×
126 cm. Walker Art Gallery.

119. Romney. "Psyche Supplicating Juno." Black chalk, 101.3 × 124.2 cm. Walker Art Gallery.

120. Romney. "Psyche by the Water of the Styx." Black chalk, 101.6 × 126.4 cm. Walker Art Gallery.

121. Romney. "Psyche Being Rowed across the Styx." Pen and ink, 31.3 × 48.1 cm. Fitzwilliam Museum.

122. Richard Westall. The first Angel pleading with one of the beautiful and elegant Daughters of Men. Engraved by Charles Heath for the first tale in Thomas Moore, *The Loves of the Angels*, Second Edition, 1823, facing p. 6. Beinecke Library, Yale. Westall's drawings have not been traced.

123. Westall. The Cherub Rubi appearing to Lilis. Engraved by E. Portbury for Moore, *The Loves of the Angels*, 1823, facing p. 33. Beinecke Library, Yale.

124. Westall. The Angel
Zaraph's first sight of Nama.
Title page vignette engraved
by Heath for Moore, *The
Loves of the Angels,* 1823.
Beinecke Library, Yale.

125. Westall. Zaraph hears
Nama singing by the shore.
Engraved by Heath for
Moore, *The Loves of the
Angels,* 1823, facing p. 104.
Beinecke Library, Yale.

126. John Flaxman. Compact of Angels. Grey and brown wash, 13 × 20.9 cm., inscribed "Enoch / The [*cut off*]", "2" (or "7"). Collection of Christopher Powney. The effect is of group joining group in harmony.

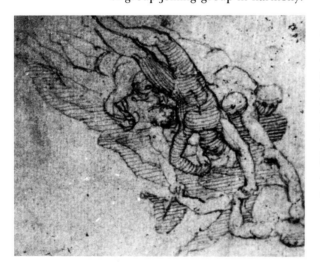

127. Flaxman. Descent of the Angels. Pencil, 11.1 × 8.9 cm., inscribed "3." University College, London. The straight-line style of shading, not used elsewhere in Flaxman's *Enoch* designs, was used by Flaxman about 1793 for direct transfer to copper when his designs were engraved. Plates 127–29 may be regarded, perhaps, not as variants of one design but as different states of the action.

128. Flaxman. Descent of
the Angels. Pen and wash,
23 × 28.5 cm., not inscribed.
Victoria & Albert Museum.
A much clearer and finer
sketch, the shading in delicate wash modeling; the effect is much more that of
the impetuous flight of men
being arrested by the sight
of something below.

129. Flaxman. Descent of
the Angels. Ink and grey
wash over pencil, 16.8 ×
23.4 cm., inscribed "Enoch /
Descent of the Angels."
University College, London.
A much clearer variant
of Plate 127, with solid
shadows, greater definition
of individuals; in particular,
one impulsive figure at bottom has broken free of the
group.

130. Flaxman. Angels descending to the Daughters of
Men. Pencil and ink with dark brown wash shading, 13.7
× 24.3 cm., inscribed "Angels descending to the
daughters of Men" and "3" (top left; "3" is erased at top
right). Fitzwilliam Museum.

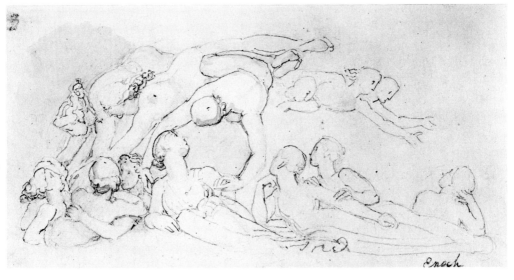

131. Flaxman. Angels descending to the Daughters of
Men. Pencil, pen and wash, 10.4 × 22.9 cm., inscribed
"Enoch" (bottom right), perhaps "red" by the Regency
debutante (fourth woman from the right), and "3[del]"
(top left). Huntington Library. A more finished version of
Plate 130, with the emphasis now upon the women, who
are more nearly contemporary.

132. Flaxman. Angels descending to the Daughters of
Men. Ink and wash over pencil, 16.7 × 23 cm., inscribed
"Angels descending to the daughters of men / Enoch."
University College, London. A much more finished and
crowded development of Plate 130.

133. Flaxman. The Daughters of Men attacked by
Angels. Ink and pencil, 7.6 × 9.5 cm., not inscribed.
University College, London. The three sketches may be
intended for separate designs.

134. Flaxman. Two Angels disputing over one of the Daughters of Men. Pencil and pen, 11 × 11.6 cm., not inscribed. University College, London. There is no description in *The Book of Enoch* of quarrels over women, but the angels there *are* set in contention at God's command.

135. Flaxman. Raphael casting the Watcher Azazyel into darkness. Ink and grey wash, 12.1 × 10.5 cm., inscribed "Assrael[?]" University College, London.

136. Flaxman. Michael driving the Watchers beneath the earth. Pen and wash, 6.8 × 6.8 cm., not inscribed. University College, London.

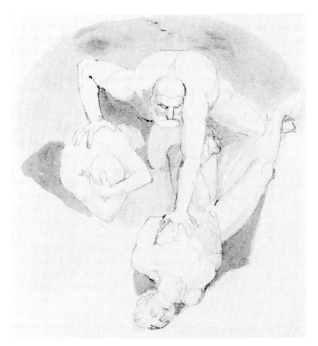

137. Flaxman. Michael binding the Watchers beneath the earth. Ink and grey wash over pencil, 14.6 × 13.7 cm., not inscribed. University College, London.

138. Flaxman. Watchers imprisoned beneath the earth. Ink, grey wash, and pencil, 8.2 × 8.5 cm., not inscribed. University College, London. The smaller of the two figures is difficult to account for from the text of *The Book of Enoch;* perhaps he is a mere man beside a Watcher.

139. Blake. A Watcher surrounded by four Daughters of
Men. Pencil, 52.7 × 36.9 cm., inscribed "Book of / Enoch"
and numbered "1. Enoch," on paper watermarked with
an elaborate crest. Rosenwald collection, U.S. National Gallery of Art. A bearded hero, with an heroic penis, is surrounded
by four women whose breasts are emphasized.

140. Blake. A Watcher seducing a Daughter of Men, with
two offspring. Pencil, 52.7 × 37 cm., inscribed "from the
Book of Enoch" and "2. Enoch," on paper watermarked
"W ELGAR / 1796." Rosenwald collection.

141. Blake. Two Watchers descending to a Daughter of
Men. Pencil, 52.7 × 37 cm., inscribed "from the Book of
Enoch" and "3. Enoch," on paper watermarked "W
ELGAR / 1796." Rosenwald collection. The orgiastic implications are made plain by the carefully emphasized
vulva of the woman and the giant, light-giving phalli of
the men.

142. Blake. Two Daughters of Men with a prone figure.
Pencil, 52.7 × 37 cm., inscribed "B. of Enoch," "4," "102"
(very faint), and "[Nº 27 *del*] Nº 26 next [?] at p. 43," on
paper watermarked with the same elaborate crest as in
Plate 139. Rosenwald collection. The "Nº 26" (&c) inscription does not seem to be related to *The Book of Enoch,*
trans. Richard Laurence (1821). There are similar enigmatic page references on Blake's designs for Dante
(1824-27) and for Bunyan (c. 1824), all owned by Linnell.

143. Blake. Enoch before the throne of One great in glory. Pencil, 52.7 × 37.1 cm., inscribed "Book of / Enoch," on paper watermarked with the same elaborate crest as in Plates 139, 142. Rosenwald collection.

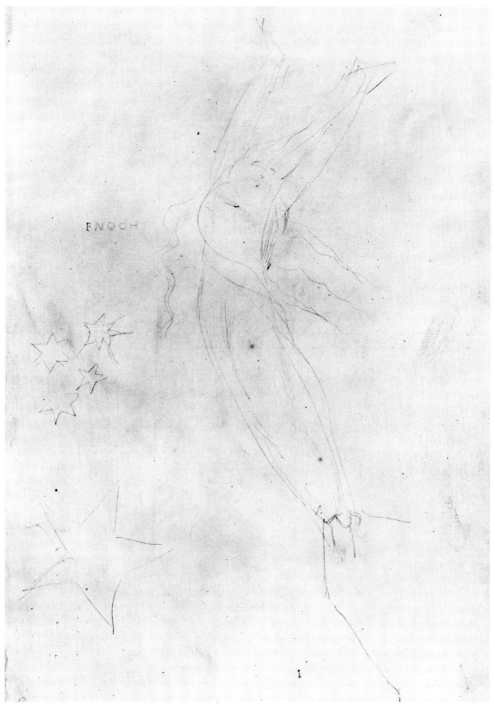

144. Blake. A Watcher punished. Pencil, 52 × 36.5 cm.,
inscribed "ENOCH" (middle left) and "Enoch" (bottom
left), on paper watermarked "W ELGAR / 1796." Grenville Winthrop Bequest, Fogg Art Museum, Harvard University. A figure tethered by the ankles soars upward between stars.

I

MOTIFS

Beginning with Joseph Wicksteed's study of the *Job* designs in 1910, most commentaries on Blake's art have centered on the meaning of individual motifs. Our awareness of Blake's pictorial vocabulary has developed at a rapid pace over the last ten years, and the resulting increase in our knowledge has permitted interpretations of his designs that take into account the relationships between motifs and the complex of meanings generated thereby. This movement toward inclusiveness has now reached out to make the study of sources—a characteristic concern of the art historian—part of iconographic studies. Blake borrowed individual motifs, subjects, and illustrative formats from a rich tradition that ranged from the work of Renaissance masters to contemporary physiognomic theories. In the act of transforming this inheritance into his own idiom, Blake not only makes use of the past but implicitly comments on it.

Blake's Visions and Re-visions of Michelangelo

Jenijoy La Belle

I T is a truth universally acknowledged that Blake is indebted to
Michelangelo for many of his giant forms. Anthony Blunt has noted
that "the motives from [Michelangelo's] work recurring in Blake's
designs are legion,"[1] and Jean Hagstrum has commented eloquently
on the ways in which the "gloomy giants of Michelangelo, not now in
action but capable, once they move, of destroying and rebuilding a
world" anticipate Blake's Triple Hecate, Urizen, Los, Albion, Newton.[2] These general observations need confirmation through the
specific tracing of individual figures from Michelangelo through the
works of Blake. An opportunity to do so is provided by a group of
seven monochrome wash drawings, now in the British Museum,
executed by Blake in the early 1780s when he was embarking on his
career as an original artist.

These drawings were copied after the engravings of the
sixteenth-century Italian artist Adam Ghisi whose small book of
seventy-three plates reproduces the Sistine frescoes. Typically,
Blake's knowledge of a Renaissance master is filtered through the
eye and hand of a fellow copy engraver. A comparison of Blake's
drawings with Michelangelo's original frescoes shows a number of
differences, but in almost every case these are Ghisi's changes, not
Blake's. Blake copied Ghisi with great exactness, making only minor,
but in some cases not insignificant, alterations in emphasis. For
Blake, Michelangelo was of course a true artist and to copy his work
with care was an almost religious duty and a chief means of absorbing into his own pictorial repertoire those figures who bore in their
lineaments some remnants of the lost works of antiquity. As Blake
wrote, "To learn the Language of Art Copy for Ever. is My Rule."[3]

Six of Blake's drawings are of figures from the lunettes above the windows on the side walls of the Sistine Chapel. For ease of reference, these figures are often identified with the Forefathers of Christ whose names are inscribed immediately above each window on tablets which separate the lunettes into two niches. However, these are often family groups or single melancholy figures who seem to have little to do with Christ's ancestors. They are to be identified with the life of man on the unredeemed earth, waiting for, yet having no knowledge of, the coming of Christ prophesied by the prophets and sibyls pictured between the spandrels over the lunettes. The seventh drawing is of one of these prophets. He is a far larger and more important figure in Michelangelo's composition than the figures in the lunettes and, unlike them, has a long iconographical tradition associated with him.

Except for omitting the moustache and slightly changing the folds along the right thigh, Blake followed Ghisi's engraving closely in his drawing of the Manasses lunette (Plate 6). For those familiar with Blake's art, a glance at this drawing will recall to the mind's eye some of Blake's designs with a general resemblance to this figure. For example, both large figures above "prophecy" on the *America* title page (Plate 7) have similar bent postures seen in profile, drapery which defines some lineaments and hides others, and, what is most important, they suggest the same sort of enervation and ennui. The figure-type appears again in Blake's representation of the poet writing in the second design to Gray's poems where the face is given more energy and presence, but with the legs crossed as in Michelangelo. As for the hood and heavy robe, Blake exaggerates it to a dark extreme in his *Night Thoughts* watercolor, page 98 of Night IX.

My point here is not that Michelangelo is the immediate source for these figures, at least not in the sense that Blake went back and looked at his early wash drawings before executing the *America* or *Night Thoughts* designs. But the drawing after Michelangelo is an important, and perhaps Blake's first, rendition of this type. Aby Warburg's concept of *pathos formulae*, recently used by Bo Lindberg in his study of the Job designs,[4] is helpful in understanding the process of initial imitation and subsequent transformation operating here. A *pathos formula* may be described as a limited range of body configurations and placements of the human form in space which communicates a definable range of mental and emotional states. These *pathos formulae* form an important part of the language of motifs in Western art, from the Renaissance to at least the nineteenth century. They are particularly significant wherever the human form is the predominant element, as it is in the work of Michelangelo and Blake. The objective is not so much to discover single sources for every posture, but rather to find the ways an individual talent first makes contact with this language of art and then changes it into his own idiom. Thus Blake learned from the Manasses lunette how to show devitalized humanity in pictorially simple profile.

Two of the drawings show a mother and child. Both are important to the development of Blake's motifs expressing the state of innocence and its relationship to the protective but potentially restrictive adult. In the drawing from the Abiud lunette (Plate 8), Blake again follows Ghisi carefully, but he does give to the faces a more anxious look, as though they were seeing in the distance—or in the future—some disturbance which makes the child cling closer to the mother, and her to the child. A similar combination of fear and protection, but with an added measure of despair, is suggested by the mother and child on the middle right margin in "Holy Thursday" in *Songs of Experience*. The same group, with a second child also clinging to the mother, appears without drapery on the *America* frontispiece (Plate 9). The impending terrors recorded by the faces in the drawing after Michelangelo have now come about, and the protective relationship is placed in the immediate context of war, destruction, and enslavement. What was in Michelangelo representative of unredeemed humanity is given in the *America* frontispiece a specifically political dimension. The mother and child are refugees suffering from horrors not specifically represented by Michelangelo, but a consequence of the same state of unredemption.

The Matthan lunette (Plate 10) includes a father, clearly delineated by Ghisi but deemphasized by Blake, or at least left unfinished. Blake seems to have been attracted by the harmonious tensions in this mother and child group with their hands and arms thrusting in opposite directions so that their gestures complement each other. The scene of course looks protective and even playful in both Ghisi and Blake. "Spring" in *Songs of Innocence* (Plate 11) eliminates the background father and turns the child about so that he is reaching for the sheep rather than for his mother. But the sense of play and of adult support for the child as he reaches out to that which he desires is maintained. In the *Night Thoughts* engravings (p.

12), the father returns, and what seems like appropriate support for the child in "Spring" is now clearly restraint. The angle of the bodies is increased, and with it a sense of tension between child and adult. In "Infant Sorrow" (Plate 12), the mother is turned toward the child again, as in Michelangelo, and reaches out to the child with the same sense of motherly affection. But now instead of responding to the mother with a complementary and unifying emotion and gesture, the child attempts to struggle away from all restraint. In the *Night Thoughts* design the child reaches out to trap a bird; here he attempts to keep from being trapped. Finally on plate 4 of *The Marriage of Heaven and Hell*, and in much the same design of the 1795 color printed drawing of "The Good and Evil Angels," the fleeing child and the restraining adult take their most dramatic form. The relationship of this design to the drawing after Michelangelo can only be seen by tracing its metamorphoses through the previous three designs. All of Blake's child and adult relationships are certainly not latent in these two family scenes from the Sistine lunettes; yet we can see how Blake's pictorial expressions of both protection and constraint were influenced by Michelangelo.

The Abia lunette (Plate 13) is one of only two among this group of drawings that have received earlier attention. Anthony Blunt has identified Ghisi's engraving as the source of the basic posture and the exaggerated musculature of Blake's Newton in the famous color printed drawing.[5] But the importance of this posture is not limited to a single work by Blake. Numerous examples can be found, showing seated figures seen from the side and reaching down with extended fingers, as in the *Night Thoughts* watercolors (VI, p. 31). We should not, however, confine this type to sideviews only. When Blake was an apprentice, his master James Basire sent him to make drawings of the sepulchral monuments in Westminster Abbey. Benjamin Heath Malkin enumerates several of these tomb-figures drawn by Blake and then comments that "these [Blake] drew in every point he could catch, frequently standing on the monument, and viewing the figures from the top."[6] Since Malkin's only source of information on Blake's early years must have been the artist himself, these words have special authority. And in the publication for which Blake made these drawings, Richard Gough's *Sepulchral Monuments in Great Britain*, there are many plates signed by Basire showing front, side, and top views of the same tomb.

Blake looked upon Michelangelo's figures as though they too

were sculptures, capable of existing in three dimensions. Thus Blake could, in effect, walk around inside the drawing and view the figure from any angle. For instance, on the title page to *Visions of the Daughters of Albion*, near the upper left margin is a front view of Michelangelo's figure, with the falling hair (only hinted at by the braid in the drawing) now emphasized and lengthened to complement the arm. While the "Newton" preserves the side view of the drawing after Michelangelo, this small figure in *Visions of the Daughters of Albion* is much closer to the lifelessness of their common antecedent. Another front view with hair falling over the face appears as Grief personified (Plate 14) in the *Night Thoughts* watercolors (V, p. 20). Here as in the "Newton" Blake has added a scroll and the compasslike formation of the fingers. Blake used a more energetic version of the same posture to represent one of the Eternals who draws a curtain between himself and the new-formed chaos on plate 15 in *The Book of Urizen*. He has the hyacinthine curls and powerful arm and back muscles of Newton. Blake also made use of the small figure, with hair blowing to the left, in the Michelangelo design. In the color printed drawing of "Pity" (Plate 45), in the figure reaching down for the babe, the hair is lengthened but the same chin, mouth, nose, eyes, and general expression are repeated. Blake combined the outstanding characteristics of the two figures from Michelangelo's design to create the Ancient of Days on the *Europe* frontispiece (Plate 15). The heavily muscled arm reaches into the abyss, and the hair and beard stream to the left. The lack of energy pictured by Michelangelo is here replaced by supreme energy, but one which will limit all energy as he creates the very world inhabited by Michelangelo's figure. Finally we come to the "Newton" (Plate 16) which in many ways seems to be the product of all the transformations of the Abia lunette I have been tracing. Blake returns to the original side view, but adds the compasses, the curls, and the intense downward gaze we have seen incorporated into this basic motif at earlier stages of its development. The mantle provides Newton with the same compositional balance and backdrop for the arm presented by the draped legs of Michelangelo's figure. Even the sense of wind blowing through the scene is maintained, albeit in a much transformed guise: the current moving from left to right, indicated by the hairlike tentacles of the polyps beneath Newton.

The so-called Solomon lunette (Plate 17) clearly does not represent the monarch. A woman, somewhat more aged in Blake's drawing than in Ghisi's engraving, draws out a ball of yarn on a skein-winder which she turns with her right foot. Blake's most unusual borrowing from this design appears in the advertisement he designed and engraved for the carpet-weaving and hosiery firm of Moore and Company. The lower section of this plate pictures contemporary eighteenth-century looms of considerable size and complexity. There are a number of children playing about these machines or working at them, including one small girl sitting on the base of the left column (Plate 18). She sits at a spinning wheel, but before her is also the very sort of antique skein-winder we see in Michelangelo and which by the eighteenth century would hardly have been normal equipment for a London weaving firm. Less bizarre but more significant are Blake's uses of the old woman, who almost immediately suggests a sibyl or one of the fates spinning out the destinies of men. She appears as a representative of toil at her spinning wheel (Plate 19) in a watercolor for Young's Night The Seventh (p. 22). Our perspective is turned toward a frontal view, but the bent posture is retained and the headdress lengthened into a mantle. The foot of the crossed leg operates the treadle much as that of Michelangelo's figure turns the winder. In Night The Fifth (p. 25) the literal context of spinning and weaving is removed, and the same ancient woman becomes a sibyl at her leaves, spinning tales of the future. A further transformation takes place in Night The Second (Plate 20) where this figure is placed within a setting of vegetative nature. Here she suggests a complex of Blake's mythological females: Tirzah, "Thou Mother of my Mortal part" in Songs of Experience; Enitharmon, the "aged Mother" of The Song of Los; and finally Blake's nature goddess Vala who frequently retains the cloak seen on the head of Michelangelo's figure. Michelangelo's spinner was not merely a pictorial source, but rapidly gained for Blake a host of conceptual associations dealt with in his poetry as much as in his designs.

Blake's most significant alterations of and additions to Ghisi's image are found in the drawing of the Aminadab lunette (Plates 21, 22). The head and shoulders are not quite as square, and the visage is more intelligent in Blake's drawing than in Ghisi's. Further, Blake has lifted the figure's gaze and lengthened a finger on the man's right hand along the cloth between his calves. The left foot is more prominent in Blake than in Ghisi because the right foot has completely receded into shadow. The most important addition is of course the legend beneath the drawing—"The Reposing Traveller." Frederick Tatham, whose notes appear on the lower margin of most of the drawings, ascribes the legend, as well as the execution of the drawing, to Blake. This is not Blake's regular manuscript hand, but rather a formal and decorative style indicating either an intention to exhibit the drawing or, what is more likely, a plan eventually to publish the design as an engraving. While still at the stage of a copy-drawing, and before any major transformation of the figure or placement in a new context, Blake has begun to identify the figure with one of his own important character-types which, as Jean Hagstrum has pointed out, is also one of Blake's own personae.[7] It must be admitted, however, that this pencil motto was probably added some time after the execution of the drawing. Indeed, the slight lean toward the left of the serif on the "g" of "Reposing" would suggest a date after 1791.[8] The inscription should remind us of both the Mental Traveller and of Blake's lines accompanying the designs to Gray's poems:

> Around the Springs of Gray my wild root weaves
> Traveller repose & Dream among my leaves.
>
> (E 473)

We are all travelers through the world of experience. Like the figure from Michelangelo, like Blake himself, we should pause to dream or have visions of art and poetry.

Blake's pictorial uses for the Reposing Traveller lead us in two directions. One of the earliest transformations is a pencil sketch on the verso of the Job drawing in the Tate Gallery preparatory for the large separate print. Here the figure is given a shepherd's staff and placed in a landscape; yet even in this slight sketch, Blake imparts a sense of visionary activity during physical repose. This figure appears again in another minor work, an unpublished drawing formerly in the Graham Robertson Collection (Plate 23). The shepherd has changed little and again has between his calves a rounded object which Martin Butlin has identified as a lyre in the Job verso sketch.[9] This motif, replacing the drapery and hands in Michelangelo's design, further identifies this character with Blake's singer-poet-visionaries. Of much greater importance is his later transformation into a representation of Christ in the tempera painting "Christ Blessing Little Children," also in the Tate Gallery. He does not look at the children, but, like the Reposing Traveller, his eyes turn upward and beyond the present scene to indicate the visionary state into which he enfolds his youthful audience. The left foot is less prominent, and the compositional role played by the pointing finger and falling cloth in the copy-drawing is fulfilled by a child.

Elsewhere Blake has developed the sinister qualities latent in the Reposing Traveller. For these, it seems as though he may have turned back to the heavy and stupefied figure in Ghisi's engraving, rather than his more enlightened second-self in his own copy-drawing. Clearly, there are Urizenic possibilities in the foot position and the massive knees. The imprisoned Ugolino-like figure dominating the design in plate 16 of *The Marriage of Heaven and Hell* retains the heavy legs crossed at the ankles. But the torso has been contracted out of view, and the head rests directly above the "V" formed by the legs. The upward-turned eyes are filled with anxiety. In the *Night Thoughts* watercolors (VII, p. 40) Blake uses not only the basic posture but the rugged features of the Reposing Traveller's face and in particular converts the latter into an expression of horror (Plate 24). In spite of the extreme tension of the face, the arms seem almost as relaxed as in the Reposing Traveller, although they now reach to the figure's ankles because of the lowered shoulder position. By radically decreasing the humanity of the figure, Blake has changed the Reposing Traveller into his opposite—the imprisoned traveller. In plate 7 of *Visions of the Daughters of Albion* we move even further toward the subhuman, for here we see only the top of the figure's head bent over in despair. The lineaments of the human form divine have collapsed as near as possible toward a sphere—without altogether losing those few basic outlines by which we recognize that human form. There are of course many other influences at play in the development of Blake's Urizenic figures—including others from the Sistine Chapel—but their relationship to the Reposing Traveller helps to explain their pictorial similarity to some of Blake's shepherds and poets.

The single Prophet among the drawings is Daniel (Plate 25). In the original fresco, a shadowy spirit hovers behind Daniel's left shoulder. Ghisi (Plate 26) has converted this mantled presence into a fat-cheeked baby who seems to be speaking, but Blake has closed the baby's mouth and given him a more pensive look. Daniel's mouth, however, has been opened slightly by Blake and the whole face given a more animated appearance. In Blake's drawing, the child is less the Muse, and more the audience. Daniel is seen with a heavy tablet or volume on his lap, supported by an Atlas-like putto. He turns to his right to transcribe the text onto another tablet or perhaps to write a commentary on it. The scene suggests Daniel's traditional associations with prophecy and the ability both to have and to interpret visions. St. Augustine gives Daniel particular stature among all the Old Testament Prophets as one who combined imagination and intelligence. As Augustine writes, "... and a greater prophet is he that interprets what another has seen, than he that has merely seen it."[10] One could thus almost take Daniel as the patron saint of artists who, like Blake, carefully copied and then went on to interpret "what another has seen" and painted.

On plate 10 of *The Marriage of Heaven and Hell* (Plate 27), Blake pictures the Devil with his scroll bearing the Proverbs of Hell. The scribe on the right is in general body posture and literary activity based on Michelangelo's Daniel. This association plus his energetic interest in the Devil's words and the progress of his more restricted companion suggests that he is no mere passive transcriber, but an active interpreter. The pictorial borrowings seem especially appropriate since the traditional associations with Daniel are compatible with the themes of visions and interpretations so important to *The Marriage*.

Young's *Night Thoughts* provided Blake with many opportunities to present interpreters of visions and poets at their labors. The winged scribe below the text panel in Night The Eighth, p. 38, owes his twisting posture and perhaps something of his air of intense concentration to the Daniel figure. In Night The Sixth, p. 34, the sideward twist becomes a complete profile, but the triangular stand for the tablet still evokes the Daniel (Plate 28). The single listening child has multiplied into a host of personified Arguments swarming around the interpreter's pen. Other variations on the interpreter-poet at his writing appear in *Night Thoughts*. In Night The Ninth, p. 80, there is a recasting of the group from *The Marriage of Heaven and Hell*, but it is now the central figure who twists to the right. Finally, the Daniel figure merges with other pictorial prototypes for the poet, as in the representation of Young at the beginning of the *Night Thoughts* watercolors (Night The First, p. ii). Here, as in the previous design, the inspiration is from above, and not from another's text.

My purpose here has not been to exaggerate the importance of these particular figures. Indeed, there are others from the Sistine Chapel that hold out equally interesting possibilities for investigation in terms of their impact on the development of Blake's pictorial imagination. However, these seven compositions have a unique virtue—there is for each an extant record of Blake's close study. Thus we are able to see the very beginnings of Blake's absorption of these *pathos formulae* and how even the subtlest changes are clues to later developments. We have also seen the ways in which a single figure can develop in two directions. For example, The Aminadab lunette evolves into contraries—the Reposing Traveller Poet and the imprisoned victim. As Blake transforms Michelangelo's designs, he also gives them an iconographic dimension which is wholly his own. Only with Daniel is there a preexisting conceptual context.

Blake had visions. There can be no question about that. Some of his art is an attempt to give concrete form and interpretation to those visions—the Visionary Heads are perhaps the clearest example. It is apparent that he approached Michelangelo's art in much the same way and that the usual distinction between copying another artist and envisioning one's own designs does not pertain. By tracing these re-visions of Michelangelo, I think we can have a better grasp not only of Blake's debt to the past but also of the meaning of his own visions.

NOTES

1. *The Art of William Blake* (New York: Columbia Univ. Press, 1959), p. 35.
2. *William Blake Poet and Painter* (Chicago: Univ. of Chicago Press, 1964), p. 40.
3. Annotations to *The Works of Sir Joshua Reynolds,* E 626.
4. *William Blake's Illustrations to the Book of Job* (Abo, Finland: Abo Akademi, 1973), p. 115.
5. *The Art of Blake,* p. 35.
6. *A Father's Memoirs of His Child* (London, 1806), p. xxi.
7. *Blake Poet and Painter,* p. 40.
8. See Erdman, "Dating Blake's Script: the 'g' hypothesis," *Blake Newsletter,* 3 (June, 1969), 8–13.
9. *William Blake: A Complete Catalogue of the Works in the Tate Gallery* (London: Tate Gallery, 1971), p. 28.
10. *De Genesi ad litteram* XII.ix (Patr. lat. xxxiv, col. 461). Quoted in Edgar Wind, *Michelangelo's Prophets and Sibyls* (London: Oxford Univ. Press, 1965), p. 52.

Blake and the Iconography of Cain

Leslie Tannenbaum

W H E N the Bard in *Milton* is asked at the conclusion of his song to verify the authenticity of his muse, he proclaims,

> I am Inspired! I know it is Truth! for I Sing/According to the inspiration of the Poetic Genius/Who is the eternal all-protecting Divine Humanity/To whom be Glory & Power & Dominion Evermore Amen
>
> *(Milton*, pls. 13–14; E 107)

Immediately below this proclamation is a picture of Cain fleeing the body of the murdered Abel. Clearly neither a literal illustration of any event in the Bard's song nor of anything following it, the Cain and Abel motif, as David Erdman asserts, serves an emblematic function, symbolizing the fratricide of temporal war—the following of the "detestable Gods of Priam"—that Milton rises to oppose.[1] Blake's use of a biblical allusion to comment upon what he considered to be the corrupt ideology of classical art recalls the "Preface" to *Milton*, with its defense of the "Sublime of the Bible" against the works of the "silly Greek and Latin slaves of the Sword" (E 94). This concept of the Bible as the embodiment of true imaginative vision suggests that the biblical illustration at the end of the Bard's proclamation is an iconographic seal, verifying the source of the Bard's vision as the same genius that inspired the Bible. The Cain and Abel design also suggests an even greater richness of meaning through its relation to earlier and contemporary illustrations of that biblical story. The pictorial tradition that the design invokes raises not only the theme of fratricide but also the themes of pity, wrath, and divine justice, which make the picture epitomize and illuminate the main issues raised by the Bard's song and the entire poem.

23

This strategic use of Cain and Abel in *Milton* and the appearance of the biblical myth in "The Body of Abel Found by Adam and Eve," in *The Ghost of Abel*, and in Blake's illustrated Genesis manuscript testify to the continued importance of Cain and Abel in his later works. In each work Blake creates meaning by placing himself within a tradition at the same time that he subverts and reshapes that tradition.

Among Blake's contemporaries, the Cain and Abel story was an extremely popular pictorial and literary subject, as it was capable of evoking the feelings of horror, pity, and awe inspired by the first murder and its consequences. The story was illustrated by Fuseli, James Stephanoff, C. W. Dietrich, Francesco Pieraccini, Pierre Paul Prudhon, William Hamilton, and Henry Singleton, among others. By the middle of the nineteenth century the subject of the death of Abel would become academic. In their treatment of the biblical story, artists of the late eighteenth and early nineteenth centuries were influenced by the older masters, whose works were continually being reproduced, individually and in illustrated Bibles. These earlier artists were less interested in the potential sublimity of the subject than in the devotional and moralistic possibilities. This dominant moralistic attitude was adopted by most of Blake's contemporaries, and it created, despite differences in style, an important thread in the tradition of visual motifs and themes derived from the fourth chapter of Genesis.

The majority of illustrations treating the Cain and Abel story dwell upon four main themes: the righteousness of Abel (with a typological emphasis upon his prefiguring Christ's priesthood and death); the commission of the first murder on earth; the first appearance of death in the world; and the first criminal's encounter with guilt and divine justice. Abel's righteousness was represented by the sacrifice of Cain and Abel. The two altars were shown with a sign of God's acceptance of Abel's offering and His rejection of Cain's. The former was usually represented by flames and smoke ascending to heaven, and the latter by a dormant altar or smoke arching horizontally. Sometimes God was shown hovering above Abel's altar. Marten de Vos (Plate 29) provides a typical example of this theme. The theme of the first murder is given dramatic treatment in the numerous representations of Cain assaulting his brother. Titian's version (Plate 30), which was frequently engraved, is perhaps the best known example. The concurrent theme of the first appearance of death in the world is represented either by the lone figure of the dead Abel or the figures of Adam and Eve— sometimes Adam alone—discovering or mourning their murdered son. The Finding of Abel is a motif that has no basis in the text of Genesis 4, but in Blake's time it had become a firmly entrenched tradition. Earlier masters such as Andrea Sacchi, Franz Floris, Lucas van Leyden, Philippe de Champaigne, and Carlo Lolli (Plate 31) all used it, and the numerous versions appearing in the first half of the nineteenth century suggest that this motif was the most frequently adopted one. Some early masters gave this family scene a typological as well as sentimental emphasis, as they showed Eve holding the dead Abel in a clear echo of the Pietà. However, the dominant theme was the pathos of slaughtered innocence, emphasized by the body of Abel which was usually placed in the foreground. This dwelling upon Abel's body—frequently shown as a classical nude— became increasingly important in the latter half of the eighteenth century. The fourth theme, Cain's guilt and punishment, was most often represented by the figure of Cain in flight, usually pursued by God or a symbolic representation of divine justice. Sometimes an artist would show God planting the mark upon Cain. In contrast to the pity evoked by Abel's body, the representation of Cain's confrontation with or futile attempt to escape from divine justice evokes the terror of divine wrath descending upon the guilty criminal. The subject appears in numerous biblical engravings, including the works of Benedetto Luti, Francesco Pieraccini, Gerhard Hoedt, and C. W. Dietrich (Plate 32).

In Blake's time the themes of murdered innocence and criminal guilt received the greatest amount of attention. Fuseli's separate figures of Cain and Abel, in Lavater's *Physiognomy*, provide a case in point. The prostrate nude body of Abel (Plate 33) is vigorously represented as destroyed potential. As Lavater observes in the text accompanying the two illustrations, Abel is the "first victim sacrificed to envy," whose "suffering innocence is here presented in manly and energetic traits, under the form of a Hero."[2] The picture echoes the younger Holbein's horizontal panel, "Dead Christ," in the Basel Kunstmuseum and underscores Fuseli's ties with the typological and moralistic aspects of the tradition. The figure of Cain (Plate 34) is the tailpiece to Lavater's text. Cain's crouched position and the expression on his face clearly indicate his guilt and wretchedness. The murdered innocence that Abel represents is more pathetically invoked by the nude figure of a murdered youth in Prudhon's "Divine Justice and Vengeance Pursuing Crime" (Plate 35), which was painted for the Palais de Justice in Paris. (Although the painting was not intended as a literal representation of Cain and Abel, its use of a traditional motif led viewers to assume the design's biblical context.) The contrasting figure of the fleeing Cain who wears, as Louis Réau describes it, "the bestial mask of the emperor Caracalla,"[3] makes the painting's deliberate moral purpose clear.[4] In this and other works of Blake's contemporaries that illustrate the murdered Abel and/or the guilty Cain, one usually finds a moral and emotional sympathy with Abel rather than Cain. When the paintings and etchings of the finding of Abel include Cain, they relegate him to the background, playing upon the pathos of Adam and Eve's discovery of death. A group of watercolors illustrating the finding of Abel, apparently all done on the same occasion by Blake's colleagues—A. E. Chalon (Plate 36), S. John Stump (Plate 37), Joshua Cristall (Plate 38), John Samuel Hayward (Plate 39) and Henry Pierce Bone (Plate 40)[5]—all use this compositional arrangement. These artists adopted the moral attitude of their predecessors, such as Franz Floris (Plate 41), whose depiction of the setting of the mark upon Cain is eclipsed by the scene of family mourning in the foreground; Floris emphasizes the typological as well as the moral significance of Abel's death through the lion devouring the lamb immediately behind the grieving family.

Blake most readily reveals his participation in this tradition of Cain and Abel illustration through his several versions of "The Body of Abel Found by Adam and Eve" (Plate 42)[6]—a subject derived from pictorial sources rather than from the biblical text. Combining the finding of Abel with the flight and judgment of Cain, Blake differs from his contemporaries in putting the fleeing Cain in the foreground and the figures of Adam and Eve with the body of Abel in the background. Blake focuses our attention on Cain even further by having Adam stare at Cain rather than at the dead Abel. Similarly, Eve's overhanging figure is deprived of the dignified madonnalike status familiar in other versions of this scene. Here Blake is clearly more interested in Cain's torment than the pathos of Abel's death; his figure of Cain echoes, and dramatically extends, the leg position of a sixteenth-century figure by Francesco Salviati (Plate 43) of Cain in flight from a wrathful God. The threat of arrested flight that the extended limb creates also echoes the composition of a

seventeenth-century design by Luti (Plate 44), where the fleeing
Cain's right hand and left foot are parallel to and almost touching
the extended arms of Abel's body; these details appear to rivet
Cain's limbs to Abel's. In Blake's design Cain's right foot is arrested
by the open grave that it seems to be emerging from, suggesting the
intensity of Cain's experience of death. Blake adds an even more
dramatic element to his design through the flames that emerge from
Cain's body, which are a transference of the sacrificial flames rising
from the altar in the works of Salviati and others. With this transformation of traditional iconography, Blake reiterates his concern
with Cain as a victim of divine wrath.

The implicit critique of divine justice in "The Body of Abel"
becomes even more apparent when we compare Blake's work with
that of Prudhon (Plate 35), where Blake's blood-drenched globe in
the sky—a symbol of divine wrath—finds its compositional parallel
in the moon hanging above Prudhon's Cain. Prudhon's obvious allegorical endorsement of traditional morality and the acclaim received by "Divine Justice and Vengeance" in the Paris Salon of 1808[7]
suggest that Blake's 1809 version mentioned in his *Descriptive
Catalogue* (E 539) may have been a direct reaction to Prudhon's
painting, which was engraved several times during that period.[8]
Whether or not Blake saw these prints, it becomes clear that he goes
beyond the sentimentality and the moralizations of his contemporaries to depict the imaginative significance of the biblical event.
Like Adam we become shocked to see that Cain is a human sacrifice
to a vindictive God, tyrannized over not only by wrath but by pity as
well—indicated in Blake's design by Eve's encircling arms, echoing
the form of the bloody sphere in the sky. Within Blake's own iconography, Eve's representation of the principle of pity is underscored
by the resemblance of her gesture to that of the figure cradling the
child in Blake's earlier color print, "Pity" (Plate 45).

These issues, the relationship between wrath and pity and the
potentially oppressive nature of both principles, reappear in the
Bard's song in *Milton*, where the Cain and Abel motif underscores
them. In plate 12 Cain is fleeing the dead Abel, carrying a knife in
his hand (Plate 46) and extending his leg even more than he does in
"The Body of Abel," thereby emphasizing his imprisonment by his
own sense of guilt. The entire composition has almost all the elements of Salviati's design—the altar, the body of Abel, and the fleeing Cain—but in Blake's work the persecuting God is internalized,

becoming, as it were, the extended foot of Cain. The figure of Abel that we view head on, which is similar to the victim of repressed wrath in Blake's earlier "A Poison Tree," echoes not only Salviati's figure but also those of Luti and Prudhon. However, unlike those artists' representations of the fleeing Cain, and unlike Blake's own in "The Body of Abel," the two figures in *Milton*, balanced against each other, are given equal emphasis. The sacrificial altar becomes the central compositional element. In effect, the altar binds the foot of the fleeing Cain to the body of Abel, and foot imagery is significant throughout the *Milton* illustrations.[9] The altar that binds Cain to Abel in an obviously destructive relationship is contrasted to the sandal that binds Los to Blake, as well as the falling star that binds Milton to Blake in plate 14, where the shifted position of the altar emphasizes the point (Plate 47). The tyrannical brotherly tie between Cain and Abel is being contrasted to the potentially liberating brotherhood that Blake shares with Robert, Milton, and Los.[10]

The primitive quality of these small designs visually reduces the Cain and Abel motif to a hieroglyph, but this reduction in visual scale produces an intellectual magnification: we can no longer pity a pathetic nude youth nor feel horror over the criminal fleeing the wrath of God. Even more than in "The Body of Abel," we are asked to contemplate the imaginative significance of the criminal and victim bound together by a warped system of justice that separates wrath from pity, yet binds the two together. In *Milton*, Satan performs this paradoxical separation by hiding beneath a mask of pity, "Seeming a brother, being a tyrant, even thinking himself a brother/While he is murdering the just" with his self-righteousness, as he actually does to Thulloh (*Milton*, pls. 7–8, E 100–101). For Blake, this system of justice and the ransom theory of salvation that is its logical consequence constitute false atonement. In *Milton* the tragic emotions of pity and terror, which Blake's contemporaries exploited in their versions of Cain and Abel, give way to a comic vision that points beyond the system of retributive justice.

These ideas surrounding the myth of Cain and Abel are more explicitly developed in *The Ghost of Abel* (Plate 48), where the design of plate 12 of *Milton* is echoed in an interlinear design on plate 1. Cain again has a knife in his hand, and his extended leg will not permit him to flee the body of his brother. Here the altar is not in the center because the design emphasizes Adam's fallen vision, his refusal to hear Jehovah and see the principle that binds the criminal to the victim. However, the altar is represented by the sacrificial flames to the left of Abel. Significantly, to the left of the flames and above Jehovah's name is the inspirational falling star that we have seen in *Milton,* intended here as a contrast to the sacrificial fire. Again, Blake's giving Cain and Abel equal emphasis and his crude style indicate his desire to go beyond his contemporaries to explore the meaning of the pity and terror that their designs evoked.[11]

As in *Milton,* the text of *The Ghost of Abel* contains an explicit condemnation of the system of retributive justice that underlies conventional ideas about Cain and Abel.[12] Agreeing with Byron's attack on orthodox concepts of atonement, Blake asserts that the demand for vengeance is really the blood-lust of Satan. The marginal illustrations employ iconographic motifs to assert that vindictive justice must be replaced by the mutual forgiveness of sins. The illustration at the bottom of plate 2 (Plate 49) emphasizes this idea, as it shows a figure mourning over the body of Abel. Is it Adam or Cain? It is difficult to tell, and the ambiguity may be intentional, as the willingness to believe the figure is Cain will reveal the reader's willingness to accept Cain's repentance. However, the important point here is that Abel's body, which Blake's contemporaries had exploited as a source of pathos, is covered by the fur-clad figure and is replaced by the horrid finger-pointing figure of the voice of Abel's blood that flows above in a horizontal cloud. The cloud, which suggests the traditional horizontal smoke from Cain's altar, again shows Cain to be the sacrificial victim to a tyrannical concept of atonement which both Blake and Byron detested.

This interpretation of the Cain and Abel myth is developed through Blake's use of iconographic tradition in the marginal designs to *The Ghost of Abel.* The stag fleeing the lion in the left margin of the title (Plate 48)—reminiscent of Floris's lamb devoured by the lion—is paralleled by the picture on the right margin of Cain fleeing from God into a thorn bush.[13] Since the stag symbolizes Christ,[14] these two small designs anticipate the revelation within the text that the voice of divine justice that persecutes Cain is really the voice of the Antichrist. The inadequacy of divine justice is further shown in the remaining small figures on the left margins of both plates of *The Ghost of Abel;* these figures illustrate the essential point upon which the tragic vision in Byron's *Cain* turns: that Cain's temptation, his murder of Abel, and his banishment repeat the pattern of the Fall, whose effects Cain had been trying to escape throughout the play.

Blake's marginal illustrations emphasize this pattern both to reiterate Byron's attack on divine justice and to criticize the limitations of Byron's vision. The designs belong to the tradition of serial illustrations of the life of Adam and Eve that would have been familiar to the young Blake in the engravings of Lucas van Leyden. Lucas's series consists of (1) the creation of Eve, (2) God's announcement of the first prohibition to Adam and Eve, (3) the eating from the tree of knowledge, (4) the expulsion from Eden, (5) Cain slaying Abel, and (6) Adam and Eve discovering Abel's body. Blake's series in *The Ghost of Abel* shows, on plate 1 (Plate 48), (1) the unfallen Adam and Eve beneath the tree of knowledge, (2) an angel descending to announce the first prohibition to a seated Adam, and (3) the eating from the tree of knowledge; and on plate 2 (Plate 49), (4) Cain planting seeds, (5) Cain slaying Abel (grabbing his brother's hair as he does in Salvator Rosa's design), (6) Cain attempting to defend himself before God, and (7) Adam and Eve under the tree again, but this time with the serpent wound around it. This imagery underlines Blake's concern that the cycles of fallen history would end only when divine mercy overcomes divine justice. Such a victory does occur within the text of Blake's poem, whose dramatic action comments upon the cyclical pattern depicted in the marginal illustrations. In *The Ghost of Abel,* as in *Milton,* tragedy gives way to comedy, and Blake's poetic text criticizes and extends Byron's tragic vision by proclaiming a new definition of atonement. Blake goes beyond the ransom theory of salvation by interpreting Christ's sacrifice as the sacrifice of Selfhood.

In his use of the Cain and Abel motif to redefine atonement, Blake transforms the typology of that biblical tale, which traditionally sees the martyrdom of the righteous Abel as the promise of redemption through the shedding of Christ's blood. In contrast to this stress upon physical death and the ransom theory of atonement, Blake posits the setting of the mark upon Cain as the symbol of true atonement, atonement through the forgiveness of sins. This idea is implied in *The Ghost of Abel,* but made explicit in the chapter title and illustrations to Genesis 4 in Blake's illustrated Genesis manuscript. The chapter heading reads: "How Generation & Death took possession of the Natural Man & of the Forgiveness of Sins written upon the Murderers Forehead" (E 667). Each of the two designs in the Genesis manuscript provides, respectively, a literal illustration of the two parts of the chapter title. The sketch for the headpiece (Plate 50) shows the dominion of Generation and Death over the Natural Man through the traditional subjects of the finding of Abel, on the left, and Cain's flight from divine vengeance, on the right (here represented for the first time in Blake's designs by the traditional pursuing figure in the sky). In contrast to the traditional iconography of the headpiece, the tailpiece to Genesis 4 (Plate 51) adds a totally new motif, Christ planting the mark upon Cain by kissing his forehead.

Usually, illustrations of the mark of Cain show God in his aspect of justice: He usually appears in the sky, pointing toward Cain, who holds his hand up to his brow. Blake's representing the mark as an act of divine mercy has no equivalent among Blake's contemporaries. Rather, it harks back to Marten De Vos's sympathetic depiction of Cain receiving divine judgment (Plate 52). Although De Vos's figure of God is in his traditional location among the parted clouds, Cain appears to be receiving a benediction rather than a curse, reminding us that in the biblical text the mark was placed upon Cain in response to his despair (Genesis 4:13-14). Like De Vos, Blake is less concerned with the pathos of Abel's death and the terror of divine wrath than with the special relationship between the sinner and his God: but Blake goes beyond De Vos by including the possibility of forgiveness. To represent this theme of forgiveness Blake uses New Testament iconography, having the figures of Christ and Cain suggest the parable of the Prodigal Son as depicted, for instance, in De Vos's engraving of that New Testament story (Plate 53).[15] Thus Blake's Genesis manuscript follows tradition in its typological juxtaposition of Old and New Testament themes, but radically shifts the specific themes that his predecessors and contemporaries had used in order to create a new typology—a typology that stresses reconciliation rather than propitiation as the true form of atonement.

Realizing the importance of Blake's own assertion that imitation is criticism ("Annotations to Reynolds," E 632), we find that Blake selects and extends earlier aspects of pictorial traditions in order to comment upon the more orthodox use of those traditions by his contemporaries. As a rejection of the pity and wrath embodied in contemporary versions of the death of Abel and the judgment of Cain, Blake's Cain and Abel designs subvert the essentially classical values that he saw as a corrupting influence in European art. Through his poetry and designs, Blake stated that contemporary visions of Cain and Abel evoked pity and terror only to serve the needs of public morality: at such tragic scenes "The soul drinks murder & revenge, & applauds its own holiness" (*Jerusalem*, pl. 37, E 181), sacrificing the criminal to the spectator's belief in his own virtue. Creating sympathy for Cain in his own works, Blake would remind us that the first naturally born man was also the first murderer. But more than have us recognize our own affinities with Cain, Blake would have us understand the imaginative significance of his act and its consequences. In the fallen world, man is doomed to be perpetually both murderer and victim, unless he—as Jesus tells Albion in *Jerusalem*—willingly dies for another by putting off his own Selfhood through the forgiveness of sins (*Jerusalem*, pl. 96, E 253). Blake's art accomplishes this act of self-annihilation by stripping the Cain and Abel illustrations of their traditionally moralistic trappings and reclothing them in imagery that draws upon and extends the works of earlier artists. Skillfully using tradition to cast off the rotten rags of memory by inspiration, Blake makes the redemption of the art of his age nothing less than the redemption of the entire fallen world. It is therefore appropriate that, as the traditional progenitor of the arts[16] and as the ancestor of Jesus in Blake's mythology (*Jerusalem*, pl. 62, E 210–11), Cain is the iconographic exemplar of the first promise of "Peace Brotherhood and Love" (*The Ghost of Abel*, pl. 2, E 270).

NOTES

Research for this article was accomplished during my tenure as a Summer Fellow at the Henry E. Huntington Library and Art Gallery.

1.   David V. Erdman, "The Steps (Of Dance and Stone) That Order Blake's *Milton*," *Blake Studies*, 6, No. 1 (Fall 1973), 76; and Erdman's note to plate 12[15] of *Milton* in *The Illuminated Blake*, ed. David V. Erdman (Garden City, N.Y.: Doubleday, 1974), p. 231.

2.   John Caspar Lavater, *Essays on Physiognomy*, trans. Henry Hunter (London: John Murray, 1792), II, 286.

3.   *Iconographie de L'Art Chrétien* (Paris: Presses Universitaires de France, 1957), II, pt. 1, 97.

4.   See Walter Friedlaender, *David to Delacroix*, trans. Robert Goldwater (Cambridge, Mass.: Harvard Univ. Press, 1966), p. 57.

5.   Since all of these artists were members of The Sketching Society (also called The Society for the Study of Epic and Pastoral Design) founded by Chalon and his brother, it would appear that all of these watercolor

sketches were done at one of the Society's evening meetings. The fact that they are collected—in the Huntington Library's Kitto Bible—would further support this idea, as it was the Society's policy that all of the works done during a meeting would become the property of the person who was the host for the evening. According to the Society's rules, the owner of these works could not sell these works during his lifetime without the consent of the Society. Therefore, the designs were probably sold in a block after the owner's death. (See John Lewis Roget, *A History of the Old Water-Colour Society* [London: Longmans, 1891], I, 190, 278–81, 393–94.) Because of the close connection between The Sketching Society, The Old Water-Colour Society and the rival Associated Artists in Water Colours—of which Blake, Bone, and Chalon were members at different times (Roget, I, 270–71)—Blake was no doubt familiar with the five above-mentioned artists and/or their works.

Blake's membership in the Associated Artists in Water Colours is also noted by G. E. Bentley, Jr., in *Blake Records* (Oxford: Clarendon Press, 1969), p. 231, n. 2. Here Bentley is documenting Blake's participation in the Associated Artists' watercolor exhibition of 1812, but on p. 230 Bentley confusingly states that this same exhibition was held by the Water-Colour Society and that Blake belonged to this organization. Bentley is apparently using interchangeably the titles of what were actually two separate organizations. Since Bentley's note on p. 231 cites the same source that Roget uses, *A Catalogue of the Fifth Annual Exhibition of the Associated Painters in Water Colours* [London, 1812], which lists Blake's membership, it is clear that Blake was a member only of the Associated Artists (or Painters) in Water Colours.

6.   The four extant versions of this design, one of which is a pencil sketch, are listed in Robert Essick, "Finding List of Reproductions of Blake's Art," *Blake Newsletter,* 5, Nos. 1 and 2 (Summer and Fall 1971), 113. Since their composition is essentially the same, I discuss the color version in the Tate Gallery as being typical of this group.

7.   See Friedlaender, pp. 57–58.

8.   See Edmond and Jules de Goncourt, *L'Art du Dix-Huitième Siècle,* 3rd ed. (Paris: A Quantin, 1882–1883), II, 454.

9.   Erdman, "Steps that Order Blake's *Milton,*" pp. 77, 81.

10.   W. J. T. Mitchell, in "Style and Iconography in the Illustrations of Blake's *Milton,*" *Blake Studies,* 6, No.1 (Fall 1973), 64–69, reveals how other visual images in *Milton* stress the poem's central theme of prophetic brotherhood.

11.   Mitchell, pp. 52–57, suggests a similar interpretation of the crude style in *Milton,* seeing it both as a rejection of the highly finished commercial art that Blake detested and as Blake's attempt to communicate the process of vision.

12. The interpretation of the text of *The Ghost of Abel* used throughout this paper is more fully argued in my essay, "Lord Byron in the Wilderness: Biblical Tradition in Byron's *Cain* and Blake's *The Ghost of Abel*," *Modern Philology*, 72 (May 1975), 350–64.

13. We know the fleeing figure is Cain because, according to tradition, Cain hid in the thorns that were eventually used to crown Christ (Réau, p. 98).

14. Erdman, *The Illuminated Blake*, p. 381.

15. Anthony Blunt suggests that De Vos's "Prodigal Son" may be the source of *Jerusalem* plate 99 in "Blake's Pictorial Imagination," *Journal of the Warburg and Courtauld Institutes*, 6 (1943), 204.

16. Enoch, who built a city (Genesis 4:17), Jubal, the inventor of music (Genesis 4:21), and Tubalcain, "an instructor of every artificer in brass and iron" (Genesis 4:22) were all descendants of Cain.

Blake and the Art of the Book

Kay Parkhurst Easson

I N *Jerusalem* William Blake proclaims that "Man is adjoined to Man by his Emanative portion: / Who is Jerusalem" and, in the multiple roles of Jerusalem—state, city, woman—Blake also embodies the emanative role of the book as that which can adjoin one man (author) to many men (readers). The book as logos records human life: flesh becomes the word, the word becomes flesh.[1] It was especially the illustrated book, with its ideal union of word and design and its demand from its reader of unified perceptual skills, that constituted for Blake the language through which "every Word & Every Character" communicate the totally human, the form in which "All Human Forms" could be identified. Blake, however, found that the eighteenth-century illustrated book had failed to realize the potential of its form. Divisions existed between author, illustrator, engraver, printer, and publisher. Exigencies of reproduction took precedence over originality; imitation ruled over imagination. The illustrated book was "a form at variance with itself" because book production had degenerated into mechanization, its producers victimizing their productivity by hierarchical rivalries and corporate inhumanity. The book, a "narrow doleful form," mirrored the "narrow doleful form of man and art." Thus, just as Blake must liberate Jerusalem (state, city, woman, and book) from "narrowed perceptions" and "weak Visions of Time & Space, fix'd into furrows of death,"[2] so too must he free the illustrated book, one of the "Arts of life," from the domination of Urizen—who owns (and is) the "book of brass." To create anew both the illustrated book and its reader, to bring into relief the infinite form of the book hidden by fragmentations of its art, Blake created his method of illuminated printing. By the term "illuminated" Blake suggests his break with the historical

35

evolution of the book and a return to the integrated manuscript containing word and picture individually created with a minimum of mechanical intervention. In spite of his revolt against contemporary conventions, Blake was indebted to the illustrated book of his own day for much of the structure, even for some of the content, of his works in illuminated printing. He employed techniques of book illustration, both traditionally and innovatively, that he might explore and "Cast Out False Art" as preliminary and basis for embracing the "True Art" potential in the illustrated book. An examination of his techniques of book illustration and eighteenth-century examples of illustration will clarify both structural purpose and methodology in the illuminated books.

A comparison of Blake's works with typical eighteenth-century illustrated books reveals some of the sources available to Blake for illustrative techniques and shows points of contact between Blake's commercial career as copy engraver and his vocation as book artist. In his concern for the physical and visionary form of the book, Blake conceived of the book as a "Definite and Determinate Identity," as what twentieth-century illustrator Lynd Ward has called a "contained space" within which words and pictures can be "all carefully controlled."[3] Such integral book structure can be approached by identifying three types of traditional book illustration: decorative, textual, and full-page—each with its own characteristic functions. Although there is an overlap among these types in function, an illustrated book's structure is determined by the interaction of function and the book's physical properties, thereby establishing the quality and degree of correlation within the book's text and designs.

The label "decorative illustration" may seem paradoxical, particularly when decoration is considered "primarily to beautify the book in which it is used" and illustration is "primarily to elucidate the text or to place the reader in a better position for visualizing the events narrated."[4] Yet, if decoration or ornament is perceived not as meaningless detail, and illustration is not limited to mere literal explication, then "one cannot," as McKerrow says, "by any means always keep these two sorts of embellishment separate, for there are many things to be found in books which partake in some degree of the characteristics of both."[5] The convenience and wisdom of yoking decoration and illustration, moreover, reside in the practical need to identify certain structural relationships of a book's text and designs. These are revealed only through cognizance of decorative illustra-

tion as a type with specific functions, including enrichment, pattern
and rhythm, and perspective. Blake concisely defines the structural
functions of decorative illustration in his phrase "sublime Ornament." To Blake, ornamental or decorative illustration has a
motivating power: ornament simultaneously enriches the book and
compels the reader's attention; it entices the reader's enthusiastic
involvement with the book, and in so doing initiates the transmuta-
tion of his vision from reasoned analysis to imaginative participation.

To this end, Blake embellishes his poetry with various "minute
particulars," floral or geometric, formal or naturalistic.[6] The dominant mode, however, is natural decoration: flowers, trees, birds,
rainbows, leaves, vines, worms, and serpents. In looking at Blake's
decorative illustrations, one must heed their very exuberance and
variety. It is well known that Blake modified and diversified the
multiple copies of a single work. The decorative illustrations are
especially open to metamorphoses; these particulars are the most
"impermanent" of Blake's art, more subject to change, perhaps, because of their traditional associations with the Book of Nature. In
this context, the book is a "universal and publick Manuscript"
printed with God's "wond'rous Works."[7] Because Blake opposes
"One God, One Law," mathematical proportion, and single vision,
he likewise opposes stock printer's ornaments and exactly repeatable
pictorial statements, furnishing instead infinitely varied vegetable
forms. Blake's decorations are living ornaments in marked contrast
to the stock device (reproduced below) that closes, for example, both

the twelfth edition of Hayley's *Triumphs of Temper* (1803) and the
third volume of Hayley's *Life of Cowper* (1804). Both of Hayley's
works were printed by Joseph Seagrave, who used this small woodcut vignette without regard to the literary context in which it appears. Such insensitivity and uniform repeatability is never found in
Blake's own books. The tailpiece to *America* (Plate 54) shows Blake's
play upon stock printers' ornaments of the very type used by Seagrave. In it a serpent, with "FINIS" etched in white line on his body,
twines amidst thorny but blossoming vines. At first glance, the illustration appears conventional and ornamental in configuration and

function. However, closer inspection discloses that Blake has humanized this vegetable device: two tiny human figures people the vines. (A third human figure flies or dives out of the ornament.) This decorative illustration, with its "intimations of life," underlines the freedom implicit in *America* and calls attention to the idea that Blake, in his poetry and designs, is making repeatable statements, but statements repeatable in, and because of, their living forms. Pattern and rhythm in Blake's decorations depend as much upon cessation or interruption of pattern as upon its repetition.

Blake appeals to his reader's expectations of pattern, as when he has a bird of paradise make intermittent appearances in *Songs of Innocence and of Experience,* or when he has a river flow, again intermittently and not consistently in all copies, at the base of the *Songs,* or when he decorates *Milton* with stars and rainbows, or when he pictures a moon-arc throughout *Jerusalem.* To count the number of occurrences of these motifs may be helpful in some cases, but their intermittent and various appearance is more significant. Blake's reader establishes a familiarity with the bird, river, star, rainbow, or moon-arc, but the lack of mechanical uniformity prevents him from anticipating them as he turns a new page. When the reader does see a decoration, he can see it not as mere embellishment but as a potentially symbolic unit of the book. Variety within unity is the structural paradigm for all the illuminated books, and the reader cannot abstract general patterns from an isolated instance.

Among the many types of decorative illustrations, frames, rules, and borders have the greatest architectural and psychological importance.[8] Traditionally, these constructions tend to inflate the importance of design over text and to separate them. Baskerville's 1761 *Select Fables of Esop* is an example of a book in which the division between picture and word, necessitated by eighteenth-century printing technology, is further emphasized by framing devices. To accompany each fable with an illustration on text pages would have been an expensive procedure, so small medallion cuts representing each fable were separated from the text and combined in varying ways on a full-page plate format. Each illustration or miniature is framed and then placed within various schemes of frames and ornaments. In one of these full-page plates (Plate 55) are miniature designs within square frames at each corner of the plate; these in turn frame the center miniature, itself framed by an elaborate ornament. In this way, the collection of miniatures is more important than the relationships between individual designs and the text. Frames, rules, and borders can also alter perspective by indicating space and depth around and within the miniature. A design by Thomas Stothard from the tenth (1799) edition of Hayley's *Triumphs of Temper* (Plate 56) is an oval miniature backed by a patterned rectangle with ornamental drapery at the top. The frame increases the depth of the design, thus emphasizing the pensive woman and focusing our attention on her. By frame, rule, or border, the two-dimensional text page is complemented with a three-dimensional illusion, as in the standard motif where the design is conceived as something seen through a window. Richard Bentley, in his *Designs... for the Poems of Mr. T. Gray* (1753), makes use of a wide variety of elaborate frames. His full-page plate introducing the "Ode on the Death of a Favorite Cat" (Plate 57) compels the reader to perceive the household cat through a "window" formed "in mock solemnity by the rich culture of fashionable eighteenth-century England."[9]

Ultimately, these constructions can influence the spaces within and without the design; the space within is "not merely *de*fined but *con*fined—isolated—uninvaded. Inside lies meaning; the space outside means nothing."[10] Maria Flaxman's cave is an integral part of her design, engraved by Blake for the twelfth edition of Hayley's *Triumphs of Temper* (1803), but it also serves as a three-sided frame for the woman entering it (Plate 58). The cave surrounding Bentley's tailpiece (Plate 59) to Gray's "Ode" further emphasizes the cave as a framing device. In both cases, the cave creates an uninvaded, confined space, but it is also a spiritual center within which lies meaning. Blake, however, alters the traditional function of frames in his illustration to "The Dog" in Hayley's 1802 *Designs to a Series of Ballads* (Plate 60). Although architecturally rigid, the frame contains emblematic human figures with a representational, and potentially iconographic, significance beyond the design it surrounds. It is tempting to see Blake commenting here on the quality of Hayley's poetry: Blake's frame has more meaning than the poem it accompanies. Blake frequently manipulates meaning via frames, as when his designs frame, and sometimes dominate, the texts of Young and Gray, or when the biblical text provides a conceptual frame as in the Job designs. It is in the Job that the eighteenth-century conventions of framing devices reach their most highly developed form and transcend the practical and decorative functions to which they are usually restricted.

Blake exploits the possibilities of frames, rules, and borders in the illuminated books, and while his frames have similarities to those in other eighteenth-century books, they depart from traditional forms in their variety and structural significance. In some instances the text is framed by the design, as when two wispy trees form an arch or portal sheltering child, lamb, and poem in "The Lamb," or when a healthy, stout, thorny rose has the strength to encircle the words of "The Sick Rose." At other times Blake allows the text area to frame one side of the illustration, as in plates 16 and 24 of *The Marriage of Heaven and Hell* and in "The Little Boy lost" and "The Little Boy found" of *Songs of Innocence.* This format creates a definite boundary between word and picture. The division seems particularly appropriate for two poems about a little boy "lost in the lonely fen," and for imprisoned figures or the bestial Nebuchadnezzar in *The Marriage.* The reader cannot help the little boy, distant and alone, and it would be wise to keep one's distance from prisons and Nebuchadnezzar. A unique frame surrounding both text and design appears on pl. 30 of *Milton,* copy A, appropriately depicting the "pleasant / Mild Shadow above: beneath: & on all sides round" (E 129), the place "called Beulah" which the text describes. The minimally indicated forms moving up and around the frame are the emanations given this habitation "because the Life of Man [portrayed in the design] was too exceeding unbounded." While the conjunction of frame, text, and design may suggest a Day of Judgment, as David Erdman has pointed out,[11] at the same time it manifests "Mental forms Creating," the potential forms of creation bounding the life of man until his awakening in the full "fury of Poetic Inspiration" to bind them into a work of art. Usually a frame "finishes" a work of art; Blake's frame added to this plate in *Milton,* a poem about poets and poems, begins the work of art.

Blake also uses frames which are a part of the design itself. The trees of the frontispiece to *There is No Natural Religion* (series a) enclose on three sides the seated man and woman and the two standing youths, showing the cavelike limitations of "organic perceptions." Plate 11 of *The Marriage of Heaven and Hell* illustrates the "ancient Poets" animating "all sensible objects with Gods or Geniuses" (E 37). Their animations are framed in copy I by a cave.

As the reader looks into Blake's cave and out of his own perceptual "cave," he will come to understand that he may have been living by natural religion and has forgotten that "all deities reside in the human breast." The cave-frame of the frontispiece to *Visions of the Daughters of Albion* (Plate 61) indicates the reader's perspective; the reader gazes at and penetrates into the cave of the bound and terrified figures. The space of the design is defined by the frame, as in traditional book illustration. But given the iconographic dimensions of the cave in Blake's pictorial vocabulary, our "descent" into this frontispiece is also a descent into the enchained minds of the cave's inhabitants. Blake's *Visions* raises the question of guilt and innocence: Blake's audience, as his frontispiece indicates, should not be spared from any indictment. Each of these "cave" frames comments upon the nature of meaning: does meaning lie inside or outside? Blake, in each case, has the cave as a mediating device between reader and design, commenting on both. Thus, the frame projects meaning both within and without, giving a space to the inhabitants of the design and an indictment to the reader: "for Man has closed himself up, till he sees all things thro' narrow chinks of his cavern" (E 39). If, however, the reader can see the cave enclosure as the objective form of his own perceptual limitations, then he can cause "the inside of the cave to be infinite" and discover the meaning of Blake's illuminated books, themselves formed of words and pictures rising above the cavelike recesses of copperplates etched in relief. In Blake's own illustrated books, a traditional framing device is invested with iconographic importance, the full meaning of which becomes clear only when we see the way he has adopted and revitalized the conventions of his age.

Textual illustrations are those which are inserted into the text or connected closely to the book's format: headpiece, footpiece, tailpiece, marginal design, column picture, title page device, motto, dedication device. The traditional function of these illustrations is to underscore visually the major divisions of a book or to directly picture some specific object named therein. When illustrations merely translate word into design, the reader can conceive of text and picture as virtually identical in meaning. The written word could be replaced by the picture, or vice versa, but both together intensify and clarify meaning. J. T. Stanley's 1796 translation of Gottfried Burger's *Leonora,* with frontispiece, head, and tailpiece designed by Blake and engraved by Perry, is a good example of direct translation. Both head and tailpiece are integrated with the two-dimensional text page in "papyrus style" without background or frame. The tailpiece, however, has a slight "parchment style" effect due to the stippled background.[12] In the headpiece Blake represents the initial homecoming scene; in the tailpiece he pictures the final homecoming and the emergence of Leonora from her dream. Both designs are literal translations; however, Blake's structural sense, in reinforcing the poem's symmetrical structure by the parallel content of his designs, becomes evident when his designs are compared with those in the German text, "sewed up with the translation" in some copies of *Leonora*. The "German" headpiece, designed and engraved by J. Harding, depicts William (the chief male character in the poem) and his horse resting from the battle faintly indicated in the background—perhaps William is on his way home or has lost his way. The tailpiece, also by Harding, shows an insipid cherub sleeping beside his extinguished torch, no doubt intended to convey the end, the "extinction," of the poem. Unlike Blake's illustrations, Harding's efforts neither picture important events in the narrative nor underscore the basic structure of the poem.

In his illuminated books Blake frequently capitalizes on the equation of text and design existing in the literal translation of an image from one medium into the other. Blake executes illustrations which, on the surface, seem to have a literal equality with the text, but symbolically interrelate with it. The illustration to "The Lamb," for example, pictures the scene of the poem: child speaking to lamb. However, the intertwined bower of foliage goes beyond literal translation and connotes more than the words of the poem. In other cases, the design gives less information than the text. In Principle 4 of *All Religions Are One*, for example, the design shows a traveler; the text extends the concept of traveling to the knowledge that one can acquire on a journey and then moves from traveling to syllogistic confirmation of the existence of Poetic Genius. Then, there can be instances of complex play upon the literal equivalent. Blake's footpiece design of his cottage at Felpham, *Milton*, pl. 36, gives a literal basis for concepts developed in the text. Its cartoonlike whimsy, generically less than the epic lines it illustrates, stresses the ground (footpiece) of this world in relation to poetic inspiration.

Blake's textual illustrations should be studied with full awareness of their relationship to the traditional functions of literal illustration. This should not, however, be allowed to exclude another traditional, though less frequently discussed, function of textual illustration—the establishment of tension between text and design. In these cases the reader isolates a design to ascertain its meaning or its textual referent. Paradoxically, when the reader does this he is impelled to return to the text for meaning. Each has a share in the totality of a book's meaning; neither text nor design can alone impart as much meaning as text and design together. Plate 62 of *Jerusalem* is a good instance of this technique, for it is not only a verbal–visual pun on the book as "Human Form" with its headpiece the head of a giant, its footpiece his feet, but the giant's body is missing—replaced by the page of text he holds—so that the reader must resolve the tension and imaginatively reconstruct the bodily links between head and foot. Blake implies that books are all too frequently "analytics," their bodies (and the bodies of their authors and readers) "rent away and dissipated" in "incoherent despair." Erdman correctly identifies the giant as a victim but only sees him as one victim, Luvah. He relates the design to the lines on the plate describing Luvah's cloud which bursts forth "in streams of blood upon the heaven" when the "Lamb of God" speaks.[13] Such an interpretation seems to narrow Blake's implications. The plate refers to all victims—Los, Luvah, Albion, reader, and book. On this plate a "Giant form," which Blake displays to his public in *Jerusalem,* is painfully disembodied. In order that the reader (the tiny figure gazing up at the giant) does not become what he beholds, Blake pictures the fires of intellectual thought and "printing in the infernal method" just above the giant's feet. The potential for integration and resurrection is further indicated by the peacock feathers rayed about the giant's head. The message, evidently, is that a book, a "Giant form," can be "eyed as the peacock" or single in vision; it depends on the being who holds, reads, and creates it. To (re)create this plate humanly, one must move beyond the plate and into the whole of the *Jerusalem* it images. Together text and design will provide the entire body of narrative and reader.

Blake achieves another verbal–visual pun on traditional illustrative techniques by the text–design relationships of *America* plates 10 and 12. His depiction of Urizen on plate ten in a headpiece and Orc on plate twelve in a tailpiece not only reiterates the significance of Urizen as a sky god who with "stony roof" rules the head, the rational functions, and the significance of Orc as an earthbound rebel from the "flames of hell," but also provides contrasts basic to the structure of *America.* Each plate is juxtaposed ironically to its text: Urizen reigns over the words of Orc's self-proclamation on plate ten and Orc rises "in terrible birth" to the loud alarms of the "terrible blasts" of Albion's Angel's trumpets on plate twelve. By this ironic juxtaposition, and by the mirrored stances of the protagonists, Blake visualizes the peril of extreme positions. As E. J. Rose perceptively states, Orc and Urizen are the "double Spectres Self Accurst." Neither Urizen, "decadent and overripe," nor the "immaturity or unripeness" of Orc is a proper catalyst for freedom.[14] Moreover, the textual separation of plates 10 and 12 is equivalent to the rhetorical device of *diacope,* the separation of elements of a compound word by another word or words. Urizen and Orc are this compound, the head and tail of all revolutions. Plate 11 depicts what gets caught within the revolutionary compound: an infant in a womb-tomb of grain. While showing an infant victim of Urizen and Orc, the double spectres of fixed perception, plate 11 also declares by its womb-fertility imagery that Urizen and Orc do not have to be fixed in position. A true revolution can be had by realizing that the lines of plate 10 should be applicable to its illustration—the head, Urizen, should learn a "fiery joy." And the rebellious Orc should learn to temper his physical energies in the fires of intellect. Blake shows disapproval of war's "Fury! rage! madness!" that infest all they touch, and he states in the entirety of *America* what plates 10, 11, and 12 picture in microcosm: the true revolution must be in human perception, not in bodily combat.

A more traditional book with text-design tension is Joseph Ritson's *A Select Collection of English Songs* (1783). This work, in three volumes with seventeen plates, exemplifies the eighteenth century's methodical disposition to have symmetrical head and tailpieces, in this case preceding and following each song in identical size and shape. Given the book's comfortable structural symmetry, one might expect literal translation in the designs, but such expectations are soon confounded. While the headpiece illustrating Class I, Love-Songs, does literally depict the lover in supplication to Chloris, as related in the poem, the Class I tailpiece illustration depicts not the song it immediately follows, number 69, but number 65. In examination of the tailpiece, therefore, the reader is pulled away from the last song to find the illustration's referent, eventually realizing that the illustration not only literally renders the content of one song but figuratively emphasizes one theme of its class—pain, melancholy, or

despair at the loss of love. The Class I tailpiece is an effective closure, heightening the effect of the entire class of songs of which it is
part. The text–design tensions in Blake's illuminated books, while
far more complex than that allowed by Ritson's format, are not
without precedent in more conventional eighteenth-century illustration.

The Book of Thel is about beginnings and endings. Like Ritson, it
relies on a structural tension between head and tailpieces. Moreover,
it is a work refuting the linear concept of progression from beginning to end. Nevertheless, the reader of *Thel* is led, like Thel, to
progress in anticipation of answers at the end. The end of the book,
however, provides only the questions of Thel's own grave; Thel sees
her end, her death, but flees back into the vales of Har. The reader,
at the same instant, reaches the end of the work, but is pointed back
into it by the tongue of the tailpiece serpent. In a sense, both Thel
and the reader have beginnings and endings, yet lack conclusions, as
the relationship between the title page (Plate 62) and tailpiece indicates. The first contains a version of an architectural portal, a door
into the world of the book, conventional to the title page genre.
Thel's portal, a slender tree arching up and over the letters of the
title and the design, both opens into the book and leaves the book
open, for the tailpiece serpent and the final words of text pull Thel
and the reader back to the portal, back to the beginning. It would be
a mistake, however, to conceive of this movement as a simple cycle;
Blake opposes dull rounds. The ending of *Thel* resides in the beginning only in the sense that the achievement of the end of any exploration requires an understanding of beginnings. The balanced
structure of *Thel*—title page, one plate; Part I, two plates with headpiece and tailpiece; Part II, one plate with decoration; Part III, two
plates with headpiece and tailpiece; Part IV, one plate with
tailpiece—supports this interpretation. The movement of the "left
side" of the balance is into the book, dictated by the title page portal
and reinforced by the man with shield and pointing sword in the
headpiece to Part I, while the right side moves in a contrary direction under the guidance of the tailpiece serpent. These contrary
movements are structural equivalents to the rhetorical device of
chiasmus, a balance with inversion of one side of the balance. The
midpoint of *Thel* is the Book II plate where the Cloud describes to
Thel the potential within a marriage of contraries—Cloud and Dew
"link'd in a golden band, / ... walk united, bearing food to all ...

[their] tender flowers" (E 4). This is the emotional and visionary climax of *Thel,* and it is appropriately illustrated on the title page and underscored by the simultaneous suggestions of both innocence and experience of the tailpiece children and serpent. In the very structure of *The Book of Thel,* Blake proclaims that "Without Contraries is no progression." But progression is not merely linear, because to go from beginning to end necessitates leaving behind the beginning; progression should not be negation of beginning, but recognition of the contraries of end and beginning, life and death. In *The Book of Thel,* the reader standing at the title page portal can embrace the contraries of end and beginning. He enters the door of life via the door of death described on the last page of text. These metaphors of the life of man implicit in the structure of *Thel* also find embodiment in the frontispiece to *Jerusalem.* There the traditional portal opening to a book becomes a vision of a descent into the grave and into a labyrinthine text where the reader discovers that the door of death is simultaneously the door of rebirth into visionary perception.

Full-page illustration is structurally the most complex of the three categories of illustration, since full-page illustrations are physically detached from the text and function to separate the reader from the text he is reading. Once the detachment occurs, however, full-page illustrations can lead the reader back into the text with new perspectives and reorient his reading by way of introduction, dedication, foreshadowing, summary, or recapitulation—the traditional functions of frontispieces or full-page illustrations which preface major divisions in a book. The previously discussed full-page plate of medallion cuts in Baskerville's *Fables of Esop* (Plate 55) is a recapitulation illustration; with diagrammatic emphasis, the plate brings together and recapitulates five separate fables. The frontispiece to the first illustrated edition (1688) of *Paradise Lost,* with designs by Medina engraved by Burgess, is a standard portrait frontispiece, introducing the reader to Milton. Medina also supplies full-page designs to introduce each of the twelve books of the poem, serving to foreshadow or, in some cases, to epitomize the content of the books they precede. Such epitome designs are a summary device, bringing together several scenes in one picture and, in the conjunction, portraying actions that happen successively in the text as happening simultaneously. In the illuminated books Blake exploits the complete range of functions of full-page illustration; for example, he has many portrait frontispieces, including those to *All Religions Are One, Songs of Innocence and of Experience, Europe, The Book of Los, The Song of Los,* and *Jerusalem.* Occasionally Blake blends the function of frontispiece with title page to have portrait title pages introducing a work, as in *The Book of Urizen* and *Milton.*

Whether internal full-page designs refer us back to the preceding section of a book or direct us forward into the next, they emphatically punctuate a book, often serving as essential structural indicators. Their effect, in any given work, is determined by content, by placement, and by their iconographic relationships to the text they accompany. The full-page illustrations in *The Book of Urizen* and *Jerusalem* function antithetically. No two of the seven copies of *Urizen* have the plates in the same arrangement, mostly due to changes in the placement of the full-page designs. Despite the differing order of text plates in copies A and C of *Jerusalem,* none of the eight known copies (three of them posthumous) varies in the positions of the full-page illustrations. These designs in *Jerusalem* are strong structural indicators, each having a specific place in Blake's symmetrical work of four books in one hundred plates: a frontispiece introduces the entire work, full-page illustrations preface each chapter (and at the same time close each), and a full-page design closes the entire work. Thus, when Blake planned internal full-page illustrations in his work of the mid-1790s, he tended to vary their locations within the individual copies of the work and hence to vary the semantics of individual copies. The radical shifting of full-page plates in *Urizen* is an ironic counterpart to the rigidity Urizen attempts to impose, while the full-page illustrations to *Jerusalem* are the structural equivalents to those "distinct sharp, and wirey" (E 540) bounding lines Blake embodies in almost all his nineteenth-century productions.

The arrangement of Blake's *Europe* is constant except for the position of its two internal full-page plates—pl. 9, "Famine," and pl. 10, "Plague."[15] By analyzing the position of the plates in different copies, their varying structural relationships can be identified. Of the twelve known complete copies of *Europe,* five have the "standard" arrangement (copies D–G, and posthumous copy M) with plates 9 and 10 together in that order. In three copies (I, K–L), plates 9 and 10 are together, but they are transposed—10 preceding 9—and in a different location in copy I than in K and L. Four copies have plates 9 and 10 separated: copies A–C and H move plate 10 to a position between plates 14 and 15. The two plates depict what

Michael Tolley terms the "miseries possible to mortal men," the consequences of war.[16] Working in conjunction, plates 9 and 10 act as an extraordinarily strong interruption in the text. They interrupt the reader's participation in the text and bring the reader "down" from the symbolic and mythic realm of the text (plates 8 and 11, in the standard order) to earthborn torments.

The transposition of plates 9 and 10, in three copies, could be due to Blake's momentary perception of a causal relationship—plague resulting in eventual famine—especially in copies K and L. In copy I the two plates separate, in an odd way, the two plates of the Preludium. Plate 4 ends with the "prolific pains" of the "nameless shadowy female." Plate 5 continues her speech; she asks: "And who shall bind the infinite with an eternal band? / To compass it with swaddling bands?" Plates 9 and 10, in separating plates 4 and 5, still work to emphasize geographic and mental realms and the transposition, plate 10 following plate 4, reflects appropriately the words of plates 4 and 5—the "prolific pains" of "Plague" and the "devouring" and binding of "Famine." In copies K and L, plates 9 and 10 (transposed) appear between plates 5 and 6, at the end of the Preludium and before the Prophecy. With this placement, plates 9 and 10 shift the emphasis to the prophetic action; they answer or fulfill the Preludium's introductory remarks and show the necessity for prophecy. Since plate 9 appears next to plate 6, Blake may be correlating the dead infant in this full-page design with the living "secret child" of plate 6. The four copies of *Europe* that have plates 9 and 10 in separate locations lose the strength of the two-plate division, but even a single full-page illustration divides. In the arrangement of copies A–C and H, plate 10 forecasts and depicts the "voices of despair" in London's streets, described on plate 15. Although Blake exercises freedom in his arrangements of the full-page designs in *Europe,* he minutely articulates new expanses with each arrangement.

The Song of Los contains a complete spectrum of full-page illustrations: a frontispiece, an internal full-page plate, and a full-page closure plate—the last an unusual feature rarely found in conventional illustrated books. *The Song of Los* has both a *chiasmus* structure, similar to that of *The Book of Thel,* and an asymmetrical structure created by the full-page illustrations. The frontispiece and three plates precede the full-page divider (plate 5) and three plates (including the full-page closure design) follow it.[17] The internal symmetry is counteracted by the frontispiece, which stands outside the work and thus governs the reader's perspective on the entire work. Within this structure each full-page illustration has special functions which impart additional significance to the overall structure. The frontispiece (Plate 63) depicts a kneeling figure worshipping at a book and altar, his back to the reader. He is clothed in white in contrast to the night of "dark delusion" behind him. He is usually identified as Urizen with "his woven darkness above," a large globe (or ironically a sun) printed with chaotic, illegible markings. In copies A, B, D, and E, a triangular wedge of darkness between two rays of the globe frames the kneeling figure and approximately parallels the shape of his body. This wedge acts as a perspective cue to the reader, drawing the eye from the figure upward to the mysterious globe and into the work as a whole. While the reader is closed off from the work by the back of Urizen, he is forced by the compositional arrangement to attend to the globe and its mystery.

The frontispiece is a portrait of the artist—or rather of what the artist should not be. Urizen as author creates an incoherent world-book with the fearful potential to transform its readers into what they behold. The central full-page design on plate 5 (Plate 64) of a king and queen divides the reader's point of view from the "reality" of the Africa and Asia sections of the poem because of its fairyland suggestions. Nevertheless, since "Shakespeare's Fairies . . . are the rulers of the vegetable world," their geography is quite in accordance with the ending of Africa, where Har and Heva shrink into "reptile flesh," and with the beginning of Asia, where the Kings of that continent are depicted as carnivores in "ancient woven" dens. Thus, plate 5 concurrently divides and integrates *The Song of Los.* Plate 5 depicts a marriage, Africa and Asia should be wed, but just as all is not bliss in the fairy realm (the king looks glum and his queen sleeps), Africa and Asia are structurally divorced by this plate. The full-page closure design (Plate 65) is in some respects an inversion of the frontispiece. On plate 8, Los leans on his mallet in a frontal position facing back into the book, surveying or protecting a partially cleared globe. A directional indicator, parallel to that on the frontispiece, is formed on this plate by the triangular arrangement of Los's legs above the globe—a human frame contrasting with the frame of the dark triangle on the frontispiece. The eye of the reader now moves up from the globe to Los, hence focusing not on the globe as on the frontispiece, but on the human form. This plate is also a portrait of the artist. In this version, however, Los as author frames and creates the world-book and the reader's perspective. Thus, the last plate of the book can establish a new beginning. The reader can now reread *The Song of Los* from the imaginative perspective of Los—the contrary to the constricted, Urizenic perspective of the frontispiece.

The Song of Los gives its readers two worlds and two books: the fallen world of Africa and Asia caused by the mental state pictured on the frontispiece, and the potential world of imaginative creation embodied in the final design. As a commentary on the art of the book, the frontispiece shows the state of the eighteenth-century book as Blake knew it. He knew the eighteenth-century book as a rigid form capable of binding human potential into "finite inflexible organs," but he employed, in order to go beyond, the formal conventions of book illustration: decorative illustration, textual illustration, and full-page illustration. Blake's readers, then, by recognizing the functions of illustrated book conventions, can ascertain more completely the interrelationships of text and design by which William Blake's books are Arts of Life for the life of man.

NOTES

1.   See John Lewis, *Anatomy of Printing: The Influence of Art and History on its Design* (London: Faber and Faber, 1970), pp. 56, 81–3, for illustrations of the humanistic alphabet wherein the book as human body finds one of its most literal expressions. Lewis describes the practice of relating the form of capital letters to human proportions. See also Blake's pencil sketch of "Hebrew Characters Using the Human Form" in *Pencil Drawings by William Blake,* ed. Geoffrey Keynes (London: Nonesuch Press, 1927), no. 27.

2.   The image here has traditional associations with writing. Ernst Robert Curtius, *European Literature and the Latin Middle Ages,* trans.Willard R. Trask (New York: Pantheon, 1953), p. 313, states that as "early as Plato, we find the comparison between the dressing of a field and writing." Curtius goes on to cite the referent of "to plough" as "to write," the line of writing as "a furrow," the ink as "black seed." In this passage from *Jerusalem* (E 196), the furrows are also the incised or etched lines of the intaglio process. Blake frequently used imagery with printing or writing equivalencies: ploughing, wine-press, cave, weaving, serpent, worm.

3. "The Illustrator and the Book," *Graphic Forms: The Arts as Related to the Book* (Cambridge, Mass.: Harvard Univ. Press, 1949), p. 60.

4. Ronald B. McKerrow, *An Introduction to Bibliography for Literary Students,* 2nd printing, with corrections (Oxford: Clarendon Press, 1928), p. 109.

5. McKerrow, p. 109.

6. Ruari McLean, in *Victorian Book Design and Colour Printing,* 2nd ed. (Berkeley and Los Angeles: Univ. of California Press, 1972), esp. pp. 129–30, defines the many styles of ornament.

7. Curtius surveys the metaphor on pp. 319–26 of his work. Thomas Browne identifies nature as a universal manuscript in *Religio Laici* (1643), Pt. I, Chap. 15. In *Paradise Lost,* Bk. VIII, line 67, Raphael tells Adam that "Heav'n / Is as the Book of God before thee set, Wherein to read his wond'rous Works."

8. See Bertand H. Bronson, *Printing as an Index of Taste in Eighteenth Century England* (New York: The New York Public Library, 1958), p. 22.

9. Irene Tayler, *Blake's Illustrations to the Poems of Gray* (Princeton: Princeton Univ. Press, 1971), p. 59.

10. Bronson, p. 22.

11. *The Illuminated Blake* (Garden City, New York: Anchor, 1974), p. 249.

12. In "papyrus style," originating in ancient papyrus rolls, the design shares the same neutral ground with the written characters. In "parchment style" the design is separated from the text by a frame or border. Historically, the separation of miniature from text was heightened by the sophistication of its scenic background details. These types are discussed in Kurt Weitzmann, *Illustrations in Roll and Codex: A Study of the Origin and Method of Text Illustration* (Princeton: Princeton Univ. Press, 1947), and in David Bland, *A History of Book Illustration* (Berkeley and Los Angeles: Univ. of Calif. Press, 1969).

13. *The Illuminated Blake,* p. 341.

14. "Good-bye to Orc and All That," *Blake Studies,* 4 (1972), 135–51.

15. The designs are given these titles by George Cumberland in copy D. The arrangements of plates set forth here are based on Bentley, *Blake Books.*

16. "*Europe:* 'to those ychain'd in sleep,'" in *Blake's Visionary Forms Dramatic,* ed. David V. Erdman and John E. Grant (Princeton: Princeton Univ. Press, 1970), p. 130.

17. According to Bentley, *Blake Books,* p. 358, of the five known copies of *The Song of Los,* copies A and D have the "standard" arrangement. Copy B, foliated by Blake but now loose, once had the standard order but included impressions of "The Accusers," "Joseph of Arimathea," and *America* pl. d. Copy C has the following arrangement: 1, 8, 2–4, 6, 7, 5. I

have not considered this arrangement here since it seems to represent a mistake, not a purposeful ordering of the plates. Two frontispieces would be a highly unusual technique of book illustration, and even in his innovations, Blake observes the basic conventions of book structure. Copy E was disbound in 1903 and its present arrangement of pls. 1–3, 8, 4, 6, 5, 7 has no authority.

Physiognomy, Phrenology, and Blake's Visionary Heads

Anne K. Mellor

THE belief that physical matter, including the human body, is shaped and controlled by invisible spiritual powers was widespread in Europe and England in the late eighteenth century. Whether these unseen forces were described in terms of Mesmer's fluids, Swedenborg's correspondences, Newton's gravity, astrological influences, electricity, magnetism, or fire, their existence was commonly assumed.[1] Since belief in the presence of such invisible forces was further associated with an affirmation both of God's divine will and controlling providence and of man's free will, it powerfully opposed the implicit materialism and determinism of Locke's mechanist psychology, which held that man's intellectual and moral ideas were wholly derived from physical sensations. Blake's hostility to Locke and his sympathy for Swedenborg, Jacob Boehme, Paracelsus, and other Neoplatonist or "spiritualist" thinkers is well known. Here I wish to draw attention to the influence upon Blake's thought and art of another idealist system—Lavater's physiognomy—and of its more empirical offspring—Spurzheim's phrenology.

Johann Caspar Lavater, a Zwinglian minister and lifelong friend of Henry Fuseli, founded the so-called science of physiognomy in 1772 with the publication at Leipzig of his small treatise "On Physiognomy." By 1778, he had published his mammoth four-volume study, *Physiognomische Fragmente zur Beförderung der Menschenkenntnis und Menschenliebe.* The first English translation of this work was sponsored by Fuseli and appeared in London between 1789 and 1798. Entitled *Essays on Physiognomy, Designed to Promote the Knowledge and the Love of Mankind,* and translated by Henry Hunter, this edition was beautifully printed and lavishly illustrated in five volumes. Fuseli's contributions to this edition were great: he conceived the project, found the publisher, supervised and corrected the translation, made certain that the engravings were of the highest quality, contributed many of his own illustrations, and wrote a seminal Advertisement proclaiming the truth of the science of physiognomy. Blake certainly knew this book, since he engraved four of the plates for the first volume.[2] Moreover, Blake's earlier, enthusiastic reading[3] of Fuseli's translation of Lavater's *Aphorisms on Man* (1788) would have prepared him for Lavater's larger work, since the Aphorisms "contained, in encapsulated form, some of the underlying theories of [Lavater's] physiognomical approach."[4] And in any case, it would have been difficult for Blake to avoid his close friend Fuseli's enthusiasm for Lavater's physiognomical studies. Fuseli frequently used Lavater's physiognomic models in his art, in conjunction with Le Brun's patterns for the visual expression of the passions, as Peter Tomory has shown.[5] And Blake borrowed the figure of Abel from one of Fuseli's illustrations for Lavater's *Essays on Physiognomy*, "The Death of Abel," for his figure of Adam in his "God Creating Adam." If Blake did not actually read all five royal quarto volumes of Hunter's translation of Lavater's *Essays on Physiognomy*, he might have read one of the many abridged, cheaper translations available by 1802, perhaps the one-volume edition by his acquaintance Thomas Holcroft, which also contained Lavater's posthumous "One Hundred Physiognomical Rules."[6]

In the *Essays on Physiognomy*, Lavater laid down the axioms of his new "science": (1) man's innate moral and intellectual powers determine his outward appearance, hence (2) an observer can ascertain the character of a person by carefully studying his face, features, and form. Hunter translates Lavater's definition of his new science thus:

> By Physiognomy then I mean, the talent of discovering the interior of Man by his exterior—of perceiving by certain natural signs, what does not immediately strike the senses....Physiognomy would accordingly be, the Science of discovering the relation between the exterior and the interior—between the visible surface and the invisible spirit which it covers—between the animated, perceptible matter, and the imperceptible principle which impresses this character of life upon it—between the apparent effect, and the concealed cause which produces it.[7]

Since Lavater believed that man's moral and intellectual faculties housed themselves in the human head, his observations focused upon the shape of the skull, the form of the forehead, and the conformation and expression of the facial features. As he said, "the intellectual life, the powers of human understanding, are peculiarly manifested in the conformation and position of the bones of the head; and particularly of the forehead," while "the moral life of man discovers itself principally in the face" (L I, 17). Hence, "the face is the representative or the summary of all the three divisions. The forehead, down to the eyebrows, the mirror of intelligence: The nose and cheeks, the mirror of the moral life: The mouth and chin, the mirror of the animal life; while the eye would be the centre and summary of the whole" (L I, 18). Although he focused his attention primarily upon the face and head, Lavater also acknowledged the role of gestures, habitual movements, and even dress, housing, and furniture in the manifestation of human character. As he asserted,

> Nature forms us, but we transform her work; and this very metamorphosis becomes a second nature. Placed in a vast Universe, Man forms for himself a little separate world which he fortifies, limits, arranges according to his own fancy, and in which his image is easily to be traced. (L I, 25)

Lavater succinctly concludes, *"Our imagination operates upon our physiognomy"* (L IIIA, 182).

Lavater supported these assertions with numerous citations from biblical, classical, and modern authorities, from Solomon, Pliny, and Cicero to Montaigne, Leibnitz, and Herder, and with hundreds of character analyses based on portraits and personal observations. Throughout his writings, he insists that physiognomy is a science, that basic physiognomical perceptions (what Lavater calls "Physiognomical Tact" [L I, 93]) are universally shared, and that his empirical observations can be reduced to a set of teachable rules and a system of valid classifications. But he also argues that the physiognomist, like the artist, needs genius and intuition to do his work well. Lavater's description of the "true physiognomist" shows how much of his practice depended on innate abilities rather than on acquirable skills:

> he must have the advantage of a good figure, a well proportioned body, a delicate organization, senses capable of being easily

moved, and of faithfully transmitting to the soul the impression
of external objects; above all, he must have a quick, penetrating,
and just eye. (L I, 119–20)

Moreover, the true physiognomist must have "maturity of judgment," "a strong and lively imagination, a quick and penetrating
understanding," and the ability to create a new vocabulary capable
of expressing his discoveries in an "exact, agreeable, natural, and
intelligible" language (L I, 119–20). He must further possess sufficient knowledge of anatomy, physiology, and drawing to enable him
to communicate his observations visually. Lavater concludes,

> he must possess a soul firm, yet gentle, innocent and calm; a heart
> exempted from the dominion of the ruder passions, and all
> whose various windings are well known to himself. No one can
> comprehend the expression of generosity, can distinguish the
> signs which announce a great quality, unless he himself is gener-
> ous, animated with noble sentiments, and capable of performing
> great actions. (L I, 126)

No wonder tnat so few "true physiognomists" have appeared to
confirm or disprove Lavater's system! For, as Lavater himself confessed, "physiognomy is a poetic feeling, which perceives causes and
effects" (L IIB, 443).

Lavater's science of physiognomy was, of course, a branch of
philosophical idealism. Since Lavater believed that the physical body
manifested spiritual qualities, he held that an improvement of man's
moral character would render his body more beautiful. Ultimately,
Lavater hoped, his physiognomical studies would enable men more
quickly and correctly to assess and utilize their innate abilities, to
eliminate or curb their evil tendencies, and thus to promote the
improvement of society. As his title insists, these are essays "Designed to Promote the Knowledge and the Love of Mankind."

Later, I will discuss some possible uses of Lavater's physiognomical studies in Blake's Visionary Heads. Here we should note that
Blake, like many of his contemporaries, shared Lavater's belief that
the external form of a man reveals his internal qualities. As he wrote
in The Marriage of Heaven and Hell, "Man has no Body distinct from
his Soul for that calld Body is a portion of Soul discernd by the five
Senses, the chief inlets of Soul in this age" (E 34). And in his description of his engraving of Chaucer's Canterbury Pilgrims, Blake pro-

claimed that specific moral and intellectual traits produce specific physical features:

> Of Chaucer's characters, as described in his Canterbury Tales, some of the names or titles are altered by time, but the characters themselves for ever remain unaltered, and consequently they are the physiognomies or lineaments of universal human life, beyond which Nature never steps. Names alter, things never alter. (E 523-4)[8]

Gilchrist provides several examples of Blake's physiognomical observations. Taken by his father at the age of fourteen to be apprenticed to the stipple-engraver William Wynne Ryland, Blake refused the position, saying "I do not like the man's face: *it looks as if he will live to be hanged.*"[9] Blake responded very differently when he met Oliver Goldsmith. Gilchrist says he "mightily admired the great author's finely marked head ... and thought to himself how much *he* should like to have such a head when he grew to be a man."[10] Blake also insisted on the correlation of his own features with his personality. After describing his aggressive removal of the drunken soldier John Scolfield from his garden, his subsequent trial for sedition, and Hayley's active support, Blake assures Butts: "It is certain! that a too passive manner. inconsistent with my active physiognomy had done me much mischief   I must now express to you my conviction that all is come from the spiritual world for Good & not for Evil."[11] And Gilchrist tells us that

> Down to his latest days, Blake always avowed himself a 'Liberty Boy,' a faithful 'Son of Liberty'; and would jokingly urge in self-defense that the shape of his forehead made him a republican. "I can't help being one," he would assure Tory friends, "any more than you can help being a Tory: your forehead is larger above; mine, on the contrary, over the eyes."[12]

In this context, we might note Lavater's comment that "When *the bone of the eye* is prominent, you have the sign of a singular aptitude for mental labour, of an extraordinary sagacity for great enterprises" (L IIIB, 277), but "foreheads which are *sunk toward the under part,* that is to say, prominent in the upper, I believe ... to be stupid, cowardly, incapable of great enterprises" (L IIIB, 280). Lest we miss the point of Blake's joke and wrongly infer from his comments to his Tory friends that the accident of his being born with a forehead larger over the eyes determined his radical politics, rather than the reverse, we should remember his annotation upon Lavater's 532nd Aphorism: "the substance gives tincture to the accident & makes it physiognomic" (E 585).

Lavater's science of physiognomy spawned an even more influential progeny, the science of cranioscopy or phrenology developed by Franz Joseph Gall and Johann Caspar Spurzheim. Influenced by Lavater's studies of the head and face, Gall first recognized the primary importance of the brain to the central nervous system, to mental disease, and to human intelligence. Since Gall was convinced that an organ's function determines its anatomical structure, he carefully dissected and studied the human brain and gradually developed the four basic tenets of his psycho-physiology. They are:

(1) Moral and intellectual qualities are innate. These innate qualities or faculties are created by God, said Gall, and number twenty-seven in all. Among these fundamental qualities, Gall listed the senses of colors, mechanics, music.

(2) The functioning of these twenty-seven fundamental qualities requires organic supports. Here Gall parted company with Lavater and his spiritualist contemporaries who insisted that the soul expressed itself through the body but did not depend on it. Gall, trained as a naturalist and a doctor, insisted that "no faculty manifests itself without a material condition."[13]

(3) The brain is the organ of all faculties, tendencies and feelings; Gall called the brain "the organ of the soul." Gall's researches on the brain finally ousted the competing claims of the heart, the liver, or the thorax to be the seat of the soul or mind, and paved the way to modern psychology and neurosurgery.

(4) The brain is composed of as many organs as there are faculties, tendencies and feelings. Gall believed that each of the twenty-seven faculties had its particular location within the brain; he therefore divided up the surface of the skull into twenty-seven sections. The shape and size of the surface area in each of these sections was, for Gall, an accurate indication of the state of development of the underlying faculty or feeling. For instance, a pronounced bump on the very top of the head indicated a strongly developed capacity for religious conviction. Gall devoted his career to defining the exact location of the twenty-seven faculties and to medically diagnosing his patients in these terms.

When Gall's theories were first published in his *Anatomie et*

Physiologie du systeme nerveux in 1808, they were hailed by Goethe and Blumenbach, but they were violently opposed by the medical establishments of Paris and Vienna. They received more favorable attention in England and America, primarily because they came to those countries in the revised form developed by Johann Caspar Spurzheim, one of Gall's first pupils. Spurzheim, after studying with Gall from 1804 to 1813, moved to London in 1814 and began to publish and lecture on the science he eventually renamed "phrenology," the "science of the mind." Spurzheim expanded the number of faculties first to thirty-three, and finally to thirty-six. More importantly, he eliminated from his system those faculties that were inherently evil (Gall had noted separate faculties of "murder" and "stealing"). According to Spurzheim, all the innate faculties have some good purpose and are necessary to human survival, even though every faculty can produce abuses if it is not directed and curbed by man's free moral will. By recognizing one's inherent abilities and tendencies as recorded on one's skull at an early age, one could deliberately encourage the development of one's virtues and restrain one's vices.[14]

Spurzheim's influence in England was enormous. Already in 1803 the *Edinburgh Review* had acknowledged the new science: "Of Dr. Gall and his skulls who has not heard?"[15] And in 1807, a brief and sympathetic *Account of Dr. Gall's New Theory of Physiognomy, founded upon the Anatomy and Physiology of the Brain, and the Form of the Skull* was published anonymously in London. But the Napoleonic Wars inhibited English communication with France, and it was not until 1815, with Spurzheim's lectures and his publication of an English version of their theories entitled *The Physiognomical System of Drs. Gall and Spurzheim,* that their ideas became widely known. They were also widely denounced as "trash" and "despicable trumpery" by the *Edinburgh Review* early in 1815 and as unintelligible absurdities by a Member of the London Philosophical Society in 1816.[16] But Spurzheim's widely publicized brain-dissection in Edinburgh in the fall of 1815 converted his Scots critics, and even though he returned to Paris in 1817, his ideas spread through Great Britain. Phrenological societies were founded in Scotland and England, and when Spurzheim returned to London in 1825, his lectures were packed. Within a year, his craniological charts were sufficiently widely known to be burlesqued by Cruikshank in his *Phrenological Illustrations* (1826).

Blake read and annotated Spurzheim's *Observations on the Mani-*

festations of the Deranged Mind, or Insanity (published in 1817) and immediately took issue with Spurzheim's insistence that the soul and mind depend upon bodily organs. In the language Blake echoed in his annotations, Spurzheim had argued:

> Many physicians speak of diseases of the mind; others admit both mental and corporeal causes of insanity; a few acknowledge only corporeal diseases, and with the latter I decidedly agree. The idea of mental derangements must not, however, be confounded with mental causes. Certainly the manifestations of the mind may be deranged; but I have no idea of any disease, or of any derangement of an immaterial being itself, such as the mind or soul is. The soul cannot fall sick, any more than it can die. . . . I consider the mind in this life confined to the body, of which it makes use; that is, the powers of the mind want instruments for their manifestations or, these manifestations are dependent on the instruments; cannot appear without them; and are modified, diminished, increased, or deranged, according to the condition of the instruments or organs.[17]

Explaining why children do not contract mental diseases, Spurzheim asserted:

> The reason that children do not appear as insane, strictly speaking, in my opinion is, because their cerebral organization is too delicate, and does not bear a strong morbid affection without entirely losing its fitness for the mind and endangering life. The disturbances of the organization appear merely as organic diseases, because the functions are entirely suppressed. Later, in proportion as the brain becomes firmer, it bears morbid changes longer without becoming entirely unfit for its functions or causing death. Its functions then are only disturbed, and appear under the symptoms called insanity.[18]

Blake's annotation on this passage is aimed at the opening paragraphs I first quoted. Blake insists upon a distinction between corporeal and mental disease. The mind or soul creates and is responsible for its own state of health, just as the body creates its physical condition. Blake accepts Spurzheim's assertion that disturbances of a child's physical organization cause organic or corporeal diseases. As Blake comments, "Corporeal disease. to which I readily agree." (E 652). Blake then contradicts Spurzheim: "Diseases of the mind I pity him. Denies mental health and perfection   Stick to this all is right. But see page 152" (E 652). Blake here argues that the mind, and not the body, creates mental health as well as mental disease. If one sticks to this belief in the mind's capacity to determine its own condition, all will be well, says Blake.

Blake's additional reference is to a passage in which Spurzheim himself admits that insanity can be caused by mental disturbances. As Spurzheim says, "Whatever occupies the mind too intensely or exclusively is hurtful to the brain, and induces a state favorable to insanity, in diminishing the influence of will."[19] If the will can influence the mind's propensity to mental health or sickness, insanity is not exclusively a corporeal disease. Blake then comments at length on the passage in which Spurzheim acknowledges that religious beliefs are a powerful cause of insanity. Blake writes:

> Methodism &^{c} p. 154. Cowper came to me & said. O that I were insane always I will never rest. Can you not make me truly insane. I will never rest till I am so. O that in the bosom of God I was hid. You retain health & yet are as mad as any of us all—over us all—mad as a refuge from unbelief—from Bacon Newton & Locke. (E 652)

Blake had learned of Cowper's religious madness while preparing the plates for Hayley's *Life of Cowper*.[20] In recurrent periods of insanity, Cowper had proclaimed his conviction that he was eternally damned by God and had frequently attempted suicide. As Morton Paley suggests, Blake may have been reminded of Cowper's madness by Spurzheim's statement on the first page that "some individuals feel the most distressing anxiety, and fancy themselves objects of human persecution or victims of Divine vengeance" and again by Spurzheim's remark that "Some also are alarmed for the salvation of their souls, or even think themselves abandoned for ever by God, and condemned to hell and eternal sufferings."[21] Blake, who had himself been called mad—by Hayley, by the *Examiner* reviewer of his 1809 Exhibition, and by others—here distinguishes between true and false insanity. Cowper, because he believed in a cruel God of vengeance, had allowed the errors of his mind to lead him into mental disease and despair. Blake, who believes in a God of infinite mercy residing within the bosoms of men, is considered mad by the followers of Bacon, Newton, and Locke. But Blake's madness, as

Cowper is here made to acknowledge, is actually a form of mental health and a valid "refuge from unbelief." Blake thus insists again that only mental ideas and beliefs can cause mental health or disease.

Even though Blake disagreed with Spurzheim on the corporeal causes of insanity, he may still have been influenced by Spurzheim's specific physiognomical observations. It is unlikely that Blake read Spurzheim's *Observations on . . . Insanity* without also knowing about Spurzheim's far more famous work on physiognomy, from which his study of insanity was derived. Blake's objection to Spurzheim's view that the soul or mind cannot exist independently of the body does not invalidate Spurzheim's more fundamental contention that the organs of the brain are the instruments by means of which the mental faculties manifest themselves (S 492). Moreover, Spurzheim conceded that the soul or mind could not be equated with its physical manifestations. Rather, the soul provides the internal energy or stimulus which sets the organs of the brain in motion, and the degree of spiritual motivation or activity corresponds to the degree of the organ's development. Blake could easily have accepted Spurzheim's fundamental argument that the shape of the skull directly manifests the degrees of development of the organs of the brain lying directly beneath it and is therefore a valid external index to the spiritual activities, mental abilities, and moral character of a person.

I would now like to look at three of Blake's Visionary Heads. In these portraits, I think Blake may have been using Lavater's and Spurzheim's physiognomical observations and models to guide his pencil. Blake was asked to draw the portraits of his visionary visitors by John Varley; most of the Visionary Heads were drawn between 1819 and 1825. Varley himself had studied with approval the observations of Lavater and Spurzheim,[22] and he may have further stimulated Blake's interest in these physiognomical systems. Varley was also a committed astrologer and was preparing a lengthy treatise on the influence of the heavenly bodies on human physiognomy. Only the first of four projected parts of Varley's *Treatise on Zodiacal Physiognomy* was published; it appeared in 1828 and contained Linnell's engraving of Blake's "Ghost of a Flea." Although Varley believed that the "power of the various signs of the Zodiac" created "a great diversity in the features and complexions of the human race" and that one's zodiacal sign at birth determined one's hair and eye color, facial features, complexion, and personality, it seems to me unlikely that Blake shared this belief. In *Jerusalem,* Blake implies that the stars and planets are derived from the body of Albion. Speaking to the Jews, he writes,

> You have a tradition, that Man anciently contain in his mighty limbs all things in Heaven & Earth: this you recieve from the Druids. "But now the Starry Heavens are fled from the mighty limbs of Albion." (E 170)

Plate 25 of *Jerusalem* shows the sun, moon, and stars inscribed on the mighty human form of Albion. Blake's iconography here suggests a psychological rather than an astrological source for the shape of the human form. Nonetheless, Blake shared Varley's belief in the immaterial causes of human physiognomy and was happy to oblige his friend and disciple with detailed portraits.

Let us first compare the Visionary Head of "The Man Who Taught Blake Painting in his Dreams"[23] with Spurzheim's physiognomical charts (Plates 66–68). When we set Spurzheim's phrenological models beside Blake's portrait of the man who taught him painting, we immediately notice how carefully and distinctly Blake has defined the bumps and curvatures of the forehead and skull. This suggests a reference to Spurzheim's craniological system. Since I am not a trained phrenologist, I can hardly pretend to give the correct phrenological reading of Blake's portrait. I am here concerned primarily with suggesting a possible system or methodology in terms of which one might validly interpret Blake's visionary images. With this caveat, I would like to draw attention to some of the more striking bumps on this head (Plate 69). If my numberings are correct, we might agree that Blake's painting instructor had the following qualities or mental faculties in a highly developed form.

Number 24—the organ of Locality. Spurzheim tells us that this is the ability to remember places in great detail. "This faculty measures distance, and gives notions of perspective: it makes the traveller, geographer and landscape-painter; it recollects localities and judges of symmetry....This faculty ... conceives the places occupied by external bodies" (S 368). Spurzheim's illustration (Plate 70, Fig. 2) confirms that the organ of locality coincides with the prominent bump over the inner eyes of Blake's instructor.

Number 30—the organ of Comparison. This faculty enables one to use similes and analogues (rather than syllogistic logic) in one's thought and speech. It is located in the midst of the superior part of the forehead, as Spurzheim's illustration indicates (Plate 71, Fig. 1).

Number 16—the organ of Ideality. Spurzheim identifies this faculty with the imagination, which renders people "enthusiasts" and makes them "in every thing aspire to ideality" (S 346). It is frequently found in the heads of great poets, which "are enlarged above the temples in an arched direction" (S 345), as Spurzheim's illustration of Shakespeare indicates (Plate 72, Fig. 2).

Number 32—the organ of Wit. The essence of this faculty, which elevates the "superior external parts of the forehead" (S 391), consists "in its peculiar manner of comparing, which always excites gaity and laughter" (S 392). "Jest, raillery, mockery, irony, etc., belong to this faculty" (S 392). Spurzheim illustrates this faculty with a portrait of Laurence Sterne (Plate 72, Fig. 1).

Number 20—the organ of Form. "Persons, endowed with [this faculty] in a high degree, are fond of seeing pictures" (S 359), says Spurzheim. "The conception also of the smoothness and roughness of bodies belongs to it" (S 360). Generally, this organ manifests a sensibility to the form of things. It "seems to be placed," says Spurzheim, "in the internal angle of the orbit; and if this part of the brain be much developed, it pushes the eyeball toward the external angle, that is a little outward and downward" (S 360). The eyes of Blake's painting instructor are also pushed laterally outward and upward at the outer edges; this gives his eyes a mongoloid cast. Spurzheim also comments that the Chinese whom he has met in London have had highly developed organs of form (S 359).

Number 23—the organ of Color. This is the capacity to separate and perceive the harmony of colors. It is necessary, says Spurzheim, to painters, dyers, and enamelers (S 363). This organ "is placed in the midst of the arch of the eyebrows. The external sign of a greater development of the organ of this faculty is a vaulted and round arch of the eyebrows.... In the Chinese," continues Spurzheim, "the orbitary arch is elevated in the middle, while the eyes are depressed, and it is well known they are fond of colouring" (S 364; see Plate 70, Fig. 1).

Number 25—the organ of Order. This faculty, says Spurzheim, "gives method and order in arranging objects as they are physically related.... This faculty is merely fond of putting the particulars in order according to physical considerations: as in a library, books may be arranged according to their size and form" (S 370). Although Spurzheim has not definitively located this organ, he feels that it is "probably situated outward, but not far from the organs of size and locality" (S 370).

Number 29—the organ of Language. This is the ability to learn the arbitrary signs needed to communicate ideas, reflections, sentiments, or inclinations. This organ, says Spurzheim, "makes us acquainted with arbitrary signs, has memory of them, judges of their relations, and produces a propensity to the employment of these functions" (S 387). He locates it under the eye, "in the midst of the knowing faculties, where it occupies a transverse situation" (S 383).

Number 7—the organ of Constructiveness. This is the propensity to build things. "Gall observed," remarks Spurzheim, "that those who had a particular disposition to mechanical arts presented a face of somewhat parallel form, or as large at the temples as at the cheeks" — Blake's painting instructor has such a parallel-shaped face (see Plate 73, Fig. 2)—"and consequently that a greater disposition to mechanical arts is indicated by the development of the brain at the temples" (S 318). "He found this sign," continues Spurzheim, "in great mechanicians, architects, sculptors and designers" (S 318).

Number 13—the organ of Benevolence. This organ, which is located in the "superior middle part of the forehead", *may* be accentuated in Blake's drawing (see Plate 74, Fig. 1). "This faculty . . . produces in man goodness of heart, kindness, peacefulness, mildness, benignity, benevolence, complaisance, clemency, mercifulness, compassion, humanity, hospitality, liberality, equity, cordiality, urbanity, in one word, *Christian charity*" (S 338).

In contrast to these highly developed organs of the brain, we might observe that Blake's portrait of the man who taught him painting significantly reduces the following organs (see Plates 67, 68):

Number 26—the organ of Time. This is the awareness of the chronological sequence of events and is located above the organs of locality and color.

Number 28—the organ of Tune. Located beside the organ of Time, this is the faculty of hearing the harmonies of sounds.

Number 27—the organ of Number. This is the ability to calculate and is situated at the rear of the upper eye.

Number 12—the organ of Cautiousness. This faculty, which induces circumspection, irresolution, and fear, is located above the ear, midway between the ear and the crown of the head.

Number 19—the organ of Individuality. Located in the lower center of the forehead, this is the capacity to identify persons and things, to obtain specific factual information.

According to Spurzheim's system, if I have applied it correctly, Blake's painting instructor was a highly skilled artist, with acute senses for spatial relationships, perspective, composition, proportion, shapes, textures and colors. He was highly imaginative, both in his visual designs and in his speech, which often employed metaphors or similes. He cared little for facts. Moreover, he seems to have possessed a personality highly congenial to Blake: enthusiastic, impulsive, perhaps even rash, and possibly benevolent.

If we turn now to Lavater's *Essays on Physiognomy,* we can find some confirmation for this reading of the painting instructor's character. In a general remark on foreheads, Lavater asserts that "Foreheads loaded with many angular and knotty protuberances, are the certain mark of a fiery spirit, which its own activity transports and which nothing is able to restrain" (L IIIB, 277). Commenting on eyes, Lavater says that a partially covered iris, such as that possessed by figure 3 in Lavater's plate (Plate 75) and by Blake's instructor, "is the most serene, the most profound, approaches nearest to genius" (L IIIB, 346). Summarizing his observations on eyes in his posthumously published "Physiognomical Rules," Lavater declares that "Eyes with long, sharp, especially if horizontal, corners—that is, such as do not turn downwards—with thick-skinned eyelids, which appear to cover half the pupil, are sanguine and indicative of genius."[24] The possession of a pointed chin, says Lavater, "usually passes for the sign of cunning" (L IIIB, 329). And "a nose whose ridge is broad, no matter whether straight or curved always announces superior faculties" (L IIIB, 364).

We might tentatively conclude, then, that Blake's painting instructor was a genius. He was an outstanding artist, with strongly developed senses of color, design, and texture, and an acute eye for spatial relationships. In addition he seems to have been witty, passionate, energetic, and, above all, highly imaginative. He may even have been, like Blake himself, a visionary. In his *Observations on . . . Insanity,* Spurzheim says that "Visionaries, or those who think they have communications with spirits, usually have the head elevated at the middle lateral parts of the coronal suture, between ideality and invention"[25] (i.e. between organs 16 and 33, behind 32). The man who taught Blake painting in his dreams was apparently the ideal teacher for a student of Blake's interests and aptitudes. Indeed, if we compare the portrait of Blake's instructor with the "Portrait of William Blake" attributed to John Linnell (Plate 76), the similarities between the two noses, the mouths, the arches of the eyebrows, and the configurations of the foreheads suggest that Blake's painting instructor was in fact his own imagination.[26]

Let us next look at Blake's Visionary Head of "Socrates" (Plate 77), another portrait notable for the clearly defined bumps and ridges on the forehead. Referring again to Spurzheim's phrenological system (Plate 68), we see that Blake's Socrates has the following highly developed faculties (Plate 78):

Number 30—the organ of Comparison or the faculty of using analogies, similes, parables and metaphors to persuade and affect one's listeners. Spurzheim tells us that "This organ is developed in all popular preachers beloved by the crowd, who speak by examples and parables. . . . Indeed, in order to persuade and affect, the speaker or orator must speak by analogy: he must bring spiritual things near to terrestrial objects, and compare them with each other: he must imitate the manner of the preaching of Christ. The activity of this faculty is very important. It compares the sensations and ideals of all the other faculties and points out their difference, analogy, similitude or identity" (S 388).

Number 31—the organ of Causality. This faculty which is "manifested by the development of those convolutions which occupy the upper middle and lateral parts of the forehead" (S 391; see the prominent upper forehead of Kant in Spurzheim's illustration, Plate 71, Fig. 2) desires to know the causes of events.

Number 19—the organ of Individuality. "Persons endowed with this faculty in a high degree," says Spurzheim, "are attentive to all that happens around them, to every object, to every phenomenon, to every fact; and hence also to motions. . . . This faculty moreover has knowledge of all internal faculties, and acts upon them. It desires to know all by experience, and consequently it puts every other organ in action; it wishes to hear, see, smell, taste and touch, and to know all the arts and sciences; it is fond of instruction, collects facts, and leads to practical knowledge.

I call this faculty that of *Individuality*, because it knows not only the external world in general, but also each object in its individual capacity" (S 358–9).

The possession of highly developed forms of all three of these faculties (comparison, causality, and individuality) in highly developed forms, energetically working together, "forming systems, drawing conclusions, inductions, or corollaries, and pointing out principles and laws," constitutes according to Spurzheim "the true philosophical understanding" (S 391).

In addition, Blake's Socrates seems to have enlarged organs of: *Number 24—locality* (the perception of spatial relationships between bodies); *Number 32—wit; Number 16—ideality or imagination; Number 28—tune* (the ability to hear the harmonies of sounds); *Number 29— language* (fluency in communicating one's thoughts); and *Number 20—form* (a sensibility to the shape and texture of things). *Number 13, the organ of benevolence and Christian charity,* may also be enlarged. More significant, perhaps, are the highly developed forms of organs 25: *order* (the love of arrangement and neatness) and 27: *number* (the ability to calculate).

According to Spurzheim's classifications, then, Blake's Socrates is an outstanding philosopher who is also notable for his wit, his imagination, and his linguistic and musical abilities. In addition, he is talented both in logic and in mathematics. Turning to Lavater, we discover that he devoted an entire section of his *Essays on Physiognomy* to an analysis of Socrates' facial features in an attempt to explain why this "wisest and best of men had such an ugly physiognomy" (L I, 168). Lavater argues that Socrates had *corrected* the originally negative tendencies of his personality, and that this great effort of will rendered him an even more noble character. The "spacious vault" of Socrates' forehead, asserts Lavater, "is inhabited by a mind capable of dispelling the darkness of prejudice, of overcoming a host of obstacles" (L I, 172; Lavater is describing Rubens' portrait of Socrates), while the "short and thick nape of the neck is . . . the mark of an inflexible spirit, the expression of obstinacy" (L I, 175). Echoing Socrates himself, Lavater concludes that "men of a character strongly marked, full of energy, and whose powers exert themselves out of the common road, have usually, in their exterior taken together, something disagreeable, harsh and ambiguous" (L I, 168).[27]

A physiognomic reading of Blake's Visionary Head of "Socrates" thus conforms with the qualified approval Blake expressed for Socrates' physiognomy and philosophy in his writings and conversations. Crabb Robinson recorded Blake's response to his question whether there were any resemblance between the Genius which inspired Socrates and the Spirits which spoke to Blake:

He smiled; and for once it seemed to me as if he had a feeling of vanity gratified. "The same as in our countenances." He paused and said, "I was Socrates"—and then as if he had gone too far in that—"or a sort of brother. I must have had conversations with him. So I had with Jesus Christ. I have an obscure recollection of having been with both of them."[28]

Blake further compared Socrates to Christ: both were the victims of pernicious accusers, both were redeemers of mankind. But Blake was less sympathetic to the rationalist aspects of Socrates' thought. In *The Song of Los* (E 66), he equated Socrates' moral teachings with "an abstract Law" that leads to error. "If Morality was Christianity, Socrates was the Savior," Blake twice proclaimed (E 272, 657). But true Christianity cannot be equated with moral codes and Socrates is not the ultimate savior. The enlarged organs of order (#25) and calculation (#27) in Blake's visionary portrait of Socrates thus draw our attention to what Blake regarded as Socrates' pernicious love of logic, rational thought, and moral absolutes.

The last Visionary Head I wish to discuss, "The Man Who Built the Pyramids" (Plate 79), seems to draw primarily on Lavater's physiognomical studies. We might note in passing, however, the bulge beneath the external angle of the eyebrow which according to Spurzheim indicates a highly developed faculty of number and mathematical calculation (see Jedidiah Buxton, Plate 80, Fig. 1). The second volume of Lavater's *Essays on Physiognomy* tells us to begin our analysis of a profile head by measuring it. One should draw a horizontal line from the tip of the nose to the extremity of the hindhead and a perpendicular line from the top of the head down to the place where the chin joins the neck (Plate 81). His preparatory sketches for this drawing in the *Blake-Varley Sketchbook* (Plate 82) indicate that Blake was basing this profile on an isoceles triangle laid on its side. Geometrical calculations such as those recommended by Lavater were clearly part of Blake's conception of this portrait. In the pyramid-builder's profile, the width significantly exceeds the height. Such a head, says Lavater, "which is broader than it is long, having a contour harsh, stiff, angular and distended, announces a formidable degree of inflexibility, which is almost always accompanied with the blackest malignity. A contour lax and soft is, in the same case, the infallible mark of sensuality, weakness, indolence and voluptuousness" (L IIA, 184). Blake's pyramid-builder seems to combine in his extremely sharp nose and soft lips and receding chin both inflexible malignity and decadent sensuality. If we further divide this head into four horizontal sections as Lavater instructs us in his last volume, drawing lines at the hairline, the eyebrows, the extremity of the nose and the point of the chin, we discover more about the pyramid-builder. These four sections, says Lavater, are equal in a well-proportioned, noble character. But the sections of the pyramid-builder's head increase as we move down from his forehead. Such a disproportion, most closely shared by figure 12 in Lavater's illustration (Plate 83), indicates a "shocking brutality" and a general stupidity (L IIIB, 272).

Other comments by Lavater reinforce this initial reading of the pyramid-builder. "A retreating chin is always negative" (L IIIB, 392) while "fleshy lips have always a struggle to maintain with sensuality and indolence" (L IIIB, 397). The pyramid-builder's opened mouth, sketched to the left of his head, further identifies him as a crude sensualist. Analysing a similar mouth (Plate 84, Fig. 2), Lavater comments that it "languishes with a passion not yet extinguished by despair, and which it is determined to pursue without much delicacy as to the justice of the means . . . the under lip is extremely gross" (L IIIB, 402). Figure 3 (Plate 84), whose fleshy underlip and raised corners resemble those of the pyramid-builder, reveals, says Lavater, "the gaiety and malignity of an indelicate voluptuary, who loves indulgence, and sacrifices every thing to pleasure" (L IIIB, 402). The pyramid-builder's generally brutal physiognomy is further accentuated by his complexion which, as Blake noted in his preparatory sketches, is "a Shiny Black." Lavater cited approvingly the argument of a German physiognomist that a white countenance "generally speaking, pleases the eye; black, on the contrary, excites gloomy and unpleasant ideas" (L IIIA, 84). In sum, then, Blake's pyramid-builder is skilled at calculation and engineering, but is a cruel taskmaster and a crude, self-indulgent sensualist.

A physiognomic analysis of "The Man who Built the Pyramids" according to Lavater's principles and observations thus coincides with Blake's general views of Egypt, the Egyptians, and the pyramids expressed elsewhere in his writings and art. Blake consistently associated the land of the pyramids with the fallen world of bondage and misery, as both Albert S. Roe and S. Foster Damon have shown.[29] Blake links both Egypt and Babylon with Ulro; they are Urizen-dominated lands of materialism, repressive laws and mathematical systems. In *Jerusalem,* Los denounces the "pyramids of pride" (E 249) which are built with the blood of the workers. As Blake writes,

... there they take up
The articulations of a mans soul, and laughing throw it down
Into the frame, then knock it out upon the plank, & souls are bak'd
In bricks to build the pyramids of Heber & Terah." (E 192)

The pyramids are further associated with the Whore of Babylon and the reign of "Mystery" in *Milton* (E 138). In this context, it seems significant that the pyramid-builder's notebook in Blake's preparatory sketch (Plate 82) is lightly sketched with pseudohieroglyphs. This might be taken as yet another sign of his commitment to "mystery" or the delusions of materialism (see the books of hieroglyphs belonging to Urizen [Title page and Plate 5, *Book of Urizen*] and Hecate ["Hecate," color printed drawing in the Tate Gallery]). Albert Roe has further noted that these hieroglyphlike characters signify "15 Degrees of Cancer ascending," in accord with John Varley's astrological charting of the pyramid-builder's birth inscribed on the lower right.[30] Can we see this as Blake's subtle jibe at Varley's belief that the material bodies in the heavens control the destinies of men?

Blake specifically condemned the art of Egypt as mere "Nature and Imitation" in his inscriptions on his *Laocoön* engraving (E 272) and as "Mathematic Form," "Eternal in the Reasoning Memory," in his comments *On Homer's Poetry & On Virgil* (E 267). That this pyramid-builder uses rigid geometrical forms in his architectural constructions is indicated by the design of his workshop or study which Blake has sketched at the left of his drawing (Plate 79). This room is based on a strict horizontal/vertical, two-dimensional axis and is decorated with minimal abstract geometrical patterns arranged in unrelieved bilateral symmetry.

When we look at these three Visionary Heads in the light of the physiognomical systems of Lavater and Spurzheim, they emerge as complex visual statements of Blake's conceptions of his painting instructor (who, since he appeared to Blake in his dreams, may be an image of the ideal artist), of Socratic philosophy, and of Egyptian art and culture. I would not want, however, to overestimate the seriousness with which Blake took these drawings; they were clearly intended to tease, tantalize, and amuse his close friends. Blake was conversant with physiognomical and phrenological concepts and vocabularies, but he used them with a light touch, to communicate his ideas jocoseriously to a circle that understood this visual language.

NOTES

1.   This historical phenomenon has been brilliantly documented by Robert Darnton in his *Mesmerism and the End of the Enlightenment in France* (Cambridge, Mass.: Harvard Univ. Press, 1968), Chaps. 1, 2 and *passim.*

2.   Blake engraved the following plates: (1) "Democritus," Vol. I, facing p. 159; (2) tailpiece for Fragment XI, Vol. I, p. 206; (3) a face similar to "Spalding," Vol. I, p. 225 (perhaps a self-portrait); and (4) "Aged Figures Gardening," Vol. I, p. 271.

3.   Blake's copiously annotated copy of Lavater's *Aphorisms on Man* is in the H. E. Huntington Library. Blake engraved the frontispiece for this translation by Fuseli.

4.   Marcia Allentuck, "Fuseli and Lavater: Physiognomical Theory and the Enlightenment," *Studies in Voltaire and the Eighteenth Century,* 55 (1967), 97.

5.   *The Life and Art of Henry Fuseli* (New York: Praeger, 1972), pp. 47–8, 51, 93, 106, 115, 122, 162–63 and pls. 64, 65.

6.   For Blake's contacts with Thomas Holcroft, see G. E. Bentley, Jr., *Blake Records* (Oxford: Clarendon Press, 1969), pp. 40, 576 and note 1. Holcroft's translation of Lavater's *Essays on Physiognomy* was first published in 3 volumes in London in 1793. A one volume abridgement of this edition was published in London later that year. Editions of this abridged version published after 1801 include a translation of Lavater's posthumous "One Hundred Physiognomical Rules." This became the most popular version and went through 15 editions by 1878.

Other English translations of the *Essays on Physiognomy* include those by the Rev. C. Moore (in 3 Vols., London, 1793–94), by George Grenville (in 4 Vols., London, 1800), and by S. Shaw (1 Vol., London, 1800).

7.   John Caspar Lavater, *Essays on Physiognomy, Designed to Promote the Knowledge and the Love of Mankind,* illustrated by more than Eight Hundred Engravings accurately copied; executed by, or under the inspection of, Thomas Holloway. Translated from the French by Henry Hunter, D. D. (London: John Murray, Vol. I, 1789; Vol. II, 1792; Vol. III, 1798), Vol. I, p. 20. All further references, unless otherwise specified, will be to this edition, hereafter cited in the text as L followed by volume and page numbers.

8. Does Blake's assertion here provide an explanation for the relatively limited number of facial features and expressions present in Blake's artistic vocabulary? Perhaps Blake is physiognomically numbering the classes of men and simplifying each face to the physiognomical type that most clearly reveals its underlying moral character.

9. Alexander Gilchrist, *Life of William Blake,* ed. Ruthven Todd (London: J. M. Dent & Sons; New York: E. P. Dutton & Co.; revised edition, 1945), p. 11.

10. Gilchrist, p. 13.

11. Letter to Thomas Butts, August 16, 1803, E 699–700.

12. Gilchrist, p. 80.

13. Franz Joseph Gall, *Sur les fonctions du cerveau et sur celle de chacune de ses parties* (Paris, 1822), Vol. I, p. 231. For an excellent brief account of Gall's theories and importance, see Erwin H. Ackerknecht, M.D., and Henri V. Vallois, M.D., *Franz Joseph Gall, Inventor of Phrenology and His Collection* (Madison, Wisconsin: Wisconsin Studies in Medical History, No. 1, 1956).

14. J. G. Spurzheim, M.D., *The Physiognomical System of Drs. Gall and Spurzheim; founded on An Anatomical and Physiological Examination of the Nervous System in General, and of the Brain in Particular; and indicating the Dispositions and Manifestations of the Mind* (London: Baldwin, Cradock and Joy, 1815, second edition), p. 515; cited hereafter as S followed by page number. A copy of this edition, now in the Bancroft Library, Berkeley, California, and originally owned by Mrs. Richard Smith, includes a shilling postcard depicting "Dr. Gall's System" and the 1/6 single sheet "Explanation of the New Physiognomical System of the Brain" reproduced here. For a sensible account of Spurzheim's influence in England and especially in America, see John D. Davies, *Phrenology: Fad and Science, A 19th-Century American Crusade* (New Haven: Yale University Press, 1955), Part One.

15. Quoted in *Phrenological Journal,* 4 (1826–27),

16. *Edinburgh Review,* 25 (1815), 268; *Three Familiar Lectures on Craniological Physiognomy, delivered before the City Philosophical Society,* by a Member (London, 1816), p. iv.

17. Johann Christoph Spurzheim, *Observations on the Deranged Manifestations of the Mind, or Insanity,* originally published in London in 1817. My references are to the facsimile reproduction of the first American edition of 1833 edited by Anthony A. Walsh (Gainesville, Florida: Scholars' Facsimiles & Reprints, 1970), pp. 75–6. Blake's annotated copy of the original edition has not been located since its annotations were transcribed by Ellis and Yeats in 1893.

18. Ibid., p. 80.

19. Ibid., p. 114.

20.   For a thoroughly documented account of Blake's knowledge of Cowper's mental illness, see Morton D. Paley, "Cowper as Blake's Spectre," *Eighteenth-Century Studies,* 1 (1967–8), 236–252.

21.   Spurzheim, *Observations on . . . Insanity,* pp. 1, 84. Cf. Paley, pp. 245–46.

22.   John Varley, *A Treatise on Zodiacal Physiognomy; illustrated with Engravings of Heads and Features; accompanied by Tables of the Time of Rising of the Twelve Signs of the Zodiac; and containing also new astrological explanations of some remarkable portions of Ancient Mythological History,* No. 1. To be completed in four parts. (London: Longman and Co., 1828), pp. 56–7.

23.   According to Martin Butlin, there are three known versions of "The Man Who Taught Blake Painting in his Dreams," two in the Tate Gallery (no. 51 is reproduced here) and one in the collection of Sir Geoffrey Keynes. These three versions "are very close to each other, even to the placing of the individual hairs and lines of shading. These do not coincide precisely enough to be the result of direct tracing but rather suggest the use of an optical aid to copying such as Cornelius Varley's Graphic Telescope. . . . The Keynes version is slightly more sensitive and may be Blake's original" (Martin Butlin, *William Blake: a complete catalogue of the works in the Tate Gallery* [London: The Tate Gallery, revised edition, 1971], p. 60).

24.   Lavater, *Essays on Physiognomy and One Hundred Physiognomical Rules,* translated by Thomas Holcroft, 15th ed. (London: William Tegg and Co., 1878), p. 464.

25.   Spurzheim, *Observations on . . . Insanity,* p. 109.

26.   The amateur phrenologist J.S. Deville also considered Blake's skull to be "representative of the imaginative faculty." For a detailed account of Deville's life mask of Blake, see *William Blake: Catalogue of the Collection in the Fitzwilliam Museum, Cambridge,* ed. David Bindman (Cambridge: Heffer, 1970), Cat. no. 55 and pls. 73–4.

27.   Throughout this passage, Lavater is echoing Socrates' descriptions of his own physiognomy (see Cicero, *Tusculan Disputations,* IV, 80, and the Scholia to Persius, IV, 24; both quoted in R. Foerster, *Scriptores Physiognomonici graeci et latini,* I, Prolegomena, p. ix).

28.   Crabb Robinson, *Diary,* selections given in Arthur Symons, *William Blake* (London: Archibald Constable and Co., 1907), p. 287.

29.   Albert S. Roe, "The Thunder of Egypt," *William Blake: Essays for S. Foster Damon,* ed. Alvin Rosenfeld (Providence, R.I.: Brown Univ. Press, 1969), pp. 158–95; and S. Foster Damon, *A Blake Dictionary* (Providence, R. I.: Brown Univ. Press, 1965), p. 116.

30.   Roe, p. 194. Unfortunately, Varley's astrological analysis of Cancer physiognomies does not appear in the only published part of his *Treatise on Zodiacal Physiognomy.*

II

DEVELOPMENT

In part because of Blake's habit of repeating similar images throughout his career, it has been all too easy to see his designs as the products of a fundamentally unchanging intellect. As a result, Blake's shifting concepts of his own role, his changing relationships to other artists living and dead, and his stylistic and technical progress have received much less attention than they deserve. The essays in the following section are based on the assumption that one of the contexts essential for understanding Blake's art is its own development.

Cataloguing William Blake

Martin Butlin

T H E oeuvre catalogue is a prime case of the establishment of minute particulars, the detailed information on the basis of which the assessment and interpretation of an artist's work must rely if these are to be anything other than speculative and self-engendering. The first essential is to establish the authenticity of each individual work of art.[1] Thus, for too long the favorite and most reproduced watercolor in the Tate Gallery was a version of the "Wise and Foolish Virgins" that is at best a product of John Linnell's family, or pupils.[2] The sentimentalization of a misunderstood Blake image had, in fact, vitiated the effect of the whole Tate Gallery collection.

Next in importance is the establishment, as far as possible, of the date of an individual work. Not only does an artist's style develop, the emotions and ideas he wishes to express also develop; indeed the two go hand in hand, combining to create an artistic personality ultimately expressed only in visual terms with an organic developing life of its own. The discovery of the meaning of a work of art, even in the limited degree to which it can be explained verbally, depends upon our placing it at the correct moment in this development.

In like manner, the context of each work must be determined where this has affected its form and hence its content: influence of other artists, sources, even art fashions must be taken into account. For no artist works in a vacuum; and Blake's origins, at a time when the advanced art of the day was the neoclassicism of even such an establishment figure as Benjamin West, and Blake's training in the fashionable world of antiquarian engravings, form an essential background to the later development not only of his style but equally of his thought.

77

The intended audience of an artist, where this can be discovered, is also of importance in determining the significance of the individual work. In some artists, for instance Blake's younger contemporary J. M. W. Turner, there is a clear distinction of intent between the works he exhibited at the Royal Academy and elsewhere, and those private works which he regarded as unsuitable for public exhibition. In the case of Blake, whose efforts at public exhibitions were rare and unsuccessful, this distinction hardly applies. But one must establish what works were executed for specific patrons and what works were final statements, what were sketches, and even what works can be regarded, from the point of view of the artist himself, as failures. A prime example is the unfinished manuscript of *Vala or the Four Zoas,* worked over to the point of unintelligibility and self-destruction: fascinating for the insight it gives into Blake's thought and methods but not to be regarded as part of the canon in the same way as are the finished illuminated books.

Finally, the actual physical state of the work must be established as closely as possible, both as an end in itself and as a source of information about other aspects of the work. Here precise size and medium can both be significant.

The establishment of these "minute particulars" also produces, almost unconsciously, an understanding of the artistic personality as a whole. One gets to know the whole through the details—a Blakean lesson that pays off in Blake scholarship, where the analysis of individual works, or groups of works (such as the illustrations to *The Book of Job,* to Dante, Milton or Gray), or of episodes in British history, have on the whole been more productive than the application of what often seem to be preconceived theories to the whole output.

The assessment of the authenticity of a work, and following that, the determination of its date, depends on two main factors: documentary evidence and a seemingly intuitive personal judgment. Contemporary records, letters, accounts, exhibition catalogues, reviews, inscriptions on the work itself, provide of course the most convincing factual evidence. The establishment of a provenance, the tracing of a work back to its original owner, is a second means. This can often be done through secondary documents such as sale catalogues and later exhibitions, or inscriptions, including the "Christie Stencil" (a combination of stenciled figures and letters that can be tied in to the auctioneer's day-books and as often as not can lead one to a sale or to the name of a previous owner).

The use of documentary evidence needs to be supplemented by what is often regarded as the "mystique of the eye." In fact, there is very little mystique about this. Essentially it is recognition based on experience and visual memory. Obviously one has to build up one's terms of reference by taking every opportunity of looking at fully documented, authenticated and, if possible, datable works. The only element involving "mystique" is that certain people do seem to be born with a better "eye" than others, just as some people, not necessarily the most musical, are born with perfect pitch.

Sometimes these two forms of assessment may conflict. A work may have a good provenance, yet not look right. A prime example is the "New Zealand" set of illustrations to *The Book of Job*.[3] Here the slightly disturbing appearance of the watercolors makes one look rather more closely at the documentary evidence. They can be traced back to the collection of Albin Martin, who emigrated to New Zealand from Great Britain, where he had been a pupil of Blake's patron John Linnell. Linnell had indeed commissioned the second set of watercolor illustrations to *The Book of Job* and had encouraged Blake to engrave them. The New Zealand set could be seen as a set of finished watercolors reduced to the size intended for the engravings as an aid in their preparation. But there already exists, in the Fitzwilliam Museum, a series of reduced-size, though freer, drawings done in preparation for the engravings. Studying Linnell's own career as an artist, moreover, one finds that he taught his children (a number of whom became painters), and presumably his other pupils, in part by setting them to copy works by other artists, including Blake.[4] Indeed Linnell himself noted, in his diary for September 12, 1821, that he had begun a copy of Blake's "Cain and Abel" which he finished on the 14th. This has led the present author to doubt the authenticity of the small replica of "Cain and Abel" in the Keynes collection—a work that in its slightly lifeless miniaturistlike delicacy reveals the same worrying features as do the New Zealand *Job* watercolors.[5]

There are certain characteristics peculiar to the cataloguing of Blake's works. He had very few patrons, the vast majority of his sales being to Thomas Butts, William Hayley, the Rev. Joseph Thomas, and John Linnell. What he did not sell, a considerable amount of his output, passed to his widow and from her to Frederick Tatham. Therefore a firm provenance, going back to an early owner, is more important and helpful than it would be in most cases. Luckily it is also easier to establish.

William Rossetti's list catalogue in the first (1863) edition of Gilchrist's *Life of William Blake* came at just the right moment, before too much had been dispersed from the early collections. Sales had begun in the 1850s but these were known to Rossetti who also, equally helpfully, recorded the main second-generation collections, those of Richard Monkton Milnes, later first Lord Houghton and father of the first Marquess of Crewe; William Stirling, later Sir William Stirling-Maxwell, Bart.; J. D., later Lord, Coleridge; C. W. Dilke; F. T. Palgrave; J. C. Strange; and Gilchrist's widow. He also records a number of dealers such as Harvey, Evans, Bohn, and Palser.

William Rossetti's own copy of the 1863 edition of Gilchrist's *Life* still exists in the Houghton Library, Harvard University, and contains a number of additions and annotations.[6] He adds, for instance, further sets of illustrations to Milton's *Comus* and *Paradise Lost* in addition to those he had listed as having been painted for Butts, indicating that they had belonged to "Chase" (Drummond Percy Chase, grandson of the Rev. Joseph Thomas[7]) and subsequently to Alfred Aspland, by whom they were lent to the exhibition at the Burlington Fine Arts Club in 1876 and sold at Sotheby's in 1885. Unfortunately, in his lists in the second (1880) edition of Gilchrist's *Life,* he omitted any reference to contemporary ownership, indicating only those works that had belonged (and might still belong) to the Butts and Linnell collections.

Both editions of Rossetti's lists are marred, moreover, by duplicated entries and misunderstood subjects. He often failed to recognise a work he saw in a sale (or perhaps, to be charitable, saw listed in a sale catalogue) as one he had already recorded in, say, the Butts collection, and his upbringing in an anarchist and free-thinking family led him to misinterpret a number of biblical and other subjects. However, his descriptions and notes on ownership are usually sufficient for one to be able to arrive at a fair idea of the nature even of lost works and, a peculiarity to be touched on later, their place in groups of works done for a particular patron at a particular time.

A rather strange criterion in assessing the authenticity of works by Blake is that quality of execution is relatively immaterial. Blake was a very uneven artist and many of his earlier works and scrappier drawings are almost totally lacking in technical merit. With the great draughtsmen of the Renaissance, Michaelangelo and Raphael, quality is the final touchstone. With Blake, one can justifiably argue that a drawing too bad to be by, say, Flaxman or Stothard can nevertheless, other things being equal, be by Blake.

Blake's designs often exist in a number of versions. Some artists rarely if ever duplicate themselves, but Blake did so quite happily, as in the case of "Queen Katharine's Dream" and the series of illustrations to *The Book of Job* and the poems of Milton. Usually, however, there was a specific reason. The first version of "The Wise and Foolish Virgins" was sold to Thomas Butts for one guinea on May 12, 1805, as one of the large group of watercolor illustrations to the Bible painted for him from 1800 to circa 1805.[8] A second version was in the Linnell collection and shows a softer, more relaxed treatment consonant with Blake's late style after Linnell became his patron in 1818. A variant of this stage in the evolution of the design was painted for William Haines of Chichester, a fellow engraver with Blake for Hayley's *Life of Romney*. Finally the President of the Royal Academy, Sir Thomas Lawrence, commissioned versions of this and "Queen Katharine's Dream" for fifteen guineas each, largely, one feels, as a matter of charity. Here the pose of the foremost Wise Virgin, as well as the treatment, is more relaxed. All four of these versions can be traced back to their original owners. All the more reason, therefore, to suspect two further versions: that in the Tate Gallery, already referred to, which is a copy of the version done for Lawrence, and that in the Santa Barbara Museum of Art, with a history back to our old friend Albin Martin, which is a copy of the Linnell version.[9]

Blake is also unusual in the way he paints works in series, as in his illustrations to the Bible (in particular *The Book of Job*) and the writings of Milton and Dante, or illustrations in which the text forms an integral part of the design, as in the cases of Young's *Night Thoughts* and the poems of Thomas Gray. Because of the limited number of Blake's patrons and the ease in tracing the provenance of most of his works, it is usually a simple matter to reassemble those series that have been dispersed and even, as has been mentioned above, to identify lost works as being from such series.

For instance, although Rossetti only listed the painting of "The Miracle of the Loaves and Fishes" among "works of unascertained method," his giving the former owner as Butts led one to guess that it must have been part of either the tempera series or the watercolor series of biblical subjects done for Butts in 1799 to 1800 and 1800 to circa 1805 respectively; when it appeared at Sotheby's on November 23, 1966, it turned out to be one of the small group of temperas painted on copper from among the first group, most of which are on canvas.

Similarly, for many years it was thought that the second set of illustrations to *Paradise Lost,* painted for Butts in 1808, only consisted of the nine designs in the Museum of Fine Arts, Boston, unlike the twelve smaller designs of 1807 painted for the Rev. Joseph Thomas and now in the Huntington Library and Art Gallery, San Marino.[10] In 1863, Rossetti listed only the nine in his main "List No. 1, Works in Colour." But, concealed in his list no. 3, "Works of Unascertained Method" and identified by the appropriate lines from *Paradise Lost* rather than direct titles, are three more works "from Mr. Butts" which can be shown to be part of the same series: "Satan Arousing the Rebel Angels" in the Victoria and Albert Museum, "Satan, Sin and Death" in the Huntington Library and Art Gallery, and "The Judgement of Adam and Eve" in the Houghton Library, Harvard University. All are close in size and style to the Boston watercolors but had been sold from the Butts collection on a different occasion. Because of the provenance and the likelihood that Blake had done a full set of twelve designs when repeating his *Paradise Lost* series it was even possible to guess, while it was still untraced in the White collection before being presented to the Houghton Library in 1966, that "The Judgement of Adam and Eve" was, like the other two, part of the same series.

A further factor linking two of the three designs with the rest of the series is the form of their signatures, a written-out "WBlake 1808," the same as occurs on all but one of the Boston watercolors. On the other hand, "Satan, Sin and Death" is signed with Blake's typical neat monogram, "WB" with a loop rising up from the foot of the "B" to enclose the letters "inv" (for *invenit*) above the "WB." It is impossible to believe that Blake would have omitted, or been allowed by his patron Butts to omit, the most dramatic subject of the entire series, a subject often treated on its own by other artists such as Hogarth, James Barry, and Fuseli. Rather, the form of the signature leads one to the conjecture that this design, on its own, may have preceded both sets of illustrations to *Paradise Lost,* though only by a year or so.

Blake seems to have changed from using his monogram "WB inv" to a written-out signature in about 1806.[11] The 1807 Huntington Library *Paradise Lost* watercolors are signed "WBlake," either preceded or followed by the date or, in five cases, with no date at all. Of the series of temperas and watercolors of biblical subjects painted for Butts, those known to have been executed between 1799 and 1805 are signed with the monogram. The only examples bearing later dates display a form of written-out signature: three of 1806, "By the Waters of Babylon" (Fogg Museum, Cambridge, Mass.), "The Repose of the Holy Family in Egypt" (Metropolitan Museum, New York), and "The Assumption of the Virgin" (Royal Collection, Windsor) are signed "WB inv," written out, and one of 1809, "The Whore of Babylon" (British Museum), which is also distinct in style from the rest of the series, is signed "WBlake inv & del."

That the changeover took place in 1806 is supported by the evidence of the illustrations to Shakespeare done in this period. Of Blake's six extra-illustrations to a Second Folio Shakespeare painted for the Rev. Joseph Thomas and now in the British Museum, those actually dated 1806 are signed with the "WB inv" monogram, as is the one undated example. The two dated 1809 are signed "WBlake." The watercolor of "The Vision of Queen Katharine" painted for Thomas Butts and dated 1807 (now in the Fitzwilliam Museum) is signed with a written-out "WB inv" (the later version painted for Sir Thomas Lawrence circa 1825 and now in the Rosenwald Collection is signed "WBlake inv," and the earlier version in the Fitzwilliam Museum, possibly of circa 1793, has the detached initials "W B"). Perhaps therefore the large "Satan, Sin and Death" was painted on its own in about 1805, when Blake was still signing with a monogram, the version in the smaller 1807 set for Thomas following it in date. When Blake came to do a second *Paradise Lost* set for Butts, he could have built it round the existing large "Satan, Sin and Death."

Blake's later signatures seem to follow the pattern established in 1806. The written-out signatures appear on the later Milton series, *On the Morning of Christ's Nativity* of 1809 and *L'Allegro and Il Penseroso* and *Paradise Regained,* both watermarked 1816, and on late temperas such as "The Ghost of a Flea" of circa 1819 and "The Body of Abel Found by Adam and Eve" (Plate 42) and "Satan Smiting Job with Sore Boils" of circa 1826–27. The Dante illustrations of 1824–27, at first sight a possible exception, are signed, when they are signed, with the initials "WB" but, although the two letters are joined as in the earlier monogram, there is no loop rising up over the letters, and the abbreviation "inv" is omitted.

However, it is perhaps tempting providence to place too great a reliance on the form of signature as an argument for dating. In the case of the large color prints, for example, the position is exceedingly complicated. Some examples are dated 1795 and all would seem to have been printed in or about that year. The eight examples listed in Blake's account with Thomas Butts of March 3, 1806, as having been delivered on July 5 or September 7, 1805, are all dated 1795 (with the possible exception of "Christ Appearing to the Apostles" at Yale, where there are only indistinct traces of what may have been a date; the rest are in the Tate Gallery)[12] and signed with the monogram (on the Tate's "House of Death" the "inv" seems to have been omitted though the loop usually enclosing it is present). Three further examples are dated 1795 but with the written-out "WBlake" ("Satan Exulting over Eve" in the Bateson collection, "Nebuchadnezzar" at Minneapolis, and "The House of Death" in the British Museum); none of these, so far as can be ascertained, was in the Butts collection. On the other hand, three further prints from the Butts collection were signed "WBlake" without a date, the signature actually being scratched into the pigments.[13] It is not certain whether Butts owned a print of "Naomi Entreating Ruth and Orpah to Return to the Land of Moab" to make up a full set of twelve subjects; he already had a watercolor of 1803 of the same subject. Of the two known prints, one is unsigned while the other, in the Victoria and Albert Museum, is inscribed "Fresco WBlake inv." Four other prints are inscribed the same way: "God Judging Adam" in the Metropolitan Museum; "Newton" belonging to the Lutheran Church in America, Philadelphia; "Hecate" in the National Gallery of Scotland; and "Christ Appearing to the Apostles" in the Rosenwald collection, National Gallery of Art, Washington; the version of "Pity" in the Metropolitan Museum, New York, appears to lack the word "Fresco" but has the written-out signature "WBlake inv." "Fresco" was the word used by Blake in his *Descriptive Catalogue* of 1809 to describe his form of tempera, which was very similar to the medium used in the color prints.

It is possible, but perhaps unjustified, to read a pattern into these apparently haphazardly varied forms of signature for similar works. It seems unlikely that Blake sold any of his large color prints except for the eleven or twelve bought by Butts; those of the others that can be traced back to an early collection passed from Mrs. Blake to Frederick Tatham, though a group was offered to Dawson Turner in a letter of June 9, 1818. Blake is known on occasion to have dated a later version of a work with the year of its original invention. The date "1795" on some of the prints may therefore merely record the date of the original printing (it is possible, though not certain, that some of the coloring by hand in watercolor was done later, perhaps just prior to the possible sale). Those prints known to have been sold to Butts in 1805 are dated 1795 with the monogram signature that Blake is known to have used up to and including 1805. The prints from the Butts collection with the written-out "WBlake" could have been sold subsequently, from 1806 onwards when no specific works were named in the accounts between Blake and Butts, at which time they could have been given the new form of signature. The "Fresco" inscriptions could have been put on anytime after 1806, perhaps in or about 1809 when Blake was using the word in his *Descriptive Catalogue*.

In the case of the large color prints it is very difficult to draw stylistic distinctions between the various works, save that some examples, including all those bought by Butts, are more finished than others. In the case of the first set of illustrations to *The Book of Job*, however, stylistic considerations support the evidence suggested by the form of signature.[14] This first set of watercolors is first documented when, on September 7, 1821, Linnell recorded that he had traced their outlines preparatory to Blake's using these drawings as the basis for a second set for Linnell. This first set was sold to Monkton Milnes from the Butts collection, and it seems reasonable from the context to accept the conclusion that they had been painted for Butts and borrowed back for the occasion. Until recently it has always been presumed that the Butts watercolors dated from only a few years before the Linnell set, but the present writer, supported independently by Bo Lindberg, has long felt that for stylistic reasons they should be dated considerably earlier, to the first decade of the 19th century. In particular their treatment, with clear outlines and relatively flat areas of generally palish color, resembles that of the biblical watercolors painted for Butts between 1800 and 1805, especially those that can be dated circa 1805. It also seemed logical that Blake, having painted one Job subject as part of the biblical series ("Job Confessing his Presumption to God" in the National Gallery of Scotland), should have followed up this series with a group of designs devoted exclusively to *The Book of Job,* or even painted them as a subgroup within the main series. Not many of the Butts *Job* watercolors are in fact signed, but designs nos. 5, "Satan Going forth" and 11, "Job's Evil Dream" (Plate 85) bear the "WB inv" monogram. On no. 10, "Job Rebuked by his Friends," however, "inv" follows the "WB." The signatures therefore, if inconsistently, support the early dating already suspected, and the very fact that the signature on no. 10 is different perhaps points to the date when Blake was abandoning the monogram for the written-out signature, circa 1805–06.

The evidence of the eye raises another problem with the Butts *Job* series. Two of the designs are very different from the rest in their rather messy, loose technique and heavy coloring. These are nos. 17, "The Vision of Christ," and 20, "Job and his Daughters" (Plate 86). One explanation is that they were painted, at least in part, by Mrs. Blake or by Thomas Butts or his son, to whom Blake gave lessons. This may be so; in particular there is some resemblance to the more heavily worked of the illustrations to Bunyan's *Pilgrim's Progress* in the Frick collection, New York, which seem to have been left unfinished by Blake and were perhaps worked over by his widow (they subsequently passed to Frederick Tatham).[15] More significant, however, is the fact that, unlike the rest of the series, they are similar in general points of style to Blake's late works. In addition they are on a different kind of paper from their companions. Most significant of all, they differ so much from their counterparts in the Linnell series that the latter cannot be based on tracings of the kind that Linnell is recorded as having made from the series as a whole in 1821.

What follows is pure conjecture, but of the kind that is perhaps justified when one has been working on the minutiae of Blake's individual works for so long. When Blake first illustrated *The Book of Job* for Thomas Butts he may have done only nineteen subjects: no title page (obviously not, as no engravings were then projected), no "Vision of Christ," and, because Butts already had a tempera version of this subject, as we shall see, no "Job and his Daughters." When he redid the series for Linnell he could have added the two new subjects and then, in gratitude to Butts for the loan of the first series, or to avoid his reproaches, repeated the two new subjects in his latest style, perhaps leaving them unfinished at his death, to be completed by his widow. Alternatively, the more sketchy nature of his late watercolor style could have led Butts or his son to strengthen their coloring.

In the final engraving of "Job and his Daughters" (Plate 87), the scene is an interior with representations of three incidents from Job's life on the wall behind the figures. In the center is God appearing to Job in the whirlwind, a scene shown in one of the other designs in both the watercolor series and the engravings. On each side are scenes not otherwise represented in the three series, the destruction of Job's servants by the Chaldeans and the destruction of Job's plowmen (by Satan, rather than by the Sabeans as in Job 1: 15). In the tempera painting (Plate 88) now in the Rosenwald collection the setting is the same, which has led to the painting being dated, from William Rossetti on, to late in Blake's career, to the time of the Job engravings, circa 1825. This late dating was reinforced by the fact that the Butts watercolor (Plate 86) shows the figure in an outdoor setting. The Linnell version (Plate 89) is a strange combination of outdoor and indoor scenes (of two related sketches of the 1820s, in the Rosenwald collection and belonging to Dr. R. E. Hemphill, the latter is definitely an outdoor scene, the former a mixture of outdoor and indoor elements; their place in the evolution of the composition is a separate, even more complex problem[16]). The tempera therefore, at first sight, seems to be Blake's final version, with an interior setting as evolved in the engraving.

However, here is a case when the physical evidence of the picture is paramount. In size, format, and above all in the actual way in which Blake's tempera medium has aged, cracking and to a certain extent darkening, the picture is at all points similar to the group of temperas on canvas of biblical subjects painted for Butts in 1799–1800, and not at all to the completely differently executed temperas of Blake's late years.[17] This physical evidence is supported by such factors, perhaps inconclusive in themselves, as the style of the figures and in particular their faces. Blake's final solution for the problem of the best setting for "Job and his Daughters" was, therefore, a return to his earliest depiction of the subject rather than the result of a gradual evolution. When painting the watercolors for Linnell and, above all, for Butts, he probably felt it necessary to do something different from the painting already owned by Butts; when it came to the engraving it was no longer so important to avoid what had always been the most satisfactory solution. Further, when Blake came to add the subject to Butts' series of watercolors (Plate 86), it was almost incumbent upon him to change the setting from the interior scene of the tempera already owned by Butts. The three incidents from Job's life appear in a break in the clouds but are only sketchily indicated, while the three daughters are no longer just passive listeners but are recording Job's words.

There remains the most important of all the distinctions between Blake and most other visual artists, the fact that he was equally creative as a writer. This is obviously of the utmost importance in interpreting the content of his work in the visual arts, a task in which the cataloguer is not directly involved though it is perhaps important, particularly for the non-Blake expert, to summarize the interpretation of an individual work. It is to be hoped, furthermore, that the facts set out in a catalogue entry will provide the scaffolding on which the interpretation can be built.

The close integration of Blake's writings and his work in the visual arts, both being the manifestation of a single "Poetic Genius," also means that the writings can sometimes be helpful in solving problems about the designs. This is obviously most true for the illustrations in Blake's illuminated books, but the case of the long-lost color print of "God Judging Adam" reflects a wider application. The full details have been set out elsewhere,[18] but, to sum up, here was a case where the appearance of the so-called "Elijah Handing on the Mantle of Inspiration to Elisha" belied its supposedly optimistic content. A faint inscription, long hidden under the mount, appeared to read "God . . . to Adam." There was a documented color print, untraced, of "God Judging Adam," and it seemed much more likely that the 1795 set of large color prints should have consisted of twelve rather than thirteen designs. The final confirmation that the "Elijah and Elisha" design, so-called since the 1860s, was in fact "God Judging Adam" came from the parallel imagery to be found in Blake's *First Book of Urizen* of the previous year.

NOTES

1. Full documentation of the works discussed in this essay will appear in my forthcoming catalogue of Blake's works, to be published by the

William Blake Trust. References to contemporary documentation, letters, etc., are not given when these are easily accessible in G. E. Bentley, Jr., *Blake Records* (Oxford: Clarendon Press, 1969), or current editions of Blake's writings.

2.   See Martin Butlin, *William Blake: A Complete Catalogue of the Works in the Tate Gallery,* 2nd ed. (London: Tate Gallery, 1971), p. 54 no. 44 and repro.

3.   This series is accepted as genuine in Laurence Binyon and Geoffrey Keynes, *Illustrations of the Book of Job by William Blake* (New York: Pierpont Morgan Library, 1935), I, 12, 47-50, the series repro. in color in fascicle 5; Philip Hofer, "Drawings by William Blake for 'The Book of Job'," *Connoisseur,* 97 (1936), 125-27; Hofer, *Illustrations of the Book of Job* (New York: Dutton, 1937), pp. 7, 9, the series repro. in color; Arnold Fawcus, "Blake's Illustrations for the Book of Job," *Times Literary Supplement* (March 15, 1974), 271-72. It is rejected by, *inter alia,* Anthony Blunt, *The Art of William Blake* (New York: Columbia Univ. Press, 1959), p. 31n.; Bo Lindberg, *William Blake's Illustrations to the Book of Job* (Abo, Finland: Abo Akademi, 1973), pp. 33-6; and David Bindman, letter in *Times Literary Supplement* (March 23, 1974), 341.

4.   See, for instance, Linnell's letter of March 16, 1831, about his children's tracings of Blake's Dante drawings (Bentley, *Blake Records,* p. 406).

5.   Geoffrey Keynes, *Blake Studies,* 2nd ed. (Oxford: Clarendon Press, 1971), pp. 145-46, repro. pl. 39.

6.   Martin Butlin, "William Rossetti's Annotations of Gilchrist's *Life of William Blake,*" *Blake Newsletter,* 2 (1968-69), 39-40; Joseph Anthony Wittreich, Jr., "Further Observations on William Rossetti's Annotations ...," *Blake Newsletter,* 3 (1969-70), 48-51.

7.   Leslie Parris, "William Blake's Mr. Thomas," *Times Literary Supplement* (Dec. 5, 1968), 1390.

8.   See Butlin, *Blake: ... Tate Gallery,* p. 54 no. 44 for all the versions of this composition and further references.

9.   See Alfred Moir, ed., *European Drawings in the Collection of the Santa Barbara Museum of Art* (Santa Barbara: Museum of Art, 1976), p. 126, repro.

10.   See Martin Butlin, "A Minute Particular Particularized: Blake's Second Set of Illustrations to *Paradise Lost,*" *Blake Newsletter,* 5 (1972-73), pp. 44-46.

11.   The following six paragraphs are a development of a suggestion first made in the article listed under note 10, where certain references to reproductions are given.

12.   See Butlin, *Blake: ... Tate Gallery,* pp. 34-41, nos. 14-18, 22-23, and also under no. 24.

13.   Butlin, *Blake: . . . Tate Gallery,* pp. 38–9, nos. 19–20; on the third work, the version of "Satan Exulting over Eve" in the collection of John Craxton, the initial "W" is absent.

14.   Blake's series of illustrations to *The Book of Job* are illustrated in color in the publication by Binyon and Keynes listed in note 3, which see for other references to the literature.

15.   Repro. in John Bunyan, *The Pilgrim's Progress,* ed. G. B. Harrison, intro. Geoffrey Keynes (New York: Limited Editions Club, 1941).

16.   See Geoffrey Keynes, *Drawings of William Blake* (New York: Dover, 1970), no. 80, repro.; Kerrison Preston, ed., *The Blake Collection of W. Graham Robertson* (London: Faber and Faber, 1952), pp. 140–41, no. 51, repro. pl. 47.

17.   For examples of each group see Butlin, *Blake: . . . Tate Gallery,* pp. 42–4, nos. 25, 26, and 28, and pp. 62–3, nos. 54–55.

18.   Martin Butlin, "Blake's 'God Judging Adam' Rediscovered," *Burlington Magazine,* 107 (1965), 86–9, the Tate example repro. p. 87 fig. 43; rpt. in Robert N. Essick, ed., *The Visionary Hand* (Los Angeles: Hennessey & Ingalls, 1973), pp. 303–10, repro. pl. 103.

Blake's Theory and Practice of Imitation

David Bindman

I F Blake made a triumphant entry into poetic creation with the *Poetical Sketches,* his entry into the visual arts was less auspicious. His very early drawings, I think it will be agreed, are poor. The forms have little sense of structure, and his command of outline is hesitant in the extreme. His acceptance as a student at the Royal Academy might be taken as a comment upon the poor standard of artistic achievement in England, but it is also clear from records that in the years following his brief period at the Royal Academy his artistic reputation was unusually high; indeed he was probably never again to receive such unqualified admiration. In later years he looked back wistfully upon his youthful reputation, and he sought ever more fruitlessly to recapture it; he exhibited his early "Penance of Jane Shore" (Plate 90) in the 1809 exhibition in order to demonstrate "that the productions of our youth and of our maturer age are equal in all essential points" (E 541), and he often comforted himself with the belief that his friends' neglect of him was due to envy of his superiority. Of this early reputation there is ample evidence. It must have meant something to have had a watercolor exhibited at the Royal Academy in his first year as an R.A. student; and according to Flaxman, writing in 1783, a Mr. Hawkins commissioned a capital drawing from Blake "for whose advantage in consideration of his great talents he seems desirous to employ his utmost interest."[1] In the following year Flaxman wrote to William Hayley that the same Hawkins was "so convinced of his uncommon talents that he is now endeavouring to raise a subscription to send him to finish his studies in Rome" and Flaxman mentioned in the same letter that "Mr Romney thinks his historical drawings rank with those of Michelangelo."[2]

The contrast between this kind of praise and the reality of the work can only be resolved by assuming that Blake's contemporaries applied quite different standards from ourselves. If we begin by looking at a recently discovered Blake drawing, probably of the "Battle of Hastings" (Plate 91),[3] we can perhaps get some idea of these standards. Apart from its woodenness, the most striking thing to an art historian is its essentially derivative nature. It belongs to a tradition which goes back to the fresco of the "Battle of Constantine" by the Raphael studio in the Vatican, for it contains on a much smaller scale a similar melée of triumphant horsemen and defeated warriors falling back in postures reminiscent of classical sculptures. As it happens, the Raphael "Battle of Constantine" was the subject of a classic article by the art historian Aby Warburg written in 1914,[4] in which he argued that the painting was a characteristic example of the dangers of the too-zealous adaptation of classical formulae, for, as he pointed out, there is virtually no figure or gesture which does not have some precedent in a sarcophagus or triumphal relief. These formulae he called *Pathosformeln,* and he had previously argued that artists of the late quattrocento had used them as a means of achieving an intensified expression of mental and physical states among the essentially static forms of their art. The principal fallen figure in Blake's battle drawing is an obvious example of a classical formula, for it is reminiscent of the famous antique dying Gaul, but probably filtered through Renaissance sources. In the recently discovered drawing of the "Great Plague of London,"[5] belonging to a History of England series of 1779–80, the group on the right is a bizarre kind of "Pietà" mixed up with a Crucifixion group. Blake worked up the composition in a more finished version of about 1784–5 (Plate 92) where it presumably forms part of a group of apocalyptic subjects, which can be associated with apocalyptic designs of the years 1780–5 by artists Blake no doubt knew personally. Mortimer's engraving of "Death on a Pale Horse" of 1781 is equally full of formulae of Renaissance and probably classical origin, and the principal dying figure in Benjamin West's drawing of the same subject of 1783 (Royal Academy) is derived directly from the celebrated "Ariadne" in the Vatican, but given a pathos which is not in the original. In a painting by George Romney of ca. 1784 (Vassar College) the pathos is also achieved by motifs from earlier masters.

These artists did not regard borrowing as shameful, but on the contrary they wore the badge of imitation with pride. In this they conformed entirely to the standards of the age, and to the precepts laid down by Reynolds, who claimed in *Discourse II* that "Invention, strictly speaking, is little more than a new combination of those images which have been previously gathered and deposited in the memory: nothing can come of nothing: he who has laid up no materials, can produce no combinations."[6] Fuseli was equally specific, in his third Academy lecture of 1800, in advocating the incorporation of figures from earlier artists into paintings: "Horace, the most judicious of critics, when treating the use of poetic words, tells his pupils that the adoption of an old word, rendered novel by a skilful construction with others, will entitle the poet to the praise of original diction. The same will be granted to the judicious adoption of figures in art." Fuseli argued in 1794 that "neither to 'copy' nor 'create' is a proper term for an art, the business of which is to imitate and invent," and in his definition of invention he returns to the word's Latin root:

> The term invention never ought to be so far misconstrued as to be confounded with that of creation, incompatible with our notions of limited being, an idea of pure astonishment, and admissable only when we mention Omnipotence: to invent is to find: to find something, presupposes its existence somewhere, implicitly or explicitly, scattered or in a mass.[7]

The admiration that Blake's early art received can be explained, therefore, by the recognition, among those artists who had aspirations toward History painting, that he understood the necessity of "the judicious adoption of figures," for this was a sign of his learning as an artist, just as the ability to quote from the classical writers was an accomplishment becoming to a serious poet. Warburg had argued, however, as had Burckhardt before him, that the Antique provided a repertoire primarily of emotive or potentially emotive gestures and forms, and that the Dionysiac element of antiquity was most fruitful but potentially the most dangerous influence.[8] But the most influential eighteenth-century treatises on art were predominantly concerned with the Apollonian heritage, appropriating many of the most seemingly Dionysiac works into their canon. Thus Winckelmann, whom Blake read as a boy, regarded the Hellenistic "Laocoön" group as the very epitome of the "edel Einfalt und stille Grösse" of the Greeks, and Mengs followed him by painting in the "Parnassus" a work of tranquility bordering upon the insipid.

Blake's friend Henry Fuseli was, in effect, the champion of a

wider conception of antiquity; he was enough of a classical scholar to
provide a real defense of the depiction of extreme emotion in painting by reference to a classical precedent both in literature and art.
Fuseli claimed Homer as his authority for the depiction of Terror in
art, and argued that "Laocoon, with his sons, will always remain a
sufficient answer to all that has been retailed in our days on the
limits of the art by tame antiquarians from tamer painters."[9] His
own art was based upon the antique—there are countless examples
of open imitation of antique forms in his paintings—and yet expresses the extremes of Homeric passion. Even at his seemingly
most extreme as in, say, the "Nightmare," Fuseli was always working
within the limits of antique types, and Nicholas Powell has traced the
ancestry of the sleeping form back through Reynolds' "Death of
Dido" and Giulio Romano to the Vatican "Ariadne" herself.[10]

One cannot, however, readily characterize Blake's early work as
either Apollonian or Dionysian. Blake's magnificent early *Job* engraving of ca. 1786 and its study in the Tate (Plate 93) bear the signs
of meditation upon the problem; the theme involves suffering and
faith in the face of adversity, and Blake has finally come down firmly
upon the side of stoic resignation rather than open anguish; as
Winckelmann says of the "Laocoön": "As the bottom of the sea lies
peaceful beneath a foaming surface, a great soul lies sedate beneath
the strife of passions in Greek figures."[11] But in the 1790s a less
restrained emotion comes to the fore, and in the *Book of Urizen*,
under the liberating influence of Fuseli's Miltonic paintings, the
protagonists express their anguish through contorted bodies and
physiognomy.

If Blake's means of expression tend to change in the 1790s,
many motifs established in his earlier years reappear in a distilled
form in the same decade. The great "Pestilence" plate in *Europe,* for
example, is in reality a conflation of motifs from the earlier compositions representing the "Great Plague of London." Similarly, the
title page of *America* and to some degree the frontispiece are derived
from a composition first known to have existed in 1784, and known
through a number of later versions, of "A Breach in a City: The
Morning after the Battle." Often we find the germ of an essentially
Blakean motif in the work of other artists. It is well known, for
example, that the frontispiece for "Asia" in the *Song of Los* is preceded by what Rossetti called the "fairy" design by Robert Blake in
the *Notebook;* but this design in turn, I believe, goes back to a

Stothard engraving of 1781 for Thomas Tickell's poem *Kensington Gardens,* a motif which may also be reflected in "Infant Joy" in *Songs of Innocence.*

Anthony Blunt has long made us familiar with Blake's indebtedness to earlier artists, particularly Renaissance and Mannerist, and he concluded essentially that the borrowings were unconscious, the outpourings of a well stocked mind, typical of an artist who had haunted print shops from an early age. But there seems to me to be evidence that Blake continued to see his art as, in one sense—although of course not exclusively—a process of imitation, but not in an obvious way. The plate in the *Book of Urizen* (Plate 94) of Los, Enitharmon, and the adolescent Orc, for example, evokes, at least for an art historian, and one may assume for many of Blake's contemporaries, two interrelated themes familiar from Renaissance paintings. In the first place, it recalls the theme of "Venus and Cupid at Vulcan's forge," but the theme of jealousy suggests also Vulcan's jealousy of Mars and Venus, here directed at the adolescent Orc. One might argue that Blake has simply recalled Renaissance prints he had seen in a print shop, but I believe there is more to it than that. In the first place, the character of Los in *The Book of Urizen* owes much to Vulcan; he is also a blacksmith and a kind of image-maker to the Gods, for it is his job to create the form of the chaotic Urizen. Furthermore, Los's jealousy, which makes him bind down Orc, exactly parallels Vulcan's in chaining Prometheus to the rock, and the Promethean nature of Orc requires no further argument. Blake is, therefore, "imitating" earlier works of art in a perfectly acceptable way, but there are potential problems in such imitation. So long as Blake accepted the widespread eighteenth-century assumption of the supremacy of Greek art—and there is every evidence that he did so in the 1790s—then Blake's practice of imitation did not present a dilemma, and this may apply equally to the incorporation of Greek mythology, as well as artistic forms. But after 1800 or so he began to turn against "the silly Greek & Latin slaves of the Sword" (E 94) and to regard Greek art and literature as Allegory rather than Inspiration; i.e., the product of Memory rather than Imagination. For Blake there was a tradition going back to Josephus at least that the writings of classical antiquity were derived from Hebraic sources, and thus stolen and perverted, and "set up by artifice against the Sublime of the Bible" (E 94); but art presented a bigger problem, for there was no surviving Hebrew art which could be regarded as a prototype for Greek sculptures. One might imagine that at this point Blake would do what Romantic theorists like Friedrich Schlegel were beginning to do in Germany, and effectively demote classical antiquity to a Pagan realm, promoting Christian art as the true model for posterity. Blake was certainly drawn to the Gothic, particularly after 1800; nonetheless, he was unable to relinquish his profound feelings for Greek art. From these apparently conflicting impulses comes one of the more bizarre artistic theories in the history of art, in which all contradictions are reconciled and only historical probability is sacrificed.

Blake's argument in *The Descriptive Catalogue* of 1809 can be reduced for the moment to the following propositions: the Jews of the Old Testament were visual artists, and their work consisted of not just the few decorative figures described in the account of the Temple of Solomon, but prototypes of all the canon of surviving antique sculpture of all ancient peoples. What we know of these Hebrew works comes entirely from ancient and especially Greek imitations. Secondly, the Hebrew prototypes were divinely inspired; and thirdly, and perhaps most important, William Blake was divinely inspired, and thus had "been taken in vision into the ancient republics, monarchies, and patriarchates of Asia, [and] has seen those wonderful originals called in the Sacred Scriptures the Cherubim" (E 521–22). The Cherubim were the originals

> from which the Greeks and Hetrurians copied Hercules, Farnese, Venus of Medicis, Apollo Belvidere, and all the grand works of ancient art. They were executed in a very superior style to those justly admired copies, being with their accompaniments terrific and grand in the highest degree. The Artist has endeavoured to emulate the grandeur of those seen in his vision, and to apply it to modern Heroes, on a smaller scale. (E 522)

Blake has claimed for himself, and for all other true artists, divine powers through the exercise of the imagination, and it is only through an apprehension of the "Originals" that such images can be given form on earth. But for all his undeniable emphasis upon the Imagination, he has left two important principles intact; first of all, Greek sculpture remains at least *primus inter pares* with works of other cultures because it is after all the best record there is of the originals. This theory also left him clear to do what he always had done in his paintings, that is, to make explicit references to classical and other formulae. Blake was able to argue that his work is not so much imitative of the antique as drawn from the same sources; thus it inevitably looks as if it is using antique forms:

> It has been said to the Artist, take the Apollo for the model of your beautiful Man and the Hercules for your strong Man, and the Dancing Fawn for your Ugly Man. Now he comes to his trial. He knows that what he does is not inferior to the grandest Antiques. Superior they cannot be, for human power cannot go beyond either what he does, or what they have done, it is the gift of God, it is inspiration and vision. He had resolved to emulate those precious remains of antiquity, he has done so and the result you behold; his ideas of strength and beauty have not been greatly different. (E 534–35)

These great Originals from which all art is derived are glimpsed again in *Jerusalem,* for they are the sculptures of Los's Halls:

> All things acted on Earth are seen in the bright Sculptures of
> Los's Halls & every Age renews its powers from these Works
> With every pathetic story possible to happen from Hate or
> Wayward Love & every sorrow & distress is carved here
> Every Affinity of Parents Marriages & Friendships are here
> In all their various combinations wrought with wondrous Art
> All that can happen to Man in his pilgrimage of seventy years. (E 159)

And they are glimpsed in visual form in the background of pl. 20 of the *Book of Job* engraving as the work of Job the artist whose pilgrimage of seventy years is revealed for the edification of his progeny in a series of ornate panels on the walls of his house. The sculptures of Los's Halls are the experiences of every man who seeks Redemption, and the works of art created by man on earth, whether by the Ancients or Moderns, are but fragmentary reflections of them.

I would like to draw some conclusions which I believe arise from the foregoing observations, which, I hasten to add, concern only a narrow aspect of Blake's artistic thought. First of all, it is clear that on the general question of imitation Blake and Reynolds are not on the opposite side of the fence, but are in some ways closer to each other than Blake and, say, his younger contemporary Palmer. Secondly, that many of the answers to questions one might ask about Blake's mature attitudes are to be found in his early work and in the work of his friends, from which he did not wholly free himself as he got older; and thirdly, and this represents a growing personal conviction, that Blake's attitudes toward art are in a profound sense eighteenth century in spirit, and are predominantly determined even to the end of his career by classical idealism.

NOTES

1.   G. E. Bentley, Jr., *Blake Records* (Oxford: Clarendon Press, 1969), p. 24.

2.   *Blake Records,* p. 27.

3.   Published by Martin Butlin, *Blake Newsletter,* 9 (Fall, 1975), 49.

4.   See E. H. Gombrich, *Aby Warburg: An Intellectual Biography* (London: Warburg Institute, 1970), pp. 177–85.

5.   Published by Martin Butlin, *Blake Newsletter,* 7 (Summer, 1973), 4.

6.   *The Works of Sir Joshua Reynolds,* ed. Edmond Malone, 2nd ed. (London, 1798), I, 28.

7.   Henry Fuseli, *Lectures on Painting* (London, 1801), Lecture III.

8.   Gombrich, *Warburg,* p. 179.

9.   *Analytical Review,* Oct., 1792; quoted in Eudo C. Mason, *The Mind of Henry Fuseli* (London: Routledge & Kegan Paul, 1951), p. 216.

10.   Nicholas Powell, *Fuseli: The Nightmare* (London: Allen Lane, 1973).

11.   Abbé Winkelmann, *Reflections on the Painting and Sculpture of the Greeks,* trans. Henry Fuseli (London, 1765), p. 30.

III

CONCEPTS

Blake's comments on other artists, his writings on the general principles of pictorial expression, and his revisionary ideas of time and space can be studied independently of any concern with artistic practice. Yet, word and deed are interdependent; and a complete picture of Blake the artist must include an understanding of those conceptual underpinnings which shaped (and were shaped by) his pictorial endeavors.

Painted Prophecies: The Tradition of Blake's Illuminated Books

Joseph Anthony Wittreich, Jr.

Blake was, even by the standards of English literature, a remarkably biblical poet. . . .

—Northrop Frye

"THE least attractive" and "most detestable" of all the scriptural books, according to D. H. Lawrence, the Book of Revelation is "the work of a second-rate mind" and "has had a greater effect on second-rate people throughout the Christian ages, than any other book in the Bible." Yet the Apocalypse, Lawrence also allows, is still a book worthy of study, "still a book to conjure with."[1] On why we should read it, or on what we stand to learn from it, Lawrence has little to say; and so for answers to these questions we must turn elsewhere—and one place to turn is Blake and his contemporary, Henry Fuseli.

A biblical poet who believed that the prophecies and gospels are all vision, all imagination, who wished to restore the Bible to its "unperverted" state (E 601, 653), Blake was, if we can believe Benjamin Heath Malkin, an avid student of the Book of Revelation.[2] This interest of Blake manifests itself in his multiple designs for John's Apocalypse (indeed, if we follow John Grant, we will want to view those designs as a sequence). This interest also manifests itself in Blake's poetry—from *The French Revolution* onward; and it may be explained as part of his larger interest, both critical and aesthetic, in the Bible. "The Old and the New Testaments," Blake was to say, "are the Great Code of Art" (*Laocoön*, E 271).

For a poet who held to such a belief, the Apocalypse would have had special appeal. "Much more excellent then all the other

101

prophecies," "the conclusion and sum of the holy scriptures in and about those things that concerne prophecy," a work of "wonderful artifice" and "singular workmanship" that, revealing "all the splendour of poetry," integrates all the arts—encomia like these suggest that the Book of Revelation best exemplifies the Bible's aesthetic system, as well as its impulse toward self-scrutiny and criticism. These encomia likewise explain the age-old tendency to regard the Bible as "the standard of all humane writings," a tendency that invariably directs attention to Revelation's aesthetic, representing it as a way of "seeing"—of keeping the "senses exercised" and of "forc[ing] open our eyes."[3] Various books of the Bible—but the Apocalypse especially—exemplify what Proclus once called "spirit-awakening books," and this is why Fuseli singled out the Apocalypse as a model for Christian art. John's method here, he says, is the proper medium of art for all those committed to purveying the truths of the spirit; in such art, the veil of eternity is rent—the sky is split open by revelation.[4]

Not just Fuseli, of course, but also England's visionary poets would have drawn Blake to prophecy and to its scriptural fulfillment in John's Apocalypse. The continued fascination of the European mind with the Apocalypse has often been noted, but just as often it has been assumed that Isaac Newton's commentary represents "the swansong of . . . a tradition" that in the arts has been "the refuge of cranks and an occasional poetic or artistic genius."[5] Among the "occasional" geniuses who turned to the Book of Revelation must be numbered Albrecht Dürer and Michelangelo, Langland, Spenser, and Milton, as well as virtually every major poet of the Romantic era. Of these artists, Milton was for Blake probably the most important influence.

In *Paradise Regained,* Milton's Jesus is emphatic about the supremacy of prophecy, all other forms being "far beneath" it (IV.363); and in this claim Jesus recalls Milton's own sentiments, expressed years before in *The Reason of Church-Government.* Here Milton writes that "in the very critical art of composition," the prophets are "incomparable"; and he singles out the Book of Revelation as a "majestick" drama, as an "eye-brightning electuary."[6] And before Milton, Spenser had been turned to the Apocalypse. When Spenser writes to Gabriel Harvey, describing his early verses as poetical visions illustrated by pictures, Harvey writes back that the Book of Revelation is a "superexcellent" model, "the verie notablest," for a poet with Spenser's ambitions.[7] Spenser abandoned those early ambitions; but clearly, they were not far from those of Blake. Blake's achievement is no less unique, to be sure; but in conception at least it had been aspired to before—by one of England's mightiest poets.

For Blake, who was as interested as Spenser and Milton before him—and as Shelley after him—in making prophecy an attribute of poetry, the Book of Revelation would have been doubly important, since here the poet and prophet, and prophet and painter, are one. As the summation of the Bible, serving as both its coda and epitome, the Apocalypse embodies a vision, and with it an aesthetic system, that earlier prophecy had only approximated. "A posy of all flowers, a vision out of all visions,"[8] the abridgement of the entire Bible, this scriptural book was also an assimilation of all literary forms—of Aeschylean tragedy and Homeric epic, of lyrics and comedies, of history, philosophy, and oratory. Yet more than just an aggregate of forms, the Book of Revelation was understood to be a "multi-media" performance—a model for what Henry Howard termed "painted prophesies."[9]

An understanding of the alliance between painting and poetry, vision and word, that occurs in prophecy extends backward into the Middle Ages and persists forward in time, through the Renaissance, into the eighteenth century and the Romantic period. If medieval Christianity consecrated the book, it also, as Ernst Curtius has shown, resolved the perennial controversy between word and picture by urging the "combination of the arts";[10] and such urgings found scriptural sanction in the idea that Revelation's prophecy, itself uniting the sister arts, was a scroll book. Thus Marjorie Reeves can speak of Joachim of Fiore's "pictorial prophesyings of new spiritual men" and of the vogue this mode of prophecy enjoyed in both the later Middle Ages and early Renaissance; and the same tradition, "not without imitators," is noted by Rupert Taylor in his study of political prophecy in England, especially during the period of the English Revolution.[11] By the time of Martin Luther certainly this alliance was a well established fact. There are three kinds of prophecy, says Luther in his 1545 Preface to the Apocalypse: Moses' kind which consists only of words, Daniel's which combines words with symbols, and John's which is purely visionary and consists only of "pictures," remaining "a concealed and dumb prophecy" until the pictures, once interpreted, are made to yield up hidden meaning.[12] Analogously, Calvin, though he demurs when it comes to providing

a commentary for the Book of Revelation, obviously has that scriptural book in mind as he distinguishes between revelation, which is
often in words, and vision, which is presented directly to the eye.[13]
And the most influential commentator of the sixteenth century,
Henry Bullinger, insists that such visions as those presented by John
of Patmos are "set forth to be looked upon . . . as . . .livyng & talkyng
images," while one early seventeenth-century commentator, William
Cowper, claimed that the Book of Revelation was simply "four pictures."[14] The assumption of all these commentators is that Christ's
vision is presented initially as a picture; for John's (and our) sakes,
that vision is preserved in a book, this time with words accompanying the pictures; and this book, in turn, is translated by John into the
Apocalypse, into its verbal icons.

The implication of all this for English art has recently been
drawn out by Ronald Paulson: "Revelation in the New Testament is
visual. . . . But in the Old Testament . . . it is aural. . . . 'Literary' England was a country that traditionally hewed to the religion and
world view that preferred the word to the image."[15] There is irony
in a Christian nation's reverting to an Old Testament way of thinking that would not have escaped Blake: Christ came, the New Testament was written as a fulfillment of the Old; the New Testament
then—prophecy as vision—should be the prophet's model. (Hebrew
law, in fact, forbade the kind of pictorial adornment that Christianity encouraged.[16]) Viewing the New Testament as a model,
moreover, meant turning to the Book of Revelation, where
prophecy is represented by a book given by Christ to John—a book
in which word and picture collaborate in the articulation of a
prophecy. That prophecy involves pictures and words, seeing and
hearing, is insisted upon by William Perkins, who explains early in
the seventeenth century that the kind of revelation experienced by
John of Patmos "is partly by vision, partly, by word";[17] and the same
supposition is made by Blake, for he writes in *The Four Zoas* that
"John *Saw* these things Reveald in Heaven / On Patmos Isle & *heard*
the Souls cry out to be deliverd / He *saw* the Harlot . . . & *saw* her
Cup" (Night VIII, E 371; italics added).

This is the tradition to which Blake subscribes; and the tradition was popularized, though it does not begin with, the various
seventeenth-century editions of Joseph Mede's *The Key of the Revelation* (see Plates 95–96). One Mr. Haydock elicited the admission that
Mede himself had entertained the idea that "those visions concern-

ing the seals were not written by Characters in letters, but being painted in certain shapes, lay hid under some covers of the Seals; which being opened, each of them in its order, appeared not to be read, but to be beheld and viewed." According to such an apprehension, Mede observes, "those words of John, *Come and see,* seem not unfitly to agree." Still, says Mede, there is evidence for believing that some parts of this prophecy are verbalized, not perhaps in simple but in representational writing. For Mede therefore, as for Haydock, the sealed book is an example of picture-prophecy conceived in such a way that the pictorial and verbal are "joyned together." Conceding this much to Haydock, Mede goes on to argue, contrary to Haydock, that John and Christ are so distanced from one another that John himself could not see into the book and so must have had it translated verbally by Christ. Thereupon, however, once this book of pictures and words is opened, it is given to John; and then John, as Christ did for him, translated the book into words for his audience.[18] At issue here is not the nature of prophecy but rather the question of how prophecy should be transmitted; at issue, too, is the nature of the book itself—what did it look like? how was it constructed, and thus what was it like once it was opened?

Adopted by Henry More (see Plate 97) and, subsequently, by most eighteenth-century commentators, Mr. Haydock's description of prophecy as a series of rolls, each to be opened in its order, provides an alternative to D. H. Lawrence's belief that the rolled up scroll "could not *actually* be opened till all seven seals are broken"; and Haydock's description clearly stands behind the eighteenth century's explanation of the book as "a roll" where each seal, when broken, presents to the viewer "certain hieroglyphic figures."[19] Samuel Langdon, for example, explains that "we may be sure that this roll consisted of a principal one, rolled inmost in the smallest size, which contained the most important matters, and was sealed separately; and of the six others rolled over it one after another, as so many covers to the principal one, each of which had also a separate seal: And so by breaking the seals of these covers, one after another, the contents of all were made known, before the inmost roll was opened." Or as Thomas Newton proposes, "we should conceive this book, that it was such a one as the ancients used, a volume or roll of a book, or more properly a volume consisting of seven volumes, so that the opening of the one seal laid open the contents only of one volume."[20]

The idea of prophecy as a scroll-book can be traced to Isaiah who says, "the heavens shall be rolled together as a scroll" (34:4). The vision itself, like its stage, was thought to be rolled as a scroll. Moreover, the seals, like the pictures they cover, are there to halt movement, though not to impede progress: they arrest attention, they force the mind into contemplation—in Blake's words, they enable the spectator to "Enter into these Images in his Imagination," to approach them "on the Fiery Chariot of his Contemplative Thought" (E 550; cf. E 545).[21] John's experience of the Revelation prophecy is like the reader's experience with Blake's illuminated books: he reads them and at the same time beholds; the pictures, though they may eventually lead him to other plates, first return him to the words of the same plate, for, as David Erdman remarks, "every graphic image in Blake's illuminations has its seed or root in the poetry."[22] And vice versa: the words instead of moving us relentlessly from one plate to the next snare our interest in the illuminations accompanying them; it might even be more in keeping with the spirit of prophecy to say that every poetic line has its seed or root in the picture accompanying it. Everything in prophecy then, everything involved in its composition, is to some purpose and bears some meaning: the quill and the stylus are ploughshares; to write and to paint is to plough up—in some cases to plough under; to etch is to burn surfaces away. The book itself is an image of, and a labyrinth leading toward, the city it would create; in the words of David Erdman, the book is "a living city of Art that would resurrect us from our graves."[23]

These are the relevant details about picture-prophecy, and many of them are focused by the exchange of letters between Haydock and Mede. Henry More, we may here note, later refined Haydock's idea of the picture-prophecy to the point of proposing that each separate vision within a prophecy has its own "Frontispiece" which, More explains, is the prophet's "contrivance" both for marking off the structural units in his prophecy and for indicating that those units "are Visions of like importance, that is, very reachingly and comprehensively Propheticall."[24] (Blake's *Milton*, of course, has seven such markers, which in *Jerusalem* are reduced to four.)

Mede is perhaps the most influential of the seventeenth-century commentators; but on the crucial detail regarding the nature of the book Haydock, rather than Mede, seems to have prevailed. This point is emphasized by various depictions of John composing (see Plate 98): "he may be busy translating his vision into verbal equivalents, but the vision he experiences through the book given to him by Christ contains both pictures and words. The tradition of picture-prophecy, then, has the effect of prodding the prophet into getting back to origins, his objective being not the translation of vision into words but the experience of vision itself, which involves pictures together with words. The visionary, as E.S. Shaffer has recently observed, "is actually seeing the events played out in the heavens."[25] The heavens are therefore a stage from which the visionary *sees* some of the time—and *hears* some of the time—a drama unfold.

Subsequent to Mede, and throughout the eighteenth century as well as today, prophecy was and is understood as we have here described it—as a collection of visionary scenes and as a form of picture-writing. For a study of Blake, obviously, the body of eighteenth-century commentary is of special importance, and so two observations about it should be made: first, it is highly derivative, relying largely on Renaissance exegesis for its conclusions; and second, as F.B. Curtis has shown, this body of commentary burgeons from 1780 to 1827 when "over eighty separate works on the prophecies and the Book of Revelation were written and published."[26] The voices of some of these commentators Blake must have heard, and they all speak more or less the same lines, believing with Isaac Newton that "the language of prophetic writings was symbolic and hieroglyphic and that their comprehension required a radically different method of interpretation."[27] Many examples may be cited; but one voice, that of George Stanley Faber, is particularly representative: "a continued hieroglyphic," the Book of Revelation exhibits "the most perfect and systematic specimens of Hebrew hieroglyphical composition" that exist in the world; "a mode of composition . . . which specifically affects hieroglyphical grandiloquence," this Book, Faber contends, "speaks by pictures quite as much as by sounds."[28]

Poets who would designate themselves prophets are, in the light of this tradition, obligated to include such scenes figuratively (as Spenser and Milton do) or quite literally (as Blake does by creating poems that are firmly ensconced in the tradition of the picture-prophecy). In the process, Spenser and Milton may raise their poems to the status of word-pictures; but Blake, observing prophetic tradition to the letter, combines pictures with words, effecting a marriage between them. Because he so assiduously observed this and other aspects of prophetic tradition, it is understandable that Blake has been called the "first great exponent" of a literary tradition wherein the roles of poet and prophet are joined in a single art—that he should even be said to represent "the first waves of the prophetic movement" in England.[29] However, these claims made for him are ones that Blake himself would have made incidentally for Spenser and quite emphatically for Milton. Yet Blake would also have seen in their similarity this difference: these other poets may make images that are *like* pictures; Blake, on the other hand, creates pictures that are an extension and a culmination of the profoundly pictorial character of his poetry. His illuminated books are, in the strictest sense, picture-prophecies. They impose pictures, once in Blake's mind, upon our own; and Blake thereby identifies himself with the prophets who, as he explains in *A Descriptive Catalogue*, reflect "what they saw in vision . . . with their imaginations and immortal organs" (E 532; cf. E 544–45). Through his pictures, Blake is able to ensure that he will speak to every kingdom and nation and language on earth; for unlike his poetry, its illuminations are composed of the universal language of visual icons, and thus they cut across the barriers imposed by a verbal idiom. Whatever his other disagreements with Isaac Newton, Blake understood that there is "a language as common amongst [the prophets] as any language is amongst the people" of different nations[30]—a language that is pictorial, iconic, and hieroglyphical. He understood, too, that no Christian document is more fully committed than the Book of Revelation is to that one objective which Blake and Karl Marx held in common—the "'complete emancipation of all human senses and qualities.'"[31]

Blake, who begins his version of the fall with the story of the closing off of the senses, would repair the ruins of the fall by opening them up again. The effect of Blake's multimedia art is to open the eye and, opening it, to guide the mind through spaces it has not traveled before: to cleanse "the doors of perception" so that everything will "appear to man as it is, infinite" (*The Marriage of Heaven and Hell,* E 39). All prophets may at times feel, like Lord Byron's Dante, that they cannot record all that crowds on their prophetic eye. Yet they try. And whatever way they resolve their dilemma (whether by mixing the various genres or by combining the arts), their objective is always the same—to overcome the limitations of their medium by devising a new optical system, an intention they accomplish by spurning the boundaries of any single form, achieving an interpenetration of the arts and, in the process, literalizing Sidney's metaphor that portrays poetry as a speaking picture. The picture energizes the poetry; and the poetry, in turn, ensures that the picture will not remain silent.

"The Man who does not know The Beginning, never can know the End of Art," Blake writes; "To recover Art has been the business of my life" (E 628; *Public Address,* E 569). The prophet, as he reaches back to origins, aspires to return poetry to that original condition in which all the arts partake of one another; by doing so, the prophet liberates himself from the limitations, and his audience from the potential monotonies, of any single art form. It has recently been said that all the arts "were originally a whole," and then argued that the history of poetry is the history of its gradual isolation from the other arts: "By the elimination of music, calligraphy, and illumination," says Octavio Paz, "poetry was reduced until it became almost exclusively an art of the intellect...mental art."[32] This is not, of course, exclusively a modern perception, but one common in eighteenth-century criticism and one that, for Blake's century, was attested to by the Bible.

The Bible, as one eighteenth-century commentator observes, uses poetry and song, in conjunction with pictorialism, "to check and divert every species of corruption" that now infects the world.[33] Such sentiments were shared by Blake, for whom poetry, painting, and music were "the three Powers ... [capable] of conversing with Paradise" (E 548). In harness with poetry, pictorialism especially could awaken the mind, helping to effect the "mind-expansion" that prophecy would induce. Every literary form is an image of reality or vision of the world; and every art form, possessing its own language, is a different mode of perception. When this is understood, the prophet's objective becomes clearer.

For the prophet, partial consciousness is no consciousness— consciousness by his definition being infinite. If Roland Barthes is right in claiming that poetry and painting represent completely different kinds of consciousness,[34] then we must conclude that poetry or painting by itself is partial consciousness at best. That in any event seems to have been Blake's conclusion. Expanding consciousness, extending it into the infinite—these objectives require a form that, transcending the limits of any one form, is capable of subsuming all perspectives; they necessitate one central form capable of embracing all others. That central form Blake understood to be prophecy—it is the ultimate model for what Angus Fletcher calls "transcendental form" and for what E.H. Gombrich calls "total form."[35] The objective of such a form is total vision. In isolation, the different art forms both represent the limits and reveal the perversions of worldly perception; in harness, however, limits are transcended and perversions repaired. For Blake then, no less than for Spenser and Milton, prophecy is the central form into which all others, literary and artistic, can be gathered; prophecy is, as Blake might say, "Ideal Form, The Universal Mold" (E 675). Blake would, of course, have found ample reason to hold to such a position as Bishop Lowth's in *Lectures on the Sacred Poetry of the Hebrews*, where prophecy is represented as excelling all other forms of poetry, both in style and in subject, or even in Lowth's *The Genealogy of Christ* where poetry and painting are placed in harness and where the visionary is described as one who sees "the sacred Forms."[36] A perfect literary microcosm, prophecy is a new creation revealing the secret of all creation, whereby order is brought out of chaos and unity is created from division.

Blake was forever, it seems, contemplating man's fall, most notably in *The Book of Urizen* and again in *The Four Zoas;* but like Milton he was less concerned with the loss of paradise than with its recovery and would certainly have agreed with his predecessor who, accounting for the public's distaste for *Paradise Regained,* remarked that his countrymen had a good sense of the loss of paradise but not an equal gusto for regaining it. In *The Four Zoas,* therefore, Blake sings of "fall into Division & ... Resurrection to Unity," of "fall into ... Decay & Death & ... Regeneration by the Resurrection" (E 297); yet even here we hear about "a Perfect Unity" and "Universal Brotherhood" (E 297) before our attention is ever turned to "fall ... Division ... Decay ... & Death." In *Jerusalem,* we look with Blake at "the Sleep of Ulro" but, like Blake, are finally concerned with "awaking to Eternal Life" (E 145). The fall is a fact, accomplished; the regaining of paradise, an aspiration not yet realized— yet one that, for Blake, could be realized through the agency of prophecy. Prophecy was, after all, devoted to "interior liberation,"[37] to mirroring this world in its sordidness and fragmentation and another world in its glory and unity. What one initially notices in Blake's illuminated books is their apparent formlessness; and many have never seen beyond that formlessness. What should be noticed, however, is that formlessness gives way to form, order emerges from disorder, fragmentation and division are swallowed up in the unity of the arts. In his effort to restore the Age of Gold, Blake has returned to origins—to the Bible; and there he finds poetry and painting integrated in prophecy. Prophecy is thus a symbol for the marriage state that prophecy itself would establish. By Blake, prophecy is therefore made into a fierce opponent of science, which not only had encouraged anatomization and fragmentation but which also was serving as an ideological justification for both.

There is suitability in the fact that *The Four Zoas,* Blake's fullest exploration of the fall, should exist as a collection of shattered fragments, should appear as a broken image of a broken world; and in the fact that *Milton* and *Jerusalem,* which still exhibit the scars and divisions of the fallen world, should bring those fragments together—should, in the very act of restoring the arts to union, be an image, magnificent and expansive and whole, of the world restored as Jerusalem. Man has left the garden, but is still in the wilderness. Blake, in these companion poems, shows man what it is to leave the wilderness—to enter the city of which both these prophecies, in their compositeness, are an image. Like all the rest of creation, the arts groan to be delivered from their fallen condition. It may be, as Bishop Lowth once remarked, that "we *at present* possess only some ruins . . . of that magnificent fabric" called prophecy.[38] Those ruins are very much in evidence in *The Four Zoas*— "that magnificent epic fragment," which as a fragment, says Herbert Marcuse, "is a cosmic transfiguration of the revolution" and which remains a fragment, it should be added, because Blake has not subjected this vision, as he will that of both *Milton* and *Jerusalem,* to "the laws of beauty, of harmony."[39] Thus when we turn to *Milton* and *Jerusalem,* we are in a *new present*—one in which the art of prophecy has been triumphantly restored. Such art subscribes to a poetics wherein the form of a work is its essence, the vehicle conveying its theme. Within the context of this poetics, therefore, the formlessness of *The Four Zoas* is as meaningful as the careful shapings of both *Milton* and *Jerusalem.*

Separation and fragmentation. The history of civilization is likewise the history of the arts that for so long have followed history into division and decay. *Resurrection to unity.* The history of the arts, of their restoration here to wholeness, Blake prophesies, will also be, *can be,* the history of civilization. This point Blake never tires of

making: "let it no more be said that Empires Encourage Arts for it is
Arts that Encourage Empires . . . [I]t is not Arts that follow & attend
upon Empire but Empire that attends upon & follows The Arts"
(*Public Address,* E 566). "Empire follows Art," Blake proclaims
(E 626). Shelley, of course, called the poet the *unacknowledged* legis-
lator of the world: *that,* for Blake, had been the sad and troubling
truth over the centuries, yet a truth that could be turned to false-
hood by *acknowledging* the poet as a prophet and, further, by
acknowledging that as a prophet he will preside over the apotheosis
of history. The prophet sees history rushing to its crisis: at the moment of crisis, a Last Judgment will occur; and in that moment,
mankind will observe the "overwhelming" of bad by good art—in
that moment, the arts will be restored—an "apocalypse of the mind"
will be succeeded by an "apocalypse . . . of national destiny."[40] The
time will be at hand. Jerusalem will be forthcoming as the poem we
have seen in our eyes.

NOTES

1. *Apocalypse* (Florence: G. Orioli, 1931), pp. 9, 15, 20, 35, 297. The
Epigraph accompanying this essay is from Frye's "Expanding Eyes," *Critical
Quarterly,* 2 (1975), 206. Michael J. Tolley makes a comment similar to
Frye's: "Blake was so steeped in biblical patterns . . . that his own patterns
were often, naturally, emanations of the biblical ones" ("Europe: to those
ychain'd in sleep," in *Blake's Visionary Forms Dramatic,* ed. David V. Erdman
and John E. Grant [Princeton: Princeton Univ. Press, 1970], p. 126).
2. See *A Father's Memoirs of His Child* (London: Printed by T. Bensley,
1806), p. xxx.
3. For these various encomia, see the following: John Bale, *The Image
of Both Churches* (1548; rpt. London: Thomas Ease [1570]), sig. Aiii[v]; James
Brocard, *The Reveled Revelation of Saint John After Divers Learned Authors*
(London: Thomas Barth, 1582), sig. B2[v]; Thomas Brightman, *The Revelation of S. John* (Leyden: Printed by John Class, 1616), p. 7; Joseph Mede, *The
Key of the Revelation,* tr. Richard More, 2nd ed. (London: Printed by Phil.
Stephens, 1650), pp. 92, 108; Robert Lowth, *Lectures on the Sacred Poetry of
the Hebrews,* tr. G. Gregory (Boston: Printed by Joseph T. Buckingham,
1815), p. 293; Isaac Newton, "Fragments from a Treatise on Revelation,"
published as Appendix A in Frank E. Manuel's *The Religion of Isaac Newton*
(Oxford: Clarendon Press, 1974), p. 107; and John Trapp, *Gods Love-*

Tokens, and the Afflicted Mans Lessons (London: Richard Badger, 1637), sig. [a], [A12].

4. "Lecture II," in *The Life and Writings of Henry Fuseli,* ed. John Knowles (3 vols.; London: Henry Colburn and Richard Bentley, 1831), II, 75. Blake and Fuseli both find in the Apocalypse a series of visions that, seen by the imaginative eye, can teach us to see with that same eye—visions, as Blake explains in *A Descriptive Catalogue,* that are not "a cloudy vapour" but that, "organized and minutely articulated," surpass anything man might see "by his mortal eye" (E 532). See also Anselm Bayly who urges epic poets, who are also prophets, to go to the Book of Revelation for instruction (*The Alliance of Musick, Poetry, and Oratory* [London: Printed for J. Stockdale, 1789], p. 267).

5. Manuel, *The Religion of Isaac Newton,* p. 89.

6. *Complete Prose Works of John Milton,* ed. Don M. Wolfe et al. (New Haven: Yale Univ. Press, and London: Oxford Univ. Press, 1953–?), I, 816, 803, 815.

7. *The Works of Edmund Spenser: A Variorum Edition,* ed. Edwin Greenlaw et al. (Baltimore: Johns Hopkins Press, 1943–57), III, 471.

8. Thomas Goodwin, *An Exposition of the Revelation* (1639), in *The Works of Thomas Goodwin* (Edinburgh: James Nichol, 1861–66), V, 33.

9. The phrase appears in *A Defensative Against the Poyson of Supposed Prophecies* (London: Printed by John Charlewood, 1620), p. 116.

10. *European Literature and the Latin Middle Ages,* tr. Willard R. Trask (New York: Pantheon Books, 1953), p. 315 (and see all of ch. 16).

11. See both Reeves's *The Influence of Prophecy in the Later Middle Ages: A Study of Joachimism* (Oxford: Clarendon Press, 1969), esp. pp. 73, 368, and Taylor's *The Political Prophecy in England* (New York: Columbia Univ. Press. 1911), p. 119.

12. "Preface to the Revelation of St. John," in *Works of Martin Luther* (Philadelphia: A.J. Holman and Castle Press, 1932), VI, 480. In his 1522 Preface, Luther observes that "there is no prophet in the Old Testament, to say nothing of the New, who deals so out and out with visions and figures" (VI, 488).

13. *Commentary on the Epistles of Paul the Apostle to the Corinthians* (Edinburgh: Calvin Translation Society, 1849), II, 366.

14. See *A Hundred Sermons upon the Apocalypse of Jesu Christ* (1557; rpt. London: John Daye, 1573), p. 1, and *Pathmos; or, A Commentary on the Revelation of Saint John* (London: Printed by George Purslow, 1619), p. 16. In Blake's century, prophecy was spoken of as something to be "written on parchment, and engraven on brass and copper" (See *Prophecies of the Reverend Christopher Love* [Boston: Samuel Hall, 1793], p. 7).

15. *Emblem and Expression: Meaning in English Art of the Eighteenth Century* (Cambridge, Mass.: Harvard Univ. Press, 1975), p. 12.

16. See John Hollander, *Vision and Resonance: Two Senses of Poetic Form* (New York: Oxford Univ. Press, 1975), p. 252.

17. *Lectures upon the Three First Chapters of the Revelation* (London: Printed by Cuthbert Burbie, 1604), sig. B2.

18. See the translator's Preface in *The Key of the Revelation*.

19. See Lawrence's *Apocalypse,* p. 141, and Samuel Langdon's *Observations on the Revelation of Jesus Christ to St. John* (Worcester, Mass.: Printed by Isaiah Thomas, 1791), p. 62.

20. See both Langdon, *Observations,* p. 62, and Newton, *Dissertations on the Prophecies, Which Have Remarkably Been Fulfilled, and at This Time are Fulfilling in the World,* 2nd ed. (London: J. and R. Tonson, 1759), p. 49. The scroll, of course, is a major symbol in Blake's pictorial art; and it is noteworthy that in "A Vision of the Last Judgment" Blake has the New Heaven and New Earth appear "as a scroll" (E 545). In this symbol, Blake allows the form of prophecy and its objective to conflate: his creation and the thing it would create are one.

21. A similar point is made by Northrop Frye in "The Road of Excess," *The Stubborn Structure: Essays on Criticism and Society* (Ithaca, N.Y.: Cornell Univ. Press, 1970), ch. 10.

22. *The Illuminated Blake* (Garden City, N.Y.: Doubleday, 1974), p. 16.

23. Ibid., p. 11; see also Curtius, *European Literature and the Latin Middle Ages,* pp. 314–15.

24. *An Explanation of the Grand Mystery of Godliness* (London: Printed for W. Morden, 1660), p. 31.

25. *"Kubla Khan" and the Fall of Jerusalem: The Mythological School in Biblical Criticism and Secular Literature 1770–1800* (Cambridge: University Press, 1975), p. 97.

26. "Blake and the Booksellers," *Blake Studies,* 6 (1974), 171.

27. See Manuel, *The Religion of Isaac Newton,* p. 87.

28. *The Sacred Calendar of Prophecy; or a Dissertation on the Prophecies* (London: Printed for C. and J. Rivington, 1828), pp. 10, 12, 15, 226. For comparable statements, see Robert Clayton, *A Dissertation on Prophecy, Wherein the Coherence and Connexion of the Prophecies in Both the Old and New Testament Are Fully Considered* (London: Reprinted for J. Watts, 1749), p. 88; Newton, *Dissertations,* pp. 3, 8; Hugh Farmer, *An Appendix to an Inquiry into the Nature and Design of Christ's Temptation in the Wilderness* (London: Printed for J. Buckland and J. Waugh, 1765), pp. 23, 25; anon., *A Key to the Mystery of the Revelation* (London: W. Goldsmith, 1785), pp. 14, 96, 209, 305; Robert Moody, *Observations on Certain Prophecies in The Book of Daniel, and the Revelation of St. John* (London: Printed for the Author, 1787), p. [5]; Langdon, *Observations,* pp. 27–28, 62; Robert Fleming, *A Discourse on the Rise and Fall of the Papacy* (Printed for Robert Fleming, 1793), p. 213; anon., *Prophetic Conjectures on the French Revolution, and Other Recent and Shortly*

Expected Events (London: Printed by W. Taylor, 1793), p. 4; James Winthrop, *An Attempt to Translate the Prophetic Part of the Apocalypse of Saint John into Familiar Language* (Boston: Printed by Belknap and Hall, 1794), pp. 3–4; James Bicheno, *The Signs of the Times; or the Dark Prophecies of Scripture Illustrated by the Application of Present Important Events* (West Springfield, Mass.: Printed by Richard Davison, 1796), p. 10; Edward King, *A Supplement to the Remarks on The Signs of the Times* (London: Printed for George Nicol, 1799), sig. A2, p. 27.

29. Sir Maurice Bowra, *The Prophetic Element* (London: English Association, 1959), p. 4.

30. "Fragments of a Treatise on Revelation," in Manuel, *The Religion of Isaac Newton*, p. 118.

31. Quoted by Herbert Marcuse, *Counter-Revolution and Revolt* (Boston: Beacon Press, 1972), p. 64.

32. *The Bow and the Lyre*, tr. Ruth L. C. Simms (New York: McGraw-Hill, 1975), pp. 256–57.

33. East Apthorp, *Of Sacred Poetry and Music* (Boston: Printed by Green and Russell, 1764), p. 16.

34. *Mythologies*, tr. Annette Lavers (1970; rpt. New York: Hill and Wang, 1972), p. 110.

35. For elucidation of these concepts, see both Fletcher, *The Transcendental Masque: An Essay on Milton's Comus* (Ithaca, N.Y.: Cornell Univ. Press, 1972), esp. ch. 4, and Gombrich, *Norm and Form: Studies in the Art of the Renaissance*, 2nd ed. (London and New York: Phaidon, 1971), esp. pp. 63, 73, 79.

36. Lowth's poem was published in London by J. Jackson in 1729; see p. 8.

37. I borrow the phrase from Paz, *The Bow and the Lyre*, p. [3].

38. *Lectures on the Sacred Poetry of the Hebrews*, p. 355.

39. *Counter-Revolution and Revolt*, pp. 103–04.

40. See Sacvan Bercovitch, "Emerson the Prophet: Romanticism, Puritanism, and Auto-American-Biography," in *Emerson: Prophecy, Metamorphosis, and Influence*, ed. David Levin (New York: Columbia Univ. Press, 1975), p. 7.

Space and Time in *Milton:*
The "Bard's Song"

Yvonne M. Carothers

B L A K E ' S well-known dissatisfaction with Lockean epistemology
goes beyond his repudiation of the notion that man is born a *tabula
rasa.* Consistent with his view that "Innate Ideas. are in Every Man
Born with him" (E 637) is his apparent adoption of Kant's view of
space and time as forms of intuition inherent in man and contributed by him to his experience. Rejecting the empiricists' view of
space and time as elements of the so-called objective universe,
Kant—and Blake—revolutionized the epistemological coordinates
of Enlightenment philosophy and aesthetics, one arguing and the
other demonstrating that space and time are integral elements of the
human mind. Thus Blake could not accept an aesthetic, typified in
Lessing's *Laocoön,* which assigns to painting and poetry distinct provinces on the basis of their affinities with empirical space and time.
He then formulated a new aesthetic, grounding it in his revolutionary views and using it to interrelate verbal and visual forms.

To locate Blake's position in the often conflicting philosophies
and aesthetics of his day, we shall look at his views on space and time
from three perspectives. First, we shall determine whether Blake's
epistemology, formulated in poetic language, may be profitably
compared and contrasted to the more discursively outlined epistemology of Kant so that we may more precisely define the natures
of Blakean space and time. Second, once we have a working definition of these natures, we shall investigate how Blake's poetic and
visual art violates the aesthetic guidelines postulated by Lessing,
whose *Laocoön* legislates the mediums most appropriate for "corporeal" and "abstract" subject matter. Third, we shall examine how

space and time function in the "Bard's Song" in *Milton,* considered by Harold Bloom an example of Blake's art at its most complex.[1]

I

Kant terms space and time the primary forms of intuition, intuition being "that through which [a mode of knowledge] is in immediate relation to [objects]."[2] These forms of intuition necessarily underlie and participate in our knowledge by allowing us loosely to organize our experience around the coordinates of space and time before the Understanding organizes it conceptually. Like the empiricists, Kant appears to ground his epistemology in sensation; and yet—here is the vital difference—he insists that these forms of intuition are not given in sensation, but are forms latent in man's mind and contributed by him to his experience.

In his discussion of space, Kant assumes that this form of intuition functions on two levels: the empirical and the pure. When functioning on the empirical level, space allows man to apprehend the forms of objects external to himself and the entire space of which they are parts. Kant then terms space a form of intuition of the outer sense, but here his terminology "outer sense" may be misleading. Granted that forms of objects are usually those of external objects, we nevertheless envision forms that represent no objects of experience—an equilateral triangle, for example. In this case, we have an instance of space as a form of intuition that manifests itself on the pure level; that is to say, the form itself does not originate in experience. Yet, should we imagine any form, whether a triangle or an object of our experience, as disappearing from our consciousness, space would still remain a form of intuition inasmuch as it is, for Kant, transcendentally ideal. Space is a form of intuition universally shared by all men, underpinning our knowledge and continuing to exist within us as a kind of voided set in the unlikely event that we ceased to inform and present objects to our consciousness.

Like space, the form of intuition called time is transcendentally ideal and operates on both the empirical and pure levels. Yet, time differs from space in its function: it does not inform objects but interrelates these forms into simultaneous or successive patterns.

These patterns, however, do not accord with some "real" object given in sensation, the *Ding an Sich* that cannot be known, but with the inner sense of the Understanding. Kant then terms time the form of intuition of the inner sense.[3]

Space and time are potential sets of all forms and interrelationships: they subsist in man until concrete manifestations testify to their existence. If these manifestations are derived from the empirical world, space and time function in accord with the laws we ascribe to that world: space may be dominated by laws governing perspective; time, by the clock. If, however, these forms and interrelationships are generated at the pure level, as in the case of the triangle, space and time accord with no external law.

Like Kant, Blake recognizes that space and time may function on two levels. Still more important for Blake is the fact that space and time are integral elements of man's mental faculties and not qualities of the empirical universe. Yet, unlike Kant, Blake does not consider the pure level of these forms as the exclusive province of mathematics. Rather, Blake substitutes the forms of art—forms that he conceives as purely intellectual—for the forms of mathematics and then constructs a purely spatiotemporal world.

The Blakean counterpart of Kant's empirical space is "Female Space," which "shrinks the Organs / Of Life till they become Finite & Itself seems Infinite" (E 103). The "Organs / Of Life" to which Blake alludes are the five senses by means of which we experience the so-called objective universe. These senses are fallen and shrunken, leaving the world immense or "Infinite" by comparison. This infinity of "Female Space" is similar to the infinite quality of space that, Kant asserts, man intuits in his experience of external objects. Blake cannot accept this infinity, however; it is an illusion of experience.

Blake disdains man's practice of relying solely on empirical experience and rejects it as a standard for the measurement of space. Instead, he claims that space is a human faculty:

> For every Space larger than a red Globule of Mans blood.
> Is visionary: and is created by the Hammer of Los
> And every Space smaller than a Globule of Mans blood. opens
> Into Eternity of which this vegetable Earth is but a shadow:
> The red Globule is the unwearied Sun by Los created
> To measure Time and Space to mortal Men. every morning.
> Bowlahoola & Allamanda are placed on each side
> Of that Pulsation & that Globule, terrible their power. (E 126)

The symbol "red Globule" functions as the standard by means of which Blake proceeds to define space. Yet, the symbol itself can be deceptive. It would be ridiculous to say that "every Space larger than a Corpuscle / Is visionary." However, part of the passage's effect derives from such a reduction: the humanist Blake asks that everyone regard spaces both larger and smaller than this basic element of life as "visionary" and as "open[ing] / Into Eternity." Still, the terms "visionary" and "open[ing] / Into Eternity" remain meaningless until the other connotations of "red Globule" are considered. This symbol is also the "unwearied Sun by Los created" and is closely associated with "that Pulsation" by means of which Blake defines time:

> Every Time less than a pulsation of the artery
> Is equal in its period & value to Six Thousand Years.
>
> For in this Period the Poets Work is Done: and all the Great
> Events of Time start forth & are concievd in such a Period
> Within a Moment: a Pulsation of the Artery. (E 126)

Here the empirical, temporal measures of one "Moment" and "Six Thousand Years" are equated through the mediation of the "Poets Work," "the unwearied Sun by Los created." Thus the "Poets Work" is the standard by means of which we define space; poetic creation alone is the measure of time: the larger dimension of a work of art may well be termed "visionary"; the work itself may "open / Into Eternity."

Blake's insistence that space and time be defined in terms of art accords with his own humanistic "System": the pure forms of intuition space and time, which reside within the "Eternal Great Humanity Divine," are championed over those intuitions adulterated by sense experience. Art supplies man with the intellectual forms necessary to transform the voided set space into a realized space; man's psychic processes determine the patterns for those forms' interrelationships—patterns that are independent of empirical time. Freed from the empirical manifestations of space and time, the artist may exult with Los that

> both Time & Space obey my will.
> I in Six Thousand Years walk up and down: for not one Moment
> Of Time is lost, nor one Event of Space unpermanent.
> But all remain: every fabric of Six Thousand Years

Remains permanent: tho' on the Earth where Satan
Fell, and was cut off all things vanish & are seen no more
They vanish not from me & mine, we guard them first & last[.]
The generations of men run on in the tide of Time
But leave their destind lineaments permanent for ever & ever. (E 116)

II

Blake's recognition that space and time belong to man's mental faculties and not to the "objective" universe profoundly influenced his manner of organizing and executing his work. Purely intellectual or artistic forms and their interrelationships become subject not to the spatiotemporal laws operative in the "objective" world but to that spatiotemporal organization created by the artist. Yet, even as Blake revolutionized man's notion of space and time, the poetic and visual arts of his own day still originated in the aesthetic dictates founded on more empirically derived notions of space and time. And exemplary of the aesthetic principles operative in the arts of the latter eighteenth and early nineteenth centuries is the *Laocoön*.

Noting that the natures of empirical time and space are analogous to the consecutive quality of discourse and the simultaneous impact of objects in painting, Lessing assigns to both the poet and the painter their respective provinces: "succession of time is the province of the poet just as space is that of the painter."[4] Implicit in this statement is the assumption that art's primary task is to imitate empirical reality. Lessing delimits the realms of both poetry and painting in order that the artist may imitate reality with a greater degree of precision.

Unlike many aestheticians of the eighteenth century, however, Lessing admits that art embraces two domains—that of reality and that of the "limitless field of our imagination" with

> the incorporeal nature of its forms, which, though varied and great in number, may exist simultaneously without concealing or damaging each other, as would the objects themselves or the natural symbols in the narrow confines of space or time.[5]

Here Lessing recognizes that the forms resident in the imagination reject "the narrow confines of space or time," but he appears not to understand that his notion of space and time is empirically derived. Unlike Blake, who does understand that empirical space and time are adulterations of the human forms, Lessing regards their empirical manifestations as definitive of reality; hence, imaginative forms appear incorporeal by contrast. He then advises the painter to represent primarily material or corporeal reality and assigns the realm of the imagination to the poet largely because of the nature of language: in his view, the "arbitrary" nature of language renders poetry the appropriate medium for expressing the "incorporeal" fantasies of the imagination.[6] Thus Lessing's venture into an artistic theory of the imagination returns to a theory of imitation.

Of course, Blake would object to Lessing's theory of the imagination on grounds that the realm of the imagination is not incorporeal. Moreover, Blake's recognition that the pure forms of intuition space and time reside in man provides him with the real coordinates, as opposed to the adulterated empirical ones, around which he can construct his art of the imagination. Working to make forms "exist simultaneously without concealing or damaging each other," Blake develops a method whereby he may interrelate the formal aspect of language with the forms of visual art: verbal-visual counterpoint.

The term "verbal-visual counterpoint" is Jean Hagstrum's; the idea is suggested in Northrop Frye's essay "Poetry and Design in William Blake": "In the longer poems there is, of course, a good deal of syncopation between design and narrative. At the bottom of Plate 8 of *Jerusalem* is a female figure harnessed to the moon: the symbol is not mentioned in the text until Plate 63."[7] Here the symbol, a verbal form, is related to a text that appears fifty-five plates earlier via the visual form on the earlier plate. In using the visual instead of the verbal form to establish relationship, Blake implicitly acknowledges that both visual and verbal forms inhabit not distinct provinces, but one province—that of the imagination. The form itself is preeminent: it defines the spatial ordinate of the imagination and acquires meaning through juxtaposition with other forms, the process of which belongs to the temporal ordinate of the imagination. In this manner, then, Blake creates an aesthetic that rejects the notion that "What oft' was thought, but ne'er so well expressed"[8] defines art, that sees the form of art as preeminent, and that presupposes a revolutionary view of space and time.

III

The coordinates of Blake's art of the imagination are forms and their interrelationships—space and psychic time. These coordinates, however, not only function as organizational principles but also comprise Blake's entire art. In his *Anatomy of Criticism,* Frye reminds us that

> Literature may have life, reality, experience, nature, imaginative truth, social conditions, or what you will for its content; but litera-ture itself is not made out of these things. Poetry can only be made out of other poems; novels out of other novels. Literature shapes itself and is not shaped externally: the *forms* of literature can no more exist outside literature than the forms of sonata and fugue and rondo can exist outside music.[9]

In order to discern how Blake's literature "shapes itself," we shall look at an example of Blake's most complex art, the "Bard's Song" in *Milton.* In our inquiry, we shall see that the content, story, or alle-gory of the "Bard's Song" is subordinate to, indeed, depends upon, the forms with which Blake constructs it. Flanked by two full plates of Milton—the title page and Plate 13—and introduced by an invo-cation to the muses, this "Song" is situated in a context whose chief purpose is to delineate and to interrelate purely artistic forms.

Blake views Milton as a paradigmatic artist and uses him to identify two major tendencies in art: one making art the hand-maiden of orthodox religions or philosophies, the other claiming the "Humanity Divine" as its proper subject matter. The Milton of *Paradise Lost* exemplifies the first tendency; the poet of *Paradise Re-gained,* the second. In the "Bard's Song," Blake depicts the struggle to renounce the self that is not autonomous and demonstrates the means, the imagination, whereby man enables his own humanity to triumph.

Frye observes in *Fearful Symmetry* that the characters of Blake's prophecies are ideographic in nature.[10] Stripped of any sensual or complex psychological life of their own, they become animated only through juxtaposition with other ideographic characters and sym-bols. Blake builds the semblance of character in much the same way as an early geometrician must have envisioned the first triangle from three lines: three pure forms are synthesized into one by the imagi-nation. Yet, unlike the line that composes part of the triangle and then becomes a line again upon the triangle's dismantling, the ideographic character does not lose its acquired significance by entering into relationships with other forms. To illustrate this accretion of forms, we shall examine two sets of relationships: the first is that set which implies the identity of Blake, the Bard, Los, and Milton; the second is the relationship of this composite four to the Satan-Palamabron dispute.

The identification of the Bard with Blake occurs implicitly in the invocation to the muses. Much in the spirit of Byron in *Don Juan,* Blake makes it evident that he is master of his poem: inspiration descends "down the Nerves of my [Blake's] right arm / From out the Portals of my Brain . . ." (E 95). He relinquishes his explicit presence only after he has introduced the subject matter of his poem, Milton. He then speaks through the Bard, who, like Blake, is the inspired narrator who vanishes behind the "Song" throughout its narration only to reappear at the end to proclaim to the incredulous Sons of Albion that

> I am Inspired! I know it is Truth! for I Sing
>
> According to the inspiration of the Poetic Genius
> Who is the eternal all-protecting Divine Humanity
> To whom be Glory & Power & Dominion Evermore Amen (E 107)

Viewed reductively, both Blake and the Bard are agents of the "Poetic Genius."

As these agents, the Bard-Blake figure has certain official affinities with the character of Los, who represents creation in time. Blake comes closest to identifying himself, the Bard, and Los when he describes the latter in the following situation:

> Loud sounds the Hammer of Los, & loud his Bellows is heard
> Before London to Hampsteads breadths & Highgates heights To
> Stratford & old Bow: & across to the Gardens of Kensington
> On Tyburns Brook: loud groans Thames beneath the iron Forge
> Of Rintrah & Palamabron of Theotorm[on] & Bromion, to forge the
>   instruments
> Of Harvest: the Plow & Harrow to pass over the Nations (E 99)

Stationing Los in London, Blake places around his character those sites that surrounded his own home on South Moulton Street and those characters (especially Theotormon and Bromion) whom he had created. Thus Blake's celebration of Los is also one of self and of the "Poetic Genius."

Finally, the implicit identification of Blake, the Bard, and Los embraces Milton. In his description of the fall of the senses (E 98), Blake depicts Los in the following stance:

> Enraged & stifled without & within: in terror & woe, he threw his
> Right Arm to the north, his left Arm to the south, & his Feet
> Stampd the nether Abyss in trembling & howling & dismay (E 96)

While it refers to Los, this description is a verbal rendering of the figure of Milton that appears on the title page (Plate 99). Here Milton appears with his back to us, his arms in the manner described above, and his head turned slightly to the right to reveal one almond-shaped eye, Blake's visual designation of a prophet.[11] The figure, whose body is carefully poised and balanced, appears somewhat unconventional in the handling of the head, which is marked by flowing hair and the singularly shaped eye. Milton's body, however, unlike the one described verbally, betrays no rage; only in the wavy forms of the cosmos that surround him can this rage be discerned. By situating this poised body within the wavy, flamelike forms, Blake indulges in something of a verbal-visual pun: this body is visually represented *inside* of or "in terror & woe"; moreover, this rage that turns outward—"Enraged . . . without"—becomes a physical locale—"the nether Abyss"—that stifles the inward man, imprisoning him "in trembling & howling & dismay." Blake's implicit suggestion that Milton and Los are so imprisoned applies also to the Bard and Blake himself, who allows Milton to enter his "left foot" (E 113). Thus all the protagonists of the "Song" constitute one character, whose "psychological imprisonment" is dramatized in the confrontation of Satan and Palamabron, who here represent mildness and rage.

To overcome the obstacles that stifle human expression, the composite four confront Urizen. We know, of course, that during the composition of *Milton* Blake was engaged in a "spiritual conflict" with the Urizenic Hayley. Milton had perverted his poetry, in Blake's opinion, by making it a handmaiden to a Urizenic god. And Los, at the beginning of the "Song," is working to combat Urizen:

> Urizen lay in darkness & solitude, in chains of the mind lock'd up
> Los siezd his Hammer & Tongs; he labourd at his resolute Anvil
> Among indefinite Druid rocks & snows of doubt & reasoning. (E 96)

Amidst the formlessness of Urizenic doubt and reasoning and under the guise of Palamabron, the composite four will confront Urizen in the Satan–Palamabron dispute.

Much has been written concerning this dispute and its probable relation to the Blake–Hayley conflict. Critics such as Bloom and Erdman, for instance, have equated Palamabron with Blake and Satan with Hayley.[12] And, indeed, several instances in the literary dispute mirror aspects of Blake's personal quarrel. Satan, described as being of "incomparable mildness," endeavors to comfort the hard-working Palamabron in much the same manner as the patron Hayley sought to comfort the industrious Blake by offering him employment at Felpham. It soon became apparent to Blake that Hayley's commissions to execute trivial works of art were stifling his genius. In a letter to Thomas Butts, the enraged Blake declares that "if a Man is the Enemy of my Spiritual Life while he pretends to be the Friend of my Corporeal. he is a Real Enemy" (E 697). This statement echoes the admonition that appears before the narration of the dispute: "Mark well my words! Corporeal Friends are Spiritual Enemies" (E 97).

Yet, it would be wiser if we would treat this equation more loosely.[13] Biography may influence art; it does not determine it. Blake further develops the conflict not after the patterns of his dispute with Hayley, but after the war in Heaven and Satan's fall in *Paradise Lost.* Angered over the question of the proprietorship of the furrows, both Palamabron and Satan call assemblies (E 102). Edenic forces side with Palamabron, and, as a result, Satan falls. The fall of Blake's Satan, the "Reasoning Negative," is an ironic reversal of the fall in Milton's poem; there the "Reasoning Negative," Nobodaddy, remains in Heaven while Satan, in whom Milton invested so much poetic energy, falls. Viewed from the Edenic perspective, the Satan of Blake's poem is truly the "Reprobate," or outcast. But, viewed from the perspective of mortals, Satan is Urizen: "His Spectre raging furious descended into its Space / Then Los & Enitharmon knew that Satan is Urizen" (E 103). Blake gives a verbal form, a space, to his creation.

The composite four have confronted Urizen in the personage of Palamabron. A figure of honest if perhaps naive intentions, Palamabron characterizes the Milton who believed that he had correctly channeled his creative powers in his attempt to "justify the ways of God to men," the Blake who accepted Hayley's "soft dissimulations of friendship," and Los who himself is the father of Satan.

Blake brings these characters, these ideographic forms, together via his own psychic time, which permits him to envision as a continuum his own quarrel with Hayley, Milton's misuse of his poetic genius, and the excesses of doubt and rage that can overwhelm and stifle the poetic genius if they are not controlled. In the "Bard's Song," both Blake and art triumph: the Satan "refusing form" at the beginning of the "Song" has been given verbal form in Urizen and organized spatially on Plate 13 (Plate 100).

It is wholly appropriate that we find Milton on the later plate considerably changed from his appearance on the title page. Although his name is nowhere explicit in the text of the "Song," Milton has, of course, been present in the composite four. He has confronted Urizen through the imaginative forms of Blake's art and conquered him. Milton now appears facing forward, holding the robes of Jesus in his right hand, wearing a halo, and revealing humility in his eyes. This divinity derives from his office as a poet of men, and his humility from the recognition of the task that Blake's art has clarified for him—the imparting not of Urizenic art but of human inspiration. Blake emphasizes Milton's new office by replacing the wavy, formless figures that surround him in the title page with the precisely delineated sun, which appears behind him on Plate 13, and whose light is repeated in the halo. The rage that may result from stifling genius has been organized and informed into the symbol of inspiration, "the unwearied Sun by Los created / To measure Time and Space to mortal Men" (E 126).

IV

Visual and verbal forms and their interrelationships—space and time—dominate Blake's art. In the "Bard's Song," Blake offers us very little "story"; here the narrative as such is largely the fabrication of critics. Frye remarks that the "instant that any critic permits himself to make a genuine comment about a poem he has begun to allegorize."[14] As critics, we should note a marked difference between the allegories we fabricate from Blake's art and those from art in which space and time operate more conventionally. In the latter case, the critic concerns himself with the interrelationships of character and circumstances in order to discover the work's governing principle. Blake's art operates inversely: the operative principles—forms and their interrelationships—are laid bare even as their total meaning remains elusive. Seen from the empirical perspective, these forms and interrelationships appear aspatial and atemporal; seen as constituting the coordinates of man's mental faculties, they comprise the world of one being—a textual Albion.

NOTES

1. *Blake's Apocalypse: A Study in Poetic Argument* (Ithaca: Cornell Univ. Press, 1970), pp. 309–10.

2. Immanuel Kant, *Critique of Pure Reason,* trans. Norman Kemp Smith (New York: St. Martin's Press, 1929), p. 65.

3. The difficulty a reader may have with Kant's distinguishing space and time on the basis of their being forms of the outer and inner senses has been anticipated by Fr. Copleston: "Inasmuch as Kant proceeds to say that time is the *a priori* formal condition of all appearances whatsoever, whereas space is the *a priori* formal condition of external appearances only, it may appear that he is contradicting himself. But his meaning is this. All representations, whether they have or have not external things as their objects, are determinations of the mind. And, as such, they belong to our internal state. Hence they must all be subject to the formal condition of inner sense or intuition, namely time. But time is thus only the mediate condition of external appearances, whereas it is the immediate condition of all internal appearance." (Frederick Copleston, S.J., *A History of Philosophy: Volume 6: Modern Philosophy: Part II: Kant* [New York: Image Books, 1964], p. 34.)

4. Gotthold Lessing, *Laocoön,* trans. Edward Allen McCormick (Indianapolis: Bobbs-Merrill, 1962), p. 91.

5. Ibid., p. 40.

6. Ibid., p. 85.

7. *The Journal of Aesthetics and Art Criticism,* 10 (1951), 41.

8. "An Essay on Criticism," *The Poems of Alexander Pope,* ed. John Butt (New Haven: Yale Univ. Press, 1963), p. 153.

9. *Anatomy of Criticism: Four Essays* (New York: Atheneum, 1969), p. 97.

10. *Fearful Symmetry: A Study of William Blake* (Princeton: Princeton Univ. Press, 1969), p. 321.

11. Jean H. Hagstrum, *William Blake: Poet and Painter* (Chicago: Univ. of Chicago Press, 1964), p. 111.

12. Cf. Bloom, *Blake's Apocalypse,* pp. 313–15; David V. Erdman, *Blake: Prophet Against Empire* (New York: Anchor Books, 1969), pp. 409, 425.

13. Along with Frye, *Fearful Symmetry,* pp. 326–27.

14. *Anatomy of Criticism,* p. 89.

Revisiting Reynold's *Discourses* and Blake's Annotations

Hazard Adams

THOUGH Blake annotated only the first eight of Reynolds' *Discourses* (in Malone's second edition of 1798), it is clear that he had read at least the fifteenth and last, the ending of which inspired him to ridicule Reynolds in verse. Reynolds concludes his last discourse with the remark: "... I should desire that the last words which I should pronounce in this Academy, and from this place, might be the name of—Michael Angelo."[1] Blake's notebook verses, entitled "A Pitiful Case," comment:

> The Villain at the Gallows tree
> When he is doomd to die
> To assuage his misery
> In Virtues praise does cry
>
> So Reynolds when he came to die
> To assuage his bitter woe:
> Thus aloud did howl & cry
> Michael Angelo Michael Angelo (E 504)

Blake treats Reynolds' final remark and perhaps the whole panegyric on Michaelangelo, which takes up much of *Discourse Fifteen*, as a hypocritical act of contrition generated by fear and misery, not by a true change of heart. For Blake, a hypocrite is someone whose position on any matter is inconsistent with itself, whose acts or particular assertions are in conflict with his fundamental philosophical stance. Hypocrisy is not merely, then, what we call pretense or deliberate charlatanism. It is any error and is as characteristic of the redeemed as of the elect.

The task I propose is to revisit the *Discourses* to determine whether it is possible to declare that the later ones ought to have softened Blake's view of Reynolds in any way or merely enforced his sense of the great gulf between them.[2] Reynolds later took up a number of matters not specifically dealt with in the first eight— genius, imagination, sculpture, architecture, the work of Gainsborough and Michaelangelo, to mention the most obvious. Still, it seems likely that by the time he had annotated eight discourses, Blake felt that he had fully enough expressed his indignation at and his fundamental philosophical differences with Reynolds. In a long note at the beginning of *Discourse Eight,* he made a kind of summary, which suggests that he had perused them all:

> Burke's treatise on the Sublime & Beautiful is founded on the Opinions of Newton & Locke on this Treatise Reynolds has grounded many of his assertions. in all his Discourses I read Burkes Treatise when very Young at the same time I read Locke on Human Understanding & Bacons Advancement of Learning on Every one of these Books I wrote my Opinions & on looking them over find that my Notes on Reynolds in this Book are exactly Similar. I felt the same Contempt & Abhorrence then; that I do now. They mock Inspiration & Vision. (E 650)

The annotations in Blake's books characteristically strike at the alleged philosophical premises of the author.

In order to revisit the later discourses, it is necessary to consider the major points of dispute in the first eight. Reynolds is not far into *Discourse One* when the first point arises. It has to do with his attempt to define the "grand style" in painting by contrasting Raphael's manner before and after he saw Michaelangelo's Sistine Chapel. He characterizes Raphael's earlier style as a "dry, Gothick, and even insipid manner, which attends to the minute accidental discriminations of particular and individual objects" (I, 9). The artist, he goes on, must improve "partial representation by the general and invariable ideas of nature" (I, 9). In these remarks, Reynolds' complaint is specifically against the artist who is merely an illusionist. He is not interested in the kind of sensuous verisimilitude that allegedly caused birds to pick at the cherries in the paintings of Zeuxis. If this were all that is *implied* by Reynolds' remarks, Blake might better have remained silent. He could hardly have quarreled with an attack on such illusionism, which gives to the artist the secondary role of servile imitator of external nature. But Reynolds grounds his complaint in a way not required by it. These grounds are not absolutely clear until the crucial *Discourse Three,* though they are implicit in the adjective "accidental," which he applies to "minute discriminations" in *Discourse One,* and to which I shall return. In *Discourse Three,* the most comprehensive of the early discourses, Reynolds expands his complaint about minute discriminations. It is not merely illusionism to which he objects, but representation of "all singular forms, local customs, particularities, and details of every kind" (III, 58). Here he displays clearly his presuppositions, which earlier lurk only in the single word "accidental," a term that we come to learn has a certain relationship to Reynolds' various concepts of nature.

If Reynolds employed the term "nature" in only one sense, what he has to say about the artist would be far clearer; but, as Roger Fry pointed out many years ago, Reynolds uses the term in more than one way. Fry notes that he uses it to denote: 1) "the sum of visible phenomena not made by artifice," 2) the Aristotelian "immanent force working in the refractory medium of matter towards the highest perfection of form," and 3) "whatever is agreeable to the affections and predispositions of the mind."[3] The first and third of these usages are clearly present in Reynolds. But in citing the second, Fry assimilates him to Aristotle rather too easily, without noting that what is present is really a mixture of Platonic and empiricist notions. This is important in Blake's quarrel with him. It is worth examining Reynolds' language with some care on the point, since Reynolds' whole conception of the grand style turns on it.

The word "accidental" is a good place to begin. It implies the location of fundamental reality beyond any of the natures enunciated by Fry. It implies that the local details of our experience are hardly real at all and that we are always seeking, like Aristotle's nature, for an ideal form. That ideal form is *there* and is the reality. As Reynolds presents it, it has a substantial quality that it lacks in Aristotle. It appears to be more like a Platonic idea. Where Reynolds connects the grand style with the improvement of "partial representation by the general and invariable ideas of nature," (I, 9) he has introduced a meaning for nature not covered by Fry's triad. Nature itself becomes the ideal substance that Aristotle said nature only endeavors to produce.

If this were the only meaning for nature that Reynolds proffers, or if he called external experience "secondary nature" or something of the sort, we would have far less difficulty with his terminology. Or if he limited the term "nature" to the world in its so-called accidental multiformity and gave the name "ideas" to what man builds up from it inductively by the process of generalization, things would be clearer. If he chose the former route, we would call Reynolds a Platonist, and, if the latter, an empiricist. As we have him, Reynolds presents us with a terminological quagmire; and we are confused about the location of ideas and of nature implied in terms like "accidental," "partial," "general," and "invariable." The whole sentence to which I have been referring is as follows:

> On the sight of the Capella Sistina, he [Raphael] immediately from a dry, Gothick, and even insipid manner, which attends to the minute accidental discriminations of particular and individual objects, assumed that grand style of painting, which improves partial representation by the general and invariable ideas of nature. (I, 9)

What Reynolds calls "partial representation" could be, from another point of view, a more *complete* representation of external nature than what he himself advocates. But from his own point of view, the more *complete* in that sense the more partial in his sense, since to be *complete* in the former sense is to introduce mere accident, which only contributes to the spectator's distraction from what is meant to be conveyed—either a Platonic form or a generalization. The term "invariable," however, leads us to believe he is probably referring here to a Platonic idea.

There is little or nothing in Plato inviting us to call his own ideas "general." The term "general" in Reynolds establishes an empirical point of view entirely different from Plato's or from Aristotle's. It suggests that ideas are built up by a rational process of induction rather than discovered as existent metaphysical forms that the accidental particulars of nature copy independent of human creative involvement. What we have in Reynolds is an attempt to force the inductive generalization from sense data to meet and become identical with the Platonic idea. This joining is implied in Reynolds' term "central form," which he advances in *Discourse Three*. "Central form," which is achieved by the grand style, is then identified with "beauty." All else is "accident" or "deformity" (III, 58). From the artist's practical point of view, search for the "central form," which Reynolds calls a "perfect state of nature" is also a search for "ideal beauty" (III, 59). There is avoidance of the Platonic criticism of poets and artists because the artistic process, as Reynolds sees it, is a rational and conceptual one and involves a transcendence of the deformed copies, deformity in this case being a surplus of accidents more often than some sort of formal strangeness.

Reynolds seems to be tied to a simple quantitative model. The artist's search for "central form" via generalization begins with "reiterated experience, and a close comparison of the objects in nature" (III, 60). Deviation from this inductive process, which operates according to the laws of associationist psychology, results in "deformity." From the artist's practical point of view the proper result must be a generalization: "The whole beauty and grandeur of the art consists, in my opinion, in being able to get above all singular forms, local customs, particularities, and details of every kind" (III, 57-8). On the other hand, from the metaphysical point of view the result is an idea: "... all the arts receive their perfection from an ideal beauty, superior to what is to be found in individual nature" (III, 53), in its eternality and invariability. But the route to it through sensible observation proceeding to abstraction is not Plato's, who does not reduce the variety of nature to the abstract idea.

One of Reynolds' problems in keeping these two ideas together is to avoid collapsing everything into the eternal, ideal perfection of the One, which is the ultimate Platonic idea. On the face of it, this would eliminate the role of the artist, who must obliterate every image he creates as he passes ever upward toward more expansive generalizations or toward the unrepresentable. Here Reynolds tries to save art, or rather his theory, by introducing the principle of several "central forms" (III, 62). These he claims to be separate and distinct from each other and yet each undeniably beautiful, that is, each contains a different ideal of beauty. He declares that each of these is based upon a class, not an individual. This view may be all right for an empirical, or even an Aristotelian, Reynolds, but it is not adequate for the Platonic Reynolds, who must quickly assert that the "highest perfection" cannot be discovered in any single class but only in "that form which is taken [abstracted] from them all" and in some way "partakes equally" of them (III, 63).

The insistence on many classes, each with its ideal of beauty, Reynolds must maintain in order to avoid the complete disappearance of the artistic image into a Platonic idea, which defies representation and renders art either false and impossible or absolutely pure, transparent allegory (in Blake's derogatory sense of the word), where the image only stands arbitrarily for an idea. But as I have noted, Reynolds' argument drives him toward the One, even as he resists. The artist is therefore to be seen as *creating* general ideas by a process of induction identical to the conceptual processes of natural philosophy. Or he is seen as struggling to *discover* the idea by a process which systematically eliminates accident from external nature until finally all the dross is removed; but were he to succeed, would not his allegorical image also have to be erased?

In neither case is the artist possessed of innate ideas; he follows a method, and it is the only method. The model of the mind is that of Locke and Hartley. The mind is a *tabula rasa,* and it operates by association. The model is spatially simple, ideas being like building blocks. The work of art is the product of a formula: "The summit of excellence seems to be an assemblage of contrary qualities, but mixed, in such proportions, that no one part is found to counteract the other" (V, 120). The imagination for Reynolds, following Burke, "is incapable of producing anything originally of itself, and can only vary and combine those ideas with which it is furnished by means of the senses" (VII, 220). It must follow from this that beauty is to be equated with symmetry and harmony in the old classical sense. Reynolds proceeds to do just that.

In such a system there is not much place for the sublime in art, even though on first impression the striving to get beyond external nature that Reynolds attributes to the grand style might be an effort toward sublimity, in one sense of the word. But the effort either destroys the image or makes the image valuable only as a purely transparent allegory: "The sublime impresses the mind at once with one great idea" (IV, 97). A great idea is, of course, for Reynolds a general idea, and a general idea is one built up or abstracted from many accidents and made into a harmony. Reynolds tries to establish a principle of beauty based on generality and really subsumes sublimity under it. Blake, on the other hand, holds to a principle of sublimity based on particularity and tends to subsume beauty. Reynolds groups the grand, the general, and the beautiful together, drains the term "sublime" of its antithetical meaning and opposes these terms with certain undesirables: "ornamental," "particular," "passionate," and "deformed."

Blake's fundamental disagreement with Reynolds can best be approached in the light of Reynolds' attempted compromise between an empirical and a Platonic stance and particularly with re-

spect to Reynolds' attack on minute particulars. It is typical of
Blake's insistence on getting to fundamental presuppositions that he
does not bother to distinguish between Reynolds' complaint against
illusionist technique and Reynolds' strictures against all use of local
detail. Blake sees at once the central issue. In *Discourse Three*
Reynolds remarks, "The wish of the genuine painter must be more
extensive: instead of endeavouring to amuse mankind with the minute neatness of his imitations, he must endeavour to improve them
by the grandeur of his ideas" (III, 52-3). Blake jumps on this with:
"Without Minute Neatness of Execution. The. Sublime cannot Exist!
Grandeur of Ideas is founded on Precision of Ideas" (E 636). Blake
does not care to note that Reynolds explains himself in a further
clause: ". . . instead of seeking praise, by deceiving the superficial
sense of the spectator, he must strive for fame, by captivating the
imagination" (III, 53). On the matter of this kind of deception,
Blake must have been in agreement with Reynolds. But for Blake
that was not the issue at hand. No doubt he had already read *Discourse One,* and the criticism of the early Raphael as attending too
much to "minute *accidental* [my italics] discrimination of particular
and individual objects," (I, 9), and saw the implication of "accidental" as fundamental. He remarks there: "minute Discrimination is
Not Accidental" (E 632). Later on, in *Discourse Three,* Reynolds carries his argument farther—much farther—and calls the "accidents"
of nature deformity, to which, of course, Blake objects violently.
Reynolds' way to justify avoiding minute, illusionist copying of nature, which he apparently instinctively dislikes and must find a reasonable argument against, is by recourse to the general or Platonic
ideas as the true reality to be copied. He does not seem to recognize
that in neither case is there any image to be copied but only an
abstract idea, so that the result can only be a naive allegory. For
Blake form must be immediately grasped, indeed imposed, by the
imagination, copied or abstracted from so-called accidental particulars or copied quixotically from Platonic forms. Blake's route is
neither the empirical nor the Platonic.

Perhaps the best single key to Blake's quarrel with Reynolds is
his annotation to Reynolds' introduction of the concept of "central
form" in *Discourse Three.* Reynolds has been discussing the "idea of
the perfect state of nature, which the artist calls the Ideal Beauty"
(III, 59). This idea Reynolds in his Platonic way calls "divine,"
though with a certain reservation. He says that it *"seems* [my italics] to

have a right to the epithet of *divine*" and it appears to be "possessed of the will and intention of the Creator" (III, 59). The artist who comes into possession of this idea succeeds. How does this occur? By means of empirical processes: ". . . it is from a reiterated experience, and a close comparison of the objects in nature, that an artist becomes possessed of the idea of that central form, if I may so express it, from which every deviation is deformity" (III, 60). Blake's response to this is that if we grant the existence of such a "central form," and Blake does not grant it ontological status—but if we should—"it does not therefore follow that all other Forms are Deformity" (E 637). The fact for Blake is that all forms are created by the mind of the poet and give shape to nature: "All Forms are Perfect in the Poets Mind. but these are not Abstracted nor Compounded from Nature but are from Imagination" (E 637). A little later on Blake denies Reynolds' "central form" entirely because it is itself an abstraction compounded from nature, and Blake at this point claims that general nature does not exist, because "Strictly Speaking All Knowledge is Particular" (E 637). This strict nominalism, however, Blake tempers when Reynolds introduces the matter of species and classes. In Reynolds' system each of these classes has a central form of its own, though of these central forms there is in turn a central form for a more inclusive class, and so on, presumably infinitely to the imageless One. Reynolds introduces the matter of species in order to halt the regress. There is, for example, a perfect human image—a form abstracted from the various types of gladiator, Apollo, Hercules, etc. (III, 63).

Blake is critical of all this. He observes that Reynolds has, in fact, abandoned the idea of one central form and introduced many (E 637). The remark that best expresses his own view is brief: "Every Class is Individual" (E 637). He is distinguishing between the artist who creates the classes of men and gives those classes individuality, as he claims Chaucer did in his particularized Canterbury pilgrims, and a class concept divested of particularity and, in Blake's mind, inevitably of any imagistic substance, substantiality being from imagination and drained out in the process of generalization from sense data. The distinction is similar to that made by Giambattista Vico in *The New Science* between "abstract" and "imaginative" universals. According to Vico, the earliest people did not have "intelligible class concepts of things."[4] They moved from particulars to universals not by a process of generalization but by a "poetic logic" that enlarges the particular into a mythic figure rather than reducing each particular to those elements it has in common with all others of its class. Blake would claim the particularity of each class or imaginative universal on the basis of the same principle of poetic apprehension rather than abstractive impoverishment, the poet's vehicle of apprehension being tropological language. Thus he would claim that each thing inhabits in its totality the class to which it belongs. Goethe tried to carry, somewhat quixotically, into modern science itself a similar principle when he displayed to Schiller a "symbolic plant."

All Blake's disagreements with Reynolds on how the artist proceeds may be referred back to this point. Blake sees the process of generalizing or abstracting from particulars as fundamentally passive and determined. It must operate mechanically according to fixed laws. It always has to end in the same place, which is for Blake a nowhere. Connected to this is Blake's vigorous objection whenever Reynolds treats artistic technique apart from imaginative conception. Indeed, Blake is so adamant on this point that he complains about Reynolds even when Reynolds deplores the separation himself. Yet strictly speaking Blake is right to complain, since for him Reynolds' position requires a distinction between thought and execution and results in a mimetic theory of a naive sort. Blake's theory of active *making* holds thought and execution together; Reynolds' theory of abstracting separates them, the process of abstraction occurring for Reynolds previous to expression in a medium. Blake's artistic act, on the other hand, requires a medium in which to *think out* the Vichean "imaginative universal." It is for Blake a characteristic of imaginative universals that they are radical creations and have no existence as concepts previous to their expression, though obviously concepts can then be abstracted from them.

The drift of Reynolds' argument is that mechanical authority and technique are worthless unless they have some grand concept behind them. The drift of Blake's annotations is that execution is the act of *creating* art and cannot really be discussed in a void of imaginative content. As usual, Blake goes to Reynolds' presuppositions rather than quarreling only with what the statements appear to say on the surface. Reynolds is, even from Blake's point of view, quite right to complain about a flashy, shallow technique: "A facility in composing,—a lively, and what is called a masterly, handling of the chalk or pencil, are, it must be confessed, captivating qualities to

young minds, and become of course the objects of their ambitions"
(I, 13). In annotating this and later remarks like it, Blake refuses to
consider that Reynolds is warning against a "facility" that is vapid,
and insists that when Reynolds talks about facility, he means real
care in execution. He calls Reynolds' remark "Supremely Insolent"
and cites the following reasons:

> Why this Sentence should be begun by the Words A Facility in
> Composing I cannot tell unless it was to cast a stigma upon Real
> facility in Composition by Assimilating it with a Pretence to &
> Imitation of Facility in Execution or are we to understand him
> to mean that Facility in Composing. is a Frivolous pursuit. A Fa-
> cility in Composing is the Greatest Power of Art & Belongs to
> None but the Greatest Artists i.e. the Most Minutely Discriminat-
> ing & Determinate. (E 632)

Blake is puzzled by Reynolds' inconsistency, but in fact they are
using the term "facility" in different senses. Blake insists that "facility" should refer to creative execution, not the execution of a copy of
a previous concept. Thus he is simply unable to imagine, or refuses
to imagine, what false facility could be. Where there is no creativity
there is no facility, since facility is defined by what it creates. If it
merely copies, it is not facility. Thus Blake can say that "Mechanical
Excellence is the Only Vehicle of Genius" (E 632) and "Execution is
the Chariot of Genius" (E 632). It is really everything. Where imagination is lacking, there is no such power. Where mechanical excellence is lacking there is no imagination. After following Reynolds'
argument for awhile, the best Blake can say of him is: "This is all
Self-Contradictory! Truth & Falshood Jumbled Together" (E 633).

The whole matter of copying and drawing from models, about
which Blake sometimes agrees and sometimes disagrees with
Reynolds, can be pushed back to the same epistemological issue.
Blake advises copying as valuable training in learning the "language
of art" and does not understand how Reynolds can agree with him
and still attack the painters of "minute particulars." It is sometimes a
matter of emphasis. Blake is always angered when Reynolds warns
against arrogant originality because Blake suspects that Reynolds
never allows anyone to trust to his own invention. Reynolds thinks,
in fact, that the young "inventor" is usually derivative and comes to
originality only through long effort. Blake, on the other hand, recognizes the young painter's need to copy as part of his apprenticeship. Reynolds sees that to do this endlessly is never to become more

than an apprentice. There is really no contradiction here, but Blake wants there to be one. Part of the problem at this point is Blake's refusal to see that Reynolds is adjusting his discourse to a certain audience. As Robert Wark has observed, "Many apparent shifts in opinion and inconsistencies in the *Discourses* dissolve at once when the passages are read in context, with due attention to the level of the student to whom they are addressed."[5] Earlier, Walter J. Hipple argued that often the supposed inconsistencies in Reynolds are actually caused by the reader's "overlooking or confounding the several stages Reynolds prescribes for the education of artists" and "juxtaposing passages without regard to the 'level' of their argumentative contexts."[6] Though Wark sees very little change in point of view or emphasis, an earlier critic, Wilson O. Clough, detects "something like a mellowing, almost a conversion."[7] These two positions, incidentally, are not necessarily antithetical, and I shall come to accept both in their ways, though I do not myself regard anything in the later Reynolds as close to a conversion.

If there is a change that would have strongly affected Blake's attitude, it would have to have occurred in Reynolds' fundamental tenets. Though Blake might well have been sensitive to a mellowing and have commented on it, it is likely that he would have treated it as a surprise or with a certain sarcasm, pointing out Reynolds' inconsistency. If a fundamental change is detectable in the later discourses it is likely to have occurred in connection with Reynolds' exposition of "genius" in *Discourse Eleven* and "imagination" in *Discourse Thirteen*.

As early as *Discourse Two* Reynolds has warned beginners not to depend on their own genius (II, 44), and Blake makes no comment on this, even though the passage summarizes Reynolds' attitude in the whole discourse. He does complain about Reynolds' later remarks, however. At the end of *Discourse Four* Reynolds states that the errors of genius are pardonable (IV, 111), and Blake argues that genius has no error (E 641). In *Discourse Six* Reynolds argues that genius is different in different times and places (VI, 152), and Blake believes that it is always and everywhere the same (E 645). In *Discourse Seven* Reynolds is sarcastic about those who wait for the call of genius (VII, 197), and Blake objects to his attitude (E 647–648). He also objects to Reynolds' remark that taste and genius are a product of learning and not innate powers.

These remarks by Reynolds on genius are all made in connection with other dominating topics. In *Discourse Eleven* Reynolds attempts an extended treatment of genius itself. Here he continues to claim that genius can err and that a work can be faultless and exhibit no genius. Blake would, of course, continue to disagree, the difference being over the nature of beauty, Reynolds treating beauty in terms of the classical theory of harmony and proportion and Blake subsuming beauty under the sublime. Reynolds continues to talk about "the Genius of mechanical performance" (XI, 43), implying that there can be such genius apart from a content, while Blake would, of course, reject the separation.

But in his argument Reynolds appears to soften his strictures against minute particulars. He concedes, "A Painter must have the power of contracting as well as dilating his sight; because, he that does not at all express particulars, expresses nothing" (XI, 43). But this, in the end, turns out to be no more than a slight softening, because Reynolds immediately adds that expression of detail alone does not prove genius and any detail that does not contribute to the expression of the "main characteristic" is "worse than useless" (XI, 44) since it draws attention from the principal point. The word "express" is employed a number of times and gives a somewhat new tone to the argument. It is joined by references to the "pleasure" of the spectator. The use of the former suggests a slight movement in a direction Blake might have welcomed. The latter, however, reveals a maintenance of the values Reynolds has held all along, for pleasure is defined not as a result of the artist's power of imitation but of his expression of the general idea. It appears that Reynolds regards the mind as fundamentally attuned to general or Platonic ideas and less to external nature. Seeing this, Blake would have been correct to conclude that fundamentally Reynolds had not changed his views by shifting the focus of his argument from the question of objective beauty to that of pleasure.

Blake would also have objected vigorously, and I think scornfully, to Reynolds' efforts to establish a principle of taste and beauty on the ground that "we are pleased" at seeing ends accomplished by seemingly inadequate means (XI, 224). This argument might have suggested to Blake that Reynolds' complaints against a certain kind of minute illusionism are merely a cover for approbation of another sort of visual trickery. The whole concept of general effect remains paramount, yet it is clear that Reynolds has tried in the later discourses to be more careful with his terms: ". . . I commend nothing for want of exactness; I mean to point out that kind of exactness which is the best . . ." (XI, 65). That kind he attempts, as we shall see, to free from imitation in a more radical way than he did heretofore.

There are statements in *Discourse Twelve* that Blake might have been compelled to comment on favorably: "I would rather wish a student, as soon as he goes abroad, to employ himself upon whatever he has been incited to by any immediate impulse, than to go sluggishly about a prescribed task" (XII, 74). Reynolds proceeds to claim that no one method is suitable to all artists and that love of method is, for many, a love of idleness (XII, 76-7). These remarks Blake might have regarded as inconsistent with earlier ones, but in fact they are not, for they are addressed not to the raw novice but to students who have advanced beyond the concerns addressed in the first discourses. All of these remarks are predicated on the idea that genius and taste are developed by study and learning and that study and learning make more possible the ability to follow out impulses successfully to artistic ends. On the matter of learning, Blake would have disagreed, claiming that taste and genius are innate. Blake and Reynolds seem to be driven to opposite extremes by the reigning system of thought and terminology at hand. Blake claims the innateness of taste and genius because he rejects the limitations put on the term "learning" as it was understood in his time to proceed by association. He chooses to throw out the concept of learning. Reynolds seeks a way to include taste and genius in the current theory of learning.

The problem reasserts itself most vigorously in Reynolds' remarks on the imagination, which occur in the important *Discourse Thirteen*. Blake has already clashed with Reynolds with respect to matters of sublimity, enthusiasm, passion, and inspiration—many of the terms Blake connects with imagination. One imagines him to have read what Reynolds had to say in *Discourse Thirteen* with skepticism. Blake had already argued that "Singular & Particular Detail" is the foundation of the sublime (E 637), while Reynolds had already called obscurity one source of it (VII, 197). Enthusiasm Reynolds had warned against when it is unaccompanied by determined systematic study, and he argued that "enthusiastick admiration seldom promotes knowledge" (III, 55). Blake connected enthusiasm directly with knowledge. Passion, too, Reynolds had found dangerous when given rein (V, 117-18), and Blake had responded, "Passion & Expression is Beauty Itself" (E 642).

The fundamental question to ask of Reynolds' *Discourse Thirteen* is whether he comes to define "imagination" as an independent mental power or merely as a special mode of operation of the reason. If the former, Blake could possibly come to agreement with him; if the latter, their disagreement would remain as fundamentally wide as ever, though Blake might detect in Reynolds' appropriation of and dwelling upon the term, along with certain other gestures, a softening.

From Blake's point of view, Reynolds starts out in a rather encouraging way. He states that whether the imagination be affected is the only test of art (XIII, 114), all other principles being tested by this one. But at once he implies that the imagination depends upon the memory, which in his view operates by the process of association (XIII, 114-15). So much, for the moment, for affect and the spectator. The artist's imagination in operation is described as follows: the artist's "animated thoughts" proceed from "the fullness of his mind, enriched with the copious stores of all the various inventions which he had ever seen, or had ever passed in his mind. These ideas are infused into his design, without any conscious effort" (XIII, 116). They should not, Reynolds warns, be overly considered and corrected or they will become commonplace. Here again is the familiar associationist theory of memory and knowledge, in which no radically creative act can be attributed to the mind. What occurs is the moving about of the elements of the memory into new combinations by a sort of *spontaneous* working, rather than a deliberate act, of the reason. It is finally a matter of unconscious (because radically foreshortened) as against conscious behavior, both operating according to the same principles. It is precisely what Blake called corporeal understanding.

In Reynolds' system reason gives way to feeling and sentiment only because it still contains them. Reynolds warns against "an unfounded distrust of the imagination and feeling, in favour of narrow, partial, confined argumentative theories," but he goes on to say that "reason, without doubt, must ultimately determine every thing; at this minute it is required to inform us when that very reason is to give way to feeling" (XIII, 116-17). This attempted paradox is not successful. In truth, imagination and feeling are, for Reynolds, determined by rational principles, the only difference being the rapidity of the unconscious process. Blake would have seen immediately that for Reynolds the imagination has no creative power and is merely a species of the corporeal understanding, possessing only the appearance of "vision."

Most of *Discourse Thirteen* is about affect and the role of the spectator. It is important to notice that Reynolds seems at the outset if not to have abandoned at least to have deemphasized in his argument against minute particulars both the empirical and the Platonic descriptions of the artistic process. Here the attack on minute copying of external nature is expanded into an attack on imitation. Painting, he now says, is "in many points of view, and strictly speaking, no imitation at all of external nature" (XIII, 119). Certainly out of its context Blake could have applauded this remark, for he could have applied his own definition of external nature—the dead primary world of Locke—to the statement, rather than Reynolds', which turns out again to be the secondary world of Plato. Reynolds argues that poetry and painting deviate from nature in order to please the imagination of the spectator, which wishes to move in a realm beyond the mundane, where its own "natural propensities" may be gratified. It is curious that on the one hand Reynolds argues that taste is learned and on the other that art is judgable by the "natural propensities" of the spectator, which are above nature. The Platonic and the general have flowed back into the argument under the new aegis of affect, and we return to the position of the early discourses after all. The ultimately natural propensities of man are resolved into a desire for "congruity, coherence, and consistency" (XIII, 123). These classical standards had already been proffered in *Discourse Seven,* but there Reynolds was still concerned with imitation. There he said:

> The natural appetite or taste of the human mind is for *Truth;* whether that truth results from the real agreement or equality of original ideas among themselves; from the agreement of the representation of any object with the thing represented; or from the correspondence of the several parts of any arrangement with each other. It is the very same taste which relishes a demonstration in geometry, that is pleased with the resemblance of a picture to an original, and touched with the harmony of music. (VII, 200)

In eliminating concern for "agreement of the representation of any object with the thing represented" Reynolds has actually gone farther toward the Platonic and general than he had before, even though he has appeared to soften his stand on the matter of minute particulars.

To Reynolds' statement above, Blake remarked: "Demonstration Similitude & Harmony are Objects of Reasoning Invention Identity & Melody are Objects of Intuition" (E 648). This remark remains symbolic of Blake's differences with the arguments of the later discourses. In *Discourse Thirteen* Reynolds speaks of artists addressing themselves to "another faculty of the mind" than reason (XIII, 126), but his own system makes that faculty only a special instance of the mind's single faculty; Blake claims the existence of a radically different faculty. Yet I can just imagine Blake concluding that Reynolds, in searching for a way to admit imagination into his system, was also trying to move to a more expansive view of mental powers. I can imagine him sensing this also in the remark that directs the painter and poet to be allowed to "dare every thing" (XIII, 125) and in the attempt in *Discourse Fifteen* to come to terms with the genius of Michaelangelo. Even the word "visionary" appears with the word "enthusiasm" in honorific contexts in *Discourse Fourteen* (XIV, 169), and Blake might have remembered a remark of his own when he discovered Reynolds distinguishing "that which addresses itself to the imagination from that which is solely addressed to the eye" (XV, 188). At the same time, Blake was not likely to forget that in Reynolds the term "imagination" is not yet emancipated from the reason and that Reynolds' complaint about the eye is merely the old complaint about minute particulars. In the end Reynolds returns to the distinction between the "narrow idea of Nature" and the "grandeur of the general ideas" (XV, 192). It is a division that for Blake had no meaning.

Involved in Blake's quarrel with Reynolds was, of course, his indignation against Reynolds as symbolic of an alien class that dominated society and in his view suppressed the very same genius that Reynolds wrote about. At the beginning of his annotations, which Blake was confident posterity would read, Blake warns the reader to expect "Nothing but Indignation & Resentment" (E 625). There is plenty of both. The warning is consistent with Blake's views about expression. Indignation was passion and expression and therefore beauty; all else would be hypocrisy and error. Yet one feels, in spite of all this by way of explanation of Blake's performance, that Blake has dealt badly with Reynolds. He deliberately refuses to recognize that at different times Reynolds is speaking about different levels of artistic sophistication when he gives advice; he does not comment on the later discourses, where Reynolds may earn at least slight redemption; and he has no sense at all that Reynolds' humility may be quite honest. Indeed, Blake's thought has no place for humility except as it is subsumed under hypocrisy, an error similar in form to subsuming imagination under reason. If one sides with Blake in his epistemological quarrel with Reynolds, one is not obliged to accept his *ad hominem* attack. In despising humility Blake also seems to have lost sight of charity. I think we can fault him for that in spite of his devil's remark that there would be no mercy, that is to say charity, if no one was poor (E 462). The devil's view is somewhat narrower than that of St. Paul.

NOTES

1. Quotations from Reynolds are all taken from *The Works of Sir Joshua Reynolds,* ed. Edmond Malone, 2nd ed. (London: Cadell and Davies, 1798). The copy of this edition with Blake's annotations is in the British Museum. The present quotation is from Discourse XV, pages 217–18. Roman numerals in parentheses refer to the discourse in which the statement may be found. Arabic numerals refer to the page.

2. The *Discourses* have been visited frequently. In addition to works specifically mentioned below, particularly worth consultation are Frederick Will, "Blake's Quarrel with Reynolds," *Journal of Aesthetics and Art Criticism,* 15 (1957), 340–49; and, principally on Reynolds, Lawrence Lipking, *The Ordering of the Arts in Eighteenth-Century England* (Princeton: Princeton Univ. Press, 1970), pp. 164–207.

3. Roger Fry, ed., *Discourses Delivered to the Students of the Royal Academy by Sir Joshua Reynolds* (London: Seeley, 1905), pp. 39–40.

4. *The New Science of Giambattista Vico,* trans. T.G. Bergin and M.H. Fisch, revised translation of the third ed. of 1744 (Ithaca: Cornell Univ. Press, 1968), pp. 115–32.

5. Robert R. Wark, ed., *Discourses on Art by Sir Joshua Reynolds* (San Marino: Huntington Library, 1959), p. xvii.

6. "General and Particular in the *Discourses* of Sir Joshua Reynolds: A Study in Method," *Journal of Aesthetics and Art Criticism,* 11 (1953), 232.

7. "Reason and Genius," *Philological Quarterly,* 23 (1944), 46–50.

Blake and the Gothic

Roger R. Easson

ANY serious examination of William Blake's graphic and poetic works will quickly bring his intensely Christian vision into focus; for Blake, it has been observed, was that rare creature in the Age of Reason, a Christian painter.[1] Much has been written on Blake's religion and on his aesthetics, but surprisingly little account has been taken of Blake's very great debt to medieval Christianity. The record is rather extensive for those who wish to catalogue Blake's contacts with the Gothic world as it was preserved in the London of Blake's time. We know, for example, that as an apprentice he was taught by James Basire who, as engraver to the Society of Antiquaries, was engaged in several publications on British antiquities. We know a good deal about Blake's early contact with the Gothic grandeur of Westminster Abbey, and Malkin informs us that Blake studied Gothic remains throughout London as well.[2] It has been remarked that Blake could have seen illuminated manuscripts in Westminster Chancery House Library, the illuminated manuscripts housed in the British Museum after 1802, the famous Bedford Hours in Joseph Johnson's printing shop, and Queen Mary's Psalter displayed in Montague House after 1795.[3] Kenneth Clark has suggested that Blake could have seen one of the greatest Romanesque manuscripts housed in the Lambeth Palace Library only a few hundred yards from his house in Lambeth.[4] And many scholars have called our attention to the Christian iconography alive in emblem books and history paintings known to Blake. But my concern here is with the larger question of Blake and the revival of interest in Gothic architecture and culture, the so-called Gothic Revival, and with that type of art which Blake usually terms "the Gothic."

The initial problem in this examination centers on the term

145

"Gothic." It is a term that has changed meaning considerably since Blake's time, due mainly to the efforts of art historians to differentiate among the various styles, periods, and traditions of the "Middle Ages." In consequence, "Gothic" for us refers most often to the culture and architecture that follows "Romanesque" and precedes "Renaissance," roughly the period between 1050 and 1450 A.D. For Blake and his contemporaries, however, such distinctions were not current. It is interesting to note that even Johnson's Dictionary in its 1799 edition does not include the word "Gothic." The term was for the most part specialist, confined to the jargon of architectural and antiquarian circles. Beyond those limits, Gothic usually meant "of or pertaining to the Goths," the early Germanic peoples who inhabited northern Europe. "Gothic" can, in fact, be seen to cover considerably more territory, culturally and artistically, in Blake's period than one might have thought.[5] Thus, at the bottom of one of Blake's earliest engravings, "Joseph of Arimathea Among the Rocks of Albion," Blake later inscribed both this title and a further identification of the figure: "This is one of the Gothic Artists who Built the Cathedrals in what we call the Dark Ages." According to Sir William Dougdale's *Monasticon Anglicanum* (1673), Joseph of Arimathea was one of the monks who came to Briton and built the clay and wattles version of the first Glastonbury Cathedral only forty-three years after the crucifixion of Christ. For Blake, the Dark Ages and the Gothic seem to have been more a state of mind than an historical period. Indeed, Blake came to see "the Gothic" as one of the great contrary forms, existing in opposition to the classical, as True Art is the contrary of False Art.

The problem of the Gothic in art is not new, and the debate over what is "medieval" and what "modern" has been going on for many years. Paul Frankl in his definitive study, *The Gothic: Literary Sources and Interpretations Through Eight Centuries,*[6] has reviewed the controversy in admirable detail; consequently I will not rehearse here the major engagements of this intellectual warfare. Rather, I will draw attention to the major themes in this lengthy exchange in order to facilitate our view of Blake's position within this larger context.

When we examine Blake's era from such a point of view, two basic trends become clear. First, as in the earlier battle between the Ancients and the Moderns in which Dryden, Temple, and Swift had participated, it is evident that a major focus of intellectual energy was on the revival of classical antiquity, expressed in architecture by the Palladian style, in painting by the neoclassical painters, and in literature by debates over classical style and modern departures from it. The discovery of Herculaneum, publications such as Stuart and Revett's *The Antiquities of Athens,* and the numerous translations of Greek and Latin classics brought ancient Greek and Roman antiquities to life for the little-traveled Blake. Oddly, England had managed to escape the immediate furor of the debate over Gothic versus classic style, so that the first publications concerning British Gothic architecture appeared only toward the middle and end of the seventeenth century. The *Monasticon Anglicanum* had only appeared from 1655–1673, and Browne Willis had published his voluminous work on the cathedrals of York from 1727–1747. Gothic, in fact, had been held in fashionable contempt by the English intelligentsia, and it was not until the fullness of the eighteenth century that it began to be considered a serious threat to accepted tastes and thus deserving of public attack.

The standardbearers of neoclassical taste maintained that that which preceded the revival of classical originals in language and art was barbaric, lacking due imitation of nature. They asserted that the decisive factor in good art was verisimilitude, as the ancients had held.[7] The material world is celebrated because it is the only reality subject to pictorial representation. The characteristic values of antiquity were erected into absolute standards of judgment. The neoclassical criteria thus became ratio, inner harmony, and intellectual clarity. The clean, geometrically defined lines of Palladian architecture, the severe styles of Adamic decoration, and, in France, the emergence of Empire style during the Napoleonic era all reflect these emphases and admirations.

By the early nineteenth century, Blake began to see the rise of the classics as a fragmentation of history. The new stress placed upon antiquity compelled a reassessment of medieval values and a division of history into two epochs, Classical Antiquity and the Middle Ages, often called pejoratively "the Dark Ages." Formerly, prior to the fifteenth-century recovery of the classics, the West had viewed the world predominantly from a perspective provided by the unchallengeable authority of the Bible. History appeared as the unfolding of God's divine plan rather than a series of "facts" to be learned from a study of the physical world or the remains of pagan antiquity. This biblical perception of time gave western man a sense of living in an Eternal Now. Events in biblical history were regarded as existing contemporaneously, not as a part of a linear progression receding infinitely into the past or extending infinitely into the future. God and Man, Christ and the Multitudes stood in the same space. The material world was considered as the active body of God, a conception reflected in the sacred buildings of the period and in the art works that adorned them. In the medieval world view, the vegetable creation was that portion of the mind of God discerned by mortal faculties. This is the Gothic reality, the conceptual foundation of Gothic art, which Blake grasped and made a central tenet of his aesthetic.

The Renaissance established a new perspective by fragmenting the Eternal Now into Greek and Roman Antiquity versus the Middle Ages. Suddenly into western awareness the concept of temporal linearism was introduced in place of Gothic simultaneity. The concept of length, hence of measurement, and consequently also of history as we know it, was the catalyst that permitted the growth of science: phenomena could now be conceived as having duration and periodicity. Verisimilitude required accurate recording of historical "facts," placed at specific points in time, and made possible the discovery of perspective as the spatial equivalent of temporal progression. The Crucifixion had now to be rendered with soldiers in Roman rather than Florentine armor; the site had to be ancient Jerusalem rather than the streets of Padua. Art was required to be in strict accord with historical fact rather than with spiritual vision. For Blake, history and allegoric fable had been created, vision and divine mystery destroyed. From a point of view consistent with Blake's statements at the beginning of *Milton*, the rise of the classics was a rebirth only in the worst sense: it was another fall from eternal vision into mortal vision. In *A Vision of the Last Judgment* (E 545) Blake says, "when they Assert that Jupiter usurped the Throne of his Father Saturn & brought on an Iron Age & Begat on Mnemosyne or Memory The Greek Muses which are not Inspiration as the Bible is. Reality was Forgot & the Vanities of Time & Space only Rememberd & calld Reality." The Fall that occurred when the revolution among the gods established the Tyrant Jupiter upon the Olympian throne and thus established the model for earthly tyrants was the same fall that occurred when Greek and Roman culture rose again in the fifteenth century to obscure the Gothic vision. "Let it. here be Noted that the Greek Fables originated in Spiritual Mystery & Real

Vision . . . Which are lost & clouded in Fable & Alegory" (E 545). Much of Blake's work in the nineteenth century is an endeavor to restore what the ancients called the Golden Age, the age before Jupiter's domination of Greek vision.

Blake suggests, as we will see in more detail later, a cycle of vision and truth, followed by a fall from vision, followed by a return to vision and truth. For him there were at least two distinct golden ages, the one that preceded the tyranny of Jupiter in the ancient world which he called the patriarchal world, and the one that preceded the rise of the classics in the modern world which he called the Gothic.

The historical perspective created by the renewed interest in the classics—we might call it the Matter of Jupiter—brought with it a loss of comprehension and understanding of the Gothic. Gothic tradition, it is true, was the subject of considerable critical study, but nearly always with the intention of enumerating its barbaric qualities. Critical and descriptive intent seemed increasingly designed to restrict, to reduce to mere fact, and to catalogue Gothic vision.

In the three hundred years that separated the rise of the classics from Blake's time, increased cultural awareness deriving from contact with the Orient, the discovery and exploration of the Americas, and the development of the spice trade made the now historically conscious European more and more aware of his geographical and cultural identity. This explosion of information together with the antiquarian's sense of history made the world of Blake's time ready for yet another restructuring of historical perspective. Publication of numerous antiquarian volumes during Blake's lifetime marked another kind of classical rebirth. Instead of the matter of Jupiter— the Greek and Roman classics—knowledge of other great civilizations of antiquity was flooding the western mind. The fragmentation now was not one of classical antiquity versus the Middle Ages, but the Persian classics, the Norse classics, the Welsh classics, the Indian classics, the British classics, the Greek and Roman classics, and the Hebrew classics—the Bible. Blake could see history as a cycle of vision: a collapse of vision followed by a rebirth of vision.

To Blake, the antiquarian and syncretic mythologizers like Bryant were extending man's horizon beyond Homer's Greece and Virgil's Rome. The civilization of ancient India came into view with Sir Charles Wilkin's translation of *The Bhag-vat-geeta or Dialogues with Kreeshna and Arjoon* in 1785, soon followed by a flurry of publications about the culture and geography of India: Thomas Maurice's *Indian Antiquities* (seven volumes, 1800), his *History of Hindostan* (1745), and *Asiatic Researches: Transactions of the Society Instituted in Bengal for Inquiring into the History and Antiquities, the Arts Sciences and Literature of Asia* (1784). Ancient England came into prominence with such works as Sharon Turner's *The History of the Anglo Saxons: Concerning the History of England from the Earliest Period to the Norman Conquest* (1799); Celtic and Druidic history with Edward Davies' *Celtic Researches on the Origin Traditions & Languages of the Ancient Britons with some Remarks on Primitive Society* (1804), and his *The Mythology and Rites of The British Druids* (1809); patriarchal religions with William Cook's *An Inquiry into Patriarchal and Druidical Religious Temples* (1755).[8]

Blake was not only a voracious reader; he apparently became a linguist as well. That his spiritual researches took him far afield we need have no doubt. We should not be surprised at finding Blake's cyclic view of history coming into play as he defines the Gothic in *A Vision of the Last Judgment* in a strictly nonlinear (i.e., nonclassical) historical perspective: "Multitudes are seen ascending from the Green fields of the blessed in which A Gothic Church is representative of true art Calld Gothic in all Ages by those who follow the Fashion" (E 549). The Gothic for Blake is an ageless representation of True Art, visionary art reified into the material world. The ancient Greeks and Romans, so dear to neoclassical writers, were seen by Blake as mere copyists of patriarchal originals that had existed long before in the great religious temples of protoantiquity—temples which Greek and Roman culture had no doubt swept away: "Rome & Greece swept Art into their maw & destroyd it   a Warlike State never can produce Art. It will Rob & Plunder & accumulate into one place, & Translate & Copy & Buy & Sell & Criticise, but not Make" (E 267). In *The Descriptive Catalogue,* Blake says of his paintings of Nelson and Pitt that they are

> compositions of a mythological cast, similar to those Apotheoses of Persian, Hindoo, and Egyptian Antiquity, which are still preserved on rude monuments, being copies from some stupendous originals now lost or perhaps buried till some happier age. The Artist having been taken in vision into the ancient republics, monarchies, and patriarchates of Asia, has seen those wonderful originals called in the Sacred Scriptures the Cherubim, which were sculptured and painted on walls of Temples, Towers, Cities,

Palaces, and erected in the highly cultivated states of Egypt, Moab, Edom, Aram, among the Rivers of Paradise. . . . (E 521–22)

The vision represented by Greek and Roman art was constricted and reduced vision, single vision. The vision of true, or Gothic, art was eternal and mythic—fourfold vision. All world views, Walter Ong says, attempt to conform to the information present in the intellectual system.[9] Where the contemporary defenders of Greek and Roman classics failed was, for Blake, in their reliance on short-sighted linear perspectives.

But Blake saw more in the Gothic than mere historical validity. He included in his understanding an increased appreciation of the perceptual states embodied in its art. Blake would have agreed with Paul Frankl:

> The answer to the question of how the contemporaries of Gothic felt about this style will only be full and resonant when we include the scholasticism and mysticism of the period, the fantastic Crusades, the poetry of Albrecht and Dante, not as beautiful background but as the Fata Morgana that hovered before men's minds and gave direction to their lives, their deeds, their writings, their sculpture and paintings, and thus also to their buildings, secular as well as sacral. If we want to express it in the style of that age we may say that the idea of the Gothic was the pillar of fire, showing the way to the pious amid the wilderness of reality of human passions.
>
> . . . everything is miracle, . . . everything is Grace, for man alone is frail. . . . Even today the great cathedrals seem to us like miracles. He who sees them as such, despite all his knowledge of their statics and rationality, sees Gothic architecture with the eyes of the Gothic.
>
> Yet, if scholars insist on getting at the root of Gothic culture . . . then the answer has to be that the root of all roots is Jesus of Nazareth. In the language of symbolism he could be identified with the pillar of fire in the desert of life, himself not 'Gothic.' . . . Gothic culture seems to be the purest and most intensive realization of the spirit contained in the New Testament.[10]

It was this spirit of Jesus that Blake urged his reader to share with him in the prefaces to *Milton* and *Jerusalem*. The Gothic represents true art, the spirit of Jesus, which is continual forgiveness of sins, and living form, which is eternal existence. The Gothic is living form, because it is not based upon linear time which stretches the living being into a space-time event in which "now" is continually being thrust into the past. In classical art, all life is a process already past or yet to be. It is the classics, those embodiments of mathematical form, "& not Goths nor Monks, that Desolate Europe with Wars" (E 267). It is the belief that the individual is finite that destroys and desolates. It is the idea that human life begins in birth and ends with death that gives death its dominion and destroys all vision of eternal existence in which the individual is the reciprocal interface between eternity and the material world. For Blake, the individual is at once eternity embodying itself into this world, and this world bodying forth into eternity.

In the "Laocoön" plate, Blake asserts that "Art is the Tree of Life. / God is Jesus. / Science is the Tree of Death. / Jesus & His Apostles & Disciples were all Artists. Their Works were destroyd by the Seven Angels of the Seven Churches in Asia. / A poet a Painter a Musician an Architect: the Man Or Woman who is not one of these is not a Christian" (E 271-72). For Blake, true art and thus the artist himself is centered upon the task of raising all men and women into a perception of eternity, into a perception of infinite life. We should take note that it was not the tree of life of which Adam and Eve ate. They ate of the tree of the knowledge of Good and Evil, which is the tree of death, or science. The fall always has had to do with the act of drawing fine distinctions, differentiating between the Good and the Evil, between heavy and light, between strong and weak, between right and wrong. Science is that aspect of life which fragments the unity of existence into a multitude of parts by cataloguing a process, by establishing a chronology, by naming plants and animals and dividing them into species and subspecies. For Blake, to become an artist is to eat of the tree of life. In no art has there ever been such an overwhelming decoration of every surface with iconographic expression as in the Gothic. Gothic art represents a concert of individual craftsmen, the encouragement of home crafts as opposed to factory-made art objects, and the community that produces a work of art for the greater glory of God as opposed to the specialized shop foreman who directs a school of apprentices.

The origins of the Gothic are, for Blake, not restricted to any one place or time. Rather, they show that the religion of Jesus is an eternal phenomenon, not subject to the approval of Pope or Caliph or Rabbi: "The antiquities of every Nation under Heaven, is no less sacred than that of the Jews. They are the same thing as Jacob Bryant, and all antiquaries have proved. How other antiquities came to be neglected and disbelieved, while those of the Jews are collected and arranged, is an enquiry, worthy of both the Antiquarian and the Divine. All had originally one language, and one religion, this was the religion of Jesus, the everlasting Gospel" (E 534).

The Gothic revival is a crucial element in the creation of Blake's poetic and pictorial aesthetic. Gothic is the spirit of vision that embraces mystery rather than allegory; perception of the infinite in everything rather than the mere surfaces of individual things; infinite imagination rather than finite reason; living form, always changing and growing, rather than mathematic form, forever static and inflexible. Blake saw his task as an attempt to reestablish the golden age, to rebuild Jerusalem in England's green and pleasant land, to guard the divine vision in time of trouble, to teach the principles of perception of the infinite to honest men who will not deny their genius or their conscience for the sake of present ease or gratification. Gothic culture was for Blake an emblem of lost vision, as fallen London and Jerusalem are emblems of the ruined city of art where the spectre of reason has gained dominion.

NOTES

1. Jean Hagstrum, "Christ's Body," *William Blake: Essays in Honour of Sir Geoffrey Keynes,* ed. Morton Paley and Michael Phillips (Oxford: Clarendon Press, 1973), p. 129.

2. Geoffrey Keynes, "The Engraver's Apprentice," *Blake Studies,* 2nd ed. (Oxford: Clarendon Press, 1971), pp. 14–30; Benjamin Heath Malkin, *A Father's Memoirs of his Child* (London, 1806), p. xxi.

3. Anne Kostelanetz Mellor, *Blake's Human Form Divine* (Berkeley: Univ. of Calif. Press, 1974), p. 133.

4. Kenneth Clark, *Blake and Visionary Art* (Glasgow: Univ. of Glasgow Press, 1973), p. 11.

5. Some suggest that the term "Gothic" was first used by Raphael, in a report addressed to Leo X dealing with works projected in Rome, and thereafter popularized by Vasari. See Kenneth Clark, *The Gothic Revival* (New York: Humanities Press, 1970), p. 13.

6. Princeton: Princeton Univ. Press, 1960.

7. Frankl, p. 241.

8. See Stuart Curran, "The Key to All Mythologies," *Shelley's Annus*

Mirabilis (San Marino, Calif.: Huntington Library, 1975), pp. 33–94 for a discussion of these publications.

    9.   Walter J. Ong, *The Presence of the Word: Some Prolegomena for Cultural and Religious History* (New York: Simon and Schuster, 1967), pp. 63ff.

    10.   Frankl, p. 234.

The "Gothicized Imagination" of "Michelangelo Blake"

Edward J. Rose

T H E R E are several milieux (historical and intellectual) for the study of Blake's art, and this is especially the case when we consider its relation to the Gothic and to Michelangelo. Many critics and scholars of Blake's work have called attention to his conscious awareness of and commitment to the Gothic, although it has not been easy to define that term as Blake understood it.[1] The well-known facts are often repeated. Mention is made of his apprenticeship and of the many hours he spent copying monuments in Westminster Abbey. We are often told that he and his master did the engravings for Richard Gough's *Sepulchral Monuments in Great Britain.* Several critics call attention to various opportunities he had, or may have had, to see medieval collections of illuminated books, urns, vases, and other such items. We all know about these experiences, but we have not really tried to explain why he is so irresistibly drawn to the Gothic and how he is able so fully to fuse his admiration for the Gothic with his unrestrained praise of Raphael and Michelangelo. All those years spent copying medieval monuments could have made even an eager apprentice hostile to the Gothic. What is it in Gothic art that so appeals to Blake, and how important to his literary and pictorial imagination is it? I hope to suggest at least some partial answers to these questions.

Blake was said by one of his earliest commentators to have a "Gothicised imagination."[2] Such a phrase does not explain, however, how Blake's imagination could also have been as deeply influenced by the art of Michelangelo as it was; for, unlike Blake, neither Michelangelo nor Raphael was an admirer of the Gothic, or so-called German, style. While it is difficult to say with absolute certainty that

155

Michelangelo was as hostile to the Gothic style as was Raphael, we
have some grounds for making assumptions about the younger artist's opinions. Raphael's displeasure arises in part from his an-
tagonism to the Goths and Vandals. He attributes what he calls the
Nordic or Germanic manner in architecture to the descendants of
the peoples who sacked Rome, a common opinion in the literature
on the Gothic. He dislikes and disapproves of the pointed arch because it has neither the load capacity nor what he believes is the
grace of the rounded Romanesque arch. He is unhappy with Gothic
ornamentation, particularly the grotesque figures used inside and
outside to support beams or decorate portals. Although the author-
ship of the letter from which Raphael's opinions come is now ques-
tioned, the fact remains that from the beginnings of the high Renaissance to the eighteenth century, the Gothic style is generally
viewed harshly and unfavorably. Vasari, who is frankly hostile to the
Gothic and who also associated the Gothic style with the Goths, is
representative of a well-established sixteenth-century attitude. In
fact, his opinions, like those of Francisco da Hollanda, most probably represent those of Michelangelo. This hostility to the Gothic is of
such long standing that Sprague Allen is prompted to remark that in
the sixth decade of the eighteenth century, the decade, of course, in
which Blake was born, "satire upon Gothicism and *chinoiserie* was
fiercest."[3]

Blake does not use the word "Gothic" often. As the *Concordance*
demonstrates, there are less than a dozen instances, almost all of
which occur in works that date after 1800: the Joseph of Arimathea
engraving, the Annotations to Reynolds' *Discourses,* the *Descriptive
Catalogue, A Vision of the Last Judgment,* and *On Homer's Poetry.* When
Reynolds writes that Albert Durer "would, probably, have been one
of the first painters of his age ... had he been initiated into those
great principles of the art, which were so well understood and prac-
tised by his contemporaries in Italy," Blake replies, "What does this
mean *'Would have been'* one of the *first Painters of his Age!* Albert Durer
Is! Not would have been! Besides. let them look at Gothic Figures &
Gothic Buildings. & not talk of Dark Ages or of Any Age! Ages are
All Equal. But Genius is Always Above The Age" (E 638). This
opinion is in keeping with the Joseph of Arimathea engraving. Beneath the picture of Joseph, based on a figure from Michelangelo's
"Martyrdom of St. Peter," Blake inscribed "This is One of the Gothic
Artists who Built the Cathedrals in what we call the Dark Ages

Wandering about in sheep skins & goat skins. of whom the World was not worthy such were the Christians in all Ages" (E 660). An intelligent historian, Blake does not approve of the term "Dark Ages" and rejects vigorously that any age is "dark." As elsewhere in his work, he denies that great artists can be ranked or that any age is greater or more capable than any other of producing great artists. Blake does not believe that the Gothic style itself is confined to a particular historical period and as a result he places himself, perhaps unconsciously, in the vanguard of the Gothic revival. Furthermore, his defense and continued admiration of Dürer is the vital link between the Gothic and Michelangelo. To Blake the Gothic revealed spiritual energy.[4]

Blake would not have approved of the Abbé de Cordemoy's anti-Gothic opinions and still less of the Abbé's disappointment in Michelangelo who, the Abbé thought, did not make use of that which was good in the Gothic Style when he completed St. Peter's.[5] Needless to say, Michelangelo would not have approved of either the Abbé or his right even to have opinions on St. Peter's. As for Michelangelo's attitude toward the Gothic, we have his caustic remarks on Antonio da Sangallo's model for St. Peter's. While Michelangelo says nothing directly about the Gothic in his letter on Sangallo's model, Vasari's version of his master's ideas makes it clear that Michelangelo did not like the German manner. "Sangallo built it closed to all light and had piled so many orders of columns, one atop the other, and with so many protruding members, spires, and details, that it resembled a Gothic work much more than a good, classic style, or the pleasing and beautiful modern manner."[6] It is difficult to understand how Vasari could have associated the Gothic style with a building "closed to all light," but then his knowledge of Gothic architecture was limited if not provincial. Besides, Italian Gothic differed from French or English. One need only compare Milan to Amiens or King's College Chapel to see the difference.

Blake's Gothic artist is unmistakably Michelangelesque, and the engraving is another effort on Blake's part to dehistorize art and to demonstrate that "Ages are All Equal." Blake's admiration for Michelangelo, Raphael, and other painters of the high Renaissance is not curbed, therefore, by the accident of *their* displeasure with the Gothic. The differing ideals of the Gothic and the high Renaissance are the contrary influences through and by which Blake's art progresses, but they are not opposites. He does not try to marry them and he does not try to view them antithetically. For great artists both the Gothic and the Grecian are simply true. Despite his aggressive and adversary stance, Blake is essentially a catholic and eclectic man. Although he revives the illuminated book, his method and his finished product are very different from that which inspired them. Blake is not a doctrinaire student of the Gothic, and he rightly does not draw a sharp distinction between the Gothic and the early Renaissance.

Blake instinctively chooses adversary positions and often defines what he likes in terms of what he does not like. The fact that the term "Gothic" was employed by Vasari, by countless other Italian artists and critics, by many German and French scholars, and by Christopher Wren and a steady stream of British artists and critics to describe what they felt was an unfortunate departure from classical lines and forms was enough to activate Blake's typical adversary response. It is the kind of response he makes to Reynolds or to any admirer of Rubens and Rembrandt. Thus, Blake *reverses* the often-repeated equation that Greek and Roman forms equal "good art," Gothic forms equal "bad art." In fact, in *A Vision of the Last Judgment,* Blake says the "Gothic Church is representative of true Art" (E 549). In England from the time of Wren to the end of the eighteenth century "Gothic" is a synonym for "tasteless," "bizarre," "rude," "grotesque," and "romantic." (The Italians had regarded it as barbaric.) Burke had declared that "smoothness" was essential to beauty; and Gothic, of course, was not smooth. But we know what Blake thought of Burke, whom (in the annotations to the *Discourses*) he condemns with Reynolds: we can easily guess what he would have thought about Burke's opinions on the Gothic. True Art, Blake observes, is "calld Gothic in All Ages. . . ."[7] Of course, Blake was not alone in his defense of the Gothic. Flaxman, Stothard, and the Society of Antiquarians were also deeply interested in Gothic art.

Blunt remarks, "To Reynolds' Aristotelian view of nature, Blake opposes a purely neo-Platonic doctrine."[8] How *pure* Blake's Neoplatonic doctrine is can be argued indefinitely, but certainly it is Neoplatonic rather than Aristotelian. Because of this pictorial Neoplatonism, which is far more important to the study of his work than any kind of literary or philosophical Neoplatonism, it is possible to see why Blake is able to draw on both Michelangelo and the Gothic without contradiction. After all, his goal is to paint the ideal form, that is, the mental, which alone is real. His case against Rubens and the Venetians gathers some of its force from these antinaturalistic attitudes. Nevertheless, there is a historical irony in all this because it is the high Renaissance that celebrates the natural and lifelike. Michelangelo himself has problems accommodating his ideal conceptions to natural forms. Furthermore, Blake's commitment (like Michelangelo's) to the formal cause, to the portrayal of the idea of man—to spiritual man rather than to vegetative or natural man— leads him to carry his Neoplatonic propensities over to the inner space of the Gothic church. He relates inner space to inner experience, to what Melville calls the "inside narrative." *Jerusalem* is his crowning achievement in this regard and the spectator-pilgrim enters with Los through a Gothic arch into the temple of the Lord, the nave of the human form which Blake conceives of after the manner of a Gothic structure. Both in architectural and individual forms, therefore, the true human experience takes place in inner space. The form, as Michelangelo insisted, was in the stone already; the artist simply exposed it. Even if the artist were to leave the sculpture unfinished it did not matter. He had been inside with his insight. The reader-spectator is told in *Jerusalem* to turn his eyes inward and in *A Vision of the Last Judgment* to enter images.[9]

Arthur Kingsley Porter, commenting on the words of the Abbot of St.-Denis, asks "In all the long centuries that have rolled by since the days of Suger, who has stood beneath the soaring vaults of a Gothic cathedral, without, however unconsciously, repeating to himself" the words the Abbot had written in the middle of the twelfth century: "... dwelling, as it were, in some strange region of the universe which neither exists entirely in the slime of the earth nor entirely in the purity of Heaven; and that, by the grace of God, I can be transported from this inferior to that higher world in an analogical manner." "It is this peculiar quality, which for lack of a better term," Kingsley Porter concludes, "we may call emotional power, that separates the Gothic from all other architectures and raises it to the supreme height."[10] There can be no doubt that it is this "emotional power" that impressed Blake, whose own work is marked by a similar spiritual energy. The Pre-Raphaelites felt the Gothicized force of Blake's work.

Blake calls this analogical mode of transportation of which Suger speaks mental travel. Los in *Jerusalem,* when he describes the nature of the Divine Analogy which redeems time, space, and history from the night thoughts of Albion, transports the reader-spectator analogically from an inferior to a higher world. Blake urges this spiritual transport upon us again when he writes in *A Vision of the Last Judgment,*

> If the Spectator could Enter into these Images in his Imagination approaching them on the Fiery Chariot of his Contemplative Thought if he could Enter into Noahs Rainbow or into his bosom or could make a Friend & Companion of one of these Images of wonder which always intreats him to leave mortal things as he must know then would he arise from his Grave then would he meet the Lord in the Air & then he would be happy. (E 550)

Architecture is sometimes described not only as formed stone or formed space, but also as formed light. Some of the most impressive characteristics of Gothic architecture can be related to the way in which light is controlled by the pinnacles, buttresses, and vertical windows, all suited to the climate of northern Europe where the sun does not move as high in the southern sky as in, for example, Italy. The shadows cast by Gothic shapes when struck by the slanting light produced effects which encouraged the long-standing belief that Gothic architecture evolved from the forest life of the Gothic tribes.[11] The ribbing in the nave, exemplified very early in England by churches such as Durham Cathedral, reinforced the parallel of the stone shapes with the living trees. (But the stone trees pointed to a higher world.) There are indications that Blake may well have accepted this analogy since it went well with his conception of the Druids. The forest theory of Gothic architecture, in fact, did not die easily.[12] In Blake's own time it was still asserted seriously as a possible source of inspiration, although the Goths and Vandals had already been replaced by the Saxons, then the Saracens, and finally the Normans as the builders of Gothic churches. At the end of *Jerusalem,* all the nations responsible for the Gothic are amalgamated in Los's furnaces with the Hebrew, a remarkable way of forming light and space if only by analogy.[13]

John Evelyn attributes the Gothic style to both the Arabs and the Goths, and Wren, later, simply calls the Gothic "Saracen"— hence the association of Gothic with Arabesque. This controversy works its way into Blake's view of the Goths and encourages once again his adversarylike reaction to established thinking: it is "The Classics, it is the Classics! & not Goths nor Monks, that Desolate Europe with Wars."[14] In the eighteenth century, the Gothic is be-

lieved to be unsuitable as a model to any who would return to nature. Blake found the rightness of his Gothicized opinions justified
by the marriage of the neoclassicist and the naturalist, a marriage in
some ways less strange than that of the Neoplatonist and naturalist
which we often see in the work of Michelangelo. Once united with
the Empiricist, the neoclassicist and naturalist formed another demonic trinity against which Blake could direct his criticism of what
he saw as a perversion of true art or even true classicism:

> Painting and Sculpture as it exists in the remains of Antiquity and
> in the works of more modern genius, is Inspiration, and cannot
> be surpassed; it is perfect and eternal. Milton, Shakspeare,
> Michael Angelo, Rafael, the finest specimens of Ancient
> Sculpture and Painting, and Architecture, Gothic, Grecian, Hin-
> doo and Egyptian, are the extent of the human mind....To sup-
> pose that Art can go beyond the finest specimens of Art that are
> now in the world, is not knowing what Art is.... [15]

Once again we see Blake's eclecticism and his refusal to rank the best
or place one age above another. The prejudice of the age was against
the Gothic and had been so for several centuries, but the tide had
been slowly turning throughout the eighteenth century. Spokesmen
for the Gothic became more influential despite neoclassical and
pro-Roman counterattacks. The vigorous defense of the Gothicists,
among whom Blake must be numbered, gave impetus to the Gothic
revival, a revival that culminated in the theories of Pugin in the
nineteenth century and established the style used in the rebuilding
of the Houses of Parliament.

The Gothic style is linear and emblematic and would have appealed to Blake on grounds of design alone, whether or not he
believed in any of the Saxon theories of origin. But perhaps what
also attracted him was the hospitality shown by the Gothic (as Blake
understood it) to the grotesque. Sir Thomas Browne's well-known
statement, "There are no Grotesques in nature," represents a view
that flourished in the Age of Reason when the word "grotesque" is
often used in the pejorative sense. Although it originally meant contrary to the natural order, it soon came to mean ridiculous or
monstrous or even unnatural. The "grotesque" was no longer simply
out of the ordinary, strange, exotic, unusual, fanciful, or extravagant. Even Ruskin and Santayana (the latter describes the grotesque
as "the suggestively monstrous") do not really express what in the

"grotesque" so appealed to Blake. Plates 25, 35, 50, 62, 78 of *Jerusalem,* for example, may be described as grotesque but not only in the modern adjectival sense of monstrous or horrifying but simply because they interrupt or go contrary to the natural order. But it is Blake's object always to go against the natural order, to follow instead the spiritual order.[16] There are many such examples in Blake's work, and we should remember his characteristic comment on his pencil drawing of nine heads, some of which are candidates for rain spouts: "All Genius varies. Thus Devils are various   Angels are all alike."[17] In the Gothic church, grotesque visions decorate portals, friezes, the bases and tops of pillars, railings, and tracery. In the eighteenth and nineteenth centuries, they take their place in the Gothic revival. Those that in the Middle Ages did not find their way into stone often decorated the illuminated page. Like Blake, Michelangelo was fond of the grotesque, and many of his works bear this out. Clements writes, "Despite widespread opinion, Michelangelo did not spurn the grotesque and probably concurred with Lomazzo's conclusion that following one's "natural reason" will assure the successful composition of grotesques, which must be orderly rather than disordered."[18] The man who knew what the reasoning quarter of man's mind could do would know what Lomazzo meant.

The decorated page of the illuminated manuscript which so influenced Blake in its organic integration of word and picture, letter and figure, was in his hands ideally suited to the grotesque. Following the illuminated manuscripts *and* Albrecht Dürer, Blake held fast to the watercolor techniques employed by the medieval artists. Although he does not seem devoted to the gouache technique, a technique that Vasari, for instance, does not distinguish from tempera, he did employ it in both watercolors and his own tempera paintings. When we look at a long series of designs such as the watercolors for the *Night Thoughts* we can appreciate how often grotesque and Gothic forms reappear, and when we leap forward to *Jerusalem* and make comparisons we see how Gothicized Blake's imagination remained. It is still pronounced in the gestures and stylized poses of the Job and Dante designs.

But Blake's devotion to the Gothic is always tempered by his boundless admiration for Michelangelo. Many of the prejudices of the Tuscan master become the axioms of the English prophet, and while some of these seem suited to a Gothicized imagination, others do not. Blake, like Michelangelo, does not believe that true vision can be equated with what Michelangelo calls "exterior vision." His concepts of "intellect" and "intellectual war" or "mental" and "mental war" have much in common with what is signified by the Italian word *intelletto,* which Michelangelo employs frequently. Michelangelo's phrase "One paints with the mind" or even Leonardo's well-known remark "painting is a mental thing" could very well have been written by Blake.[19] These views lessen the distinction which Blunt so aptly draws when he writes,

> Whereas for the writers of the Early and High Renaissance nature was the source from which all beauty was ultimately derived, however much it might be transformed by the artist's imagination, for [the] Mannerists beauty was something which was directly infused into the mind of man from the mind of God, and existed there independent of any sense-impressions. The idea in the artist's mind was the source of all the beauty in the works which he created, and his ability to give a picture of the outside world was of no importance, except insofar as it helped him to give visible expression to his idea.[20]

As Clements observes, "Michelangelo's attitude is . . . not only Neo-Platonic and neo-classic, but also Counter Reformational. In him setting becomes reduced to symbol."[21] Minimizing the role of the imitation of Nature in Michelangelo's work (a not altogether difficult feat) and overlooking the classic or neoclassic bias always present in his painting and sculpture, Blake adopted as his own Michelangelo's preference for the nude, his antipathy to both oil and portraiture, and his overwhelming emphasis upon drawing. Blake's own remarks about nakedness in the comments he makes on his own Ancient Britons painting, observations that are heightened by a Michelangelesque and scathing attack upon Rubens' Medici Cycle, echo Michelangelo, for whom all exterior trappings, including clothing, were a limitation upon the artist who sought to portray human beauty and sublimity. Blake most certainly must have expected that his own commitment would suffer from the same kind of censure that was directed at Michelangelo. The naked human form was, after all, neither to Gothic tastes nor in keeping with the spirit of the Counter-Reformation. And it certainly was not preferred by the eighteen century. But if Blake clung to Michelangelo's preference for the nude human form, he insisted even more vigor-

ously on his master's dissatisfaction with oil as a medium and his
aversion to portraiture. In the age of Gainsborough and Reynolds,
which had continued where the age of Rubens and Van Dyck
had left off, Neoplatonic predilections for the ideal form had no
place. As for Blake's frequent denunciations of oil, they are little
more than extensions of Michelangelo's own prejudice. Vasari
records, for example, that Michelangelo once said that "Oil painting
is an art for ladies, for lazy and slack persons.... "[22] Even
Michelangelo's sarcasm and aggressiveness are echoed by Blake.
Bernini, for example, felt all of Michelangelo's comments on other
artists could be reduced to four brief statements: "This is by a cunning knave. This is by a knave. This won't bother anybody. This is by
a good man."[23] Blake's highly individualistic and egocentric characteristics, which he shares with Michelangelo, are not in the spirit of
the Middle Ages. A self-proclaimed "Mental Prince" raging like Rintrah against "blockheads" is certainly Michelangelesque, but it is not
Gothic. Michelangelo's pride and individualism do not belong to the
Middle Ages, and neither do Blake's. They share Michelangelo's
legendary *terribilità,* not because of the ferocity of their criticism
when roused but because of the awe and fear which they and their
art inspire in others.[24]

One of Michelangelo's commentators, De Tolnay, thinks that
the Sistine frescos (with more than 340 human figures on the 10,000
square feet of ceiling alone) are Gothic:

> By the dynamism of the architectonic form (instead of the ra-
> tional tectonism), it has a relationship with the Gothic architec-
> tural forms. It is Gothic in the idea of the series of isolated figures
> (Prophets and Sibyls), Gothic in the differing scale of proportions
> of the figures in the same work, and Gothic in the relationship
> between the figures and the architecture—a relationship in which
> the architecture does not form the surroundings of the figures
> but is the frame which determines their places.[25]

Some of this commentary could be applied to the pages of Blake's
illuminated poems and the designs he made for Milton, the Bible,
and Dante. The determining frame, the series of isolated figures,
and the differing scale of proportions of the figures in the same
work describe many of Blake's works. The *Night Thoughts* designs
more than any other series demonstrate these characteristics. Fur-

thermore, Michelangelo's *titanismo* or *gigantismo* is also present in the *Night Thoughts*.[26] They influence Blake's conception of the giant form and the place of the giants and titans in his redactions of ancient myth. Not only do both Michelangelo and Blake idealize the art of antiquity, they never conceive of the human form as simply human. It is almost always superhuman.

Michelangelo's and Blake's emphasis upon drawing, in particular the hard, wiry line, kept them close to the linear characteristics of the Gothic style and the tempera tradition. Vasari reports that Michelangelo (like Blake after him) felt that "Poor artists cloak their poor technique with a variety of tints and shades of color." "Draw, Antonio," he wrote to Antonio Mini, "draw, Antonio, draw—don't waste time!"[27] It was not color we should look at, but "figures which show spirit and movement." To Blake Michelangelo is a great watercolorist, an idea that one of Michelangelo's biographers lends credence to when he writes of the Sistine Chapel:

> In its entire color scheme the ceiling gives the impression of an immense water-color painting. If the effect is memorable, it is because of the vivid contrasts. Some of the highlighted drapery seems like gold-embroidered brocade, even though there is no gold. . . . Gold is only simulated with other pigments. When Julius II remarked on the absence of real gold, Michelangelo lightly replied: "The prophets I have painted were poor men; they had no gold."[28]

We should recall Blake's enthusiastic response when he learned of Michelangelo's selfless labors on St. Peter's, which he did not perform for money but for love of God.

There is not much of a leap from the watercolor page to the watercolor wall and Blake's suggestion of portable frescos, which might have been influenced by Raphael's Cartoons for the Vatican tapestries, is his attempt to hit upon a middle ground.[29] It is characteristic of Blake to want to recreate the illuminated building as he had succeeded in recreating the illuminated book. And in all these attempts drawing and design take precedence (as they did with Michelangelo). Blake would not have understood his contemporary Goya's impatience with Michelangelo, "Always line—line! But where do we find these lines in nature?" Of course, we know what Blake would have said. He would have tapped his head and said, Not out there, in here. His comment on Delacroix's observation, "I open my window and look at the landscape. The idea of a line never suggests itself to me,"[30] might well have been harsher.

At the end of the eighteenth century and the beginning of the nineteenth, Blake was not really committed to the direction of the art of the next hundred years any more than he was at peace with the art of the hundred years that preceded his time. His attitudes, which coincide in countless ways with Michelangelo's revolutionary influence on the visual arts, are in the context of the eighteenth century often reactionary. When Rodin said of Michelangelo's sculpture that it was "the end-result of all Gothic thought,"[31] he could well have been describing Blake's work.

NOTES

1. The term has spawned in a small way a literature of its own. See especially Georg Germann, *Gothic Revival in Europe and Britain: Sources, Influences and Ideas,* trans. Gerald Onn (London: Lund Humphries, [1972]). See also Charles L. Eastlake, *A History of the Gothic Revival* (London: Longmans, Green, 1872); Arthur O. Lovejoy, "The First Gothic Revival and the Return to Nature," *Essays in the History of Ideas* (Baltimore: Johns Hopkins Press, 1948), pp. 136–65; and Kenneth Clark, *The Gothic Revival* (London: Constable, 1928).

2. "Gothicized Imagination" was coined by Benjamin Heath Malkin in *A Father's Memoirs of His Child* (London, 1806), pp. xvii–xli. The relevant material on Blake is reproduced by G. E. Bentley, Jr., *Blake Records* (Oxford: Clarendon Press, 1969), pp.221–31. "Michelangelo Blake" was coined by Charles Heathcote Tatham in a letter to John Linnell on behalf of himself and his son Frederick (August 2, 1824), "Can you engage Michael Angelo *Blake* to meet us . . . " (Bentley, *Blake Records,* p. 288). In the title to this essay I have regularized the spelling and omitted Tatham's emphasis on Blake.

3. B. Sprague Allen, *Tides in English Taste* (Cambridge, Mass.: Harvard Univ. Press, 1937), II, 152. For those critics who believe that "Gothic" was no longer an "abusive" term in the eighteenth century or that the "Gothicists" were the *majority* party in this continuing controversy, Allen's book and Paul Frankl's *The Gothic* (Princeton: Princeton Univ. Press, 1960) should dissuade them. For an ample discussion of the pseudo-Raphael letter on the Gothic and its text, see Frankl, *The Gothic,* pp. 271–80.

4. When Blake defines Gothic as the "living form," we must be re-

minded of his equation of the imagination with human existence itself and the Pauline distinctions he makes between the natural and spiritual bodies. The "living form" is the form of the spiritual body. The vegetable world or the natural body are of value only in that they shadow forth some facet of the eternal world or the spiritual body, that is, the vegetable world and natural body are real and meaningful only in that they reveal themselves to be members of the Divine Body and thus of the nature of God.

5. See Germann, *Gothic Revival,* p. 19. The Abbé's opinions date from the early eighteenth century.

6. See Robert J. Clements, *Michelangelo: A Self-Portrait* (New York: New York Univ. Press, 1968), p. 42.

7. *A Vision of the Last Judgment* (E 549). The passage in full reads "Multitudes are seen ascending from the Green fields of the blessed in which a Gothic Church is representative of true Art Calld Gothic in All Ages by those who follow the Fashion as that is calld which is without Shape or Fashion." The implication here appears to be that the Gothic is always in fashion because it is beyond any kind of temporary, even temporal, fashion or historically defined shape.

8. Anthony Blunt, "Blake's Pictorial Imagination," *Journal of the Warburg and Courtauld Institutes,* 6 (1943), 208.

9. E 146, 550. The images, of course, entreat "him to leave mortal things" and free him to meet the Lord. Just as "We understand a piece of wood or stone only when we see God in it" (according to John Scotus Erigena), so we only understand an image when we see God in it. The "Fiery Chariot of Contemplative Thought" is an image of wonder describing Blake's version of Michelangelo's *intelletto* (see below).

10. *Mediaeval Architecture* (New Haven: Yale Univ. Press, 1915), II, 252. See also Frankl, *The Gothic,* pp. 19–20.

11. "Shade is always Cold & never as in Rubens & the Colourists Hot & Yellowy Brown" (E 651).

12. This very old theory (it is found in the letter attributed to Raphael) is repeated many times in the eighteenth and nineteenth centuries. James Hall (1761–1832), a contemporary of Blake, in his *Essay on the Origin, History, and Principles of Gothic Architecture* (1797; 2nd ed., 1813), suggests the pliable willow withe. Given Blake's propensity for the arched willow in his designs, there is much to speculate upon in a Hall-Blake connection. Several later German critics repeat this theory, Friedrich Schlegel for one, but nothing is ever said that would connect the wicker work with the presence in Blake's work of the Nordic wicker cage which he includes effectively as a demonic parody of Los's furnace. See my essay, "Blake's Fourfold Art," *Philological Quarterly,* 49 (July, 1970), 400–23. Kenneth Clark in *The Gothic Revival,* pp. 36–37, quotes Bishop Warburton who wrote that the Goths "*struck out a new species of architecture,* unknown to

Greece or Rome, upon original principles, and *ideas much nobler* than what had given birth even to classical magnificence. For this northern people having been accustomed to worship the Deity in groves, when their religion required covered edifices, they ingeniously projected to make them resemble groves as nearly as the distance of architecture would permit."

13.   Los's furnace is, of course, a kind of kiln, and although we see him primarily as a smith he sometimes reminds us of the potter. At any rate, he does form light in an enclosed space—his furnace—into which he casts all that is to be regenerated. Los's furnace is clearly a crucible, a creative symbol which Blake opposes to the destructive wicker cage. Amalgamating the Briton, Saxon, Roman, and Norman into one nation and, we can assume by extension, one architecture, is the labor of Los.

14.   *On Homer's Poetry* (E 267). Blake's reference to Goths and Monks on this plate indicates that he associates them with an art that is contrary to the art of Greece and Rome. This comment on Homer is another version of "Empire Against Art."

15.   *A Descriptive Catalogue* (E 535). The correspondences in Blake's mind are clear: Milton is to Michelangelo as Raphael is to Shakespeare as Rubens is to Locke. Milton is Blake's literary master, Michelangelo his pictorial master. Their demonic opposites are Locke and Rubens. See my essay, "'A Most Outrageous Demon': Blake's Case Against Rubens," *Bucknell Review,* 17 (1969), 35–54; rpt. in *The Visionary Hand,* ed. Robert N. Essick (Los Angeles: Hennessey & Ingalls, 1973), pp. 311–36.

16.   It is possible to find grotesques of all sorts in Blake's work. Figures and beasts in the *Night Thoughts* designs and much of the border and interlinear decorations in any of the illuminated books could qualify, but it is designs like plates 35 and 50 of *Jerusalem* that illustrate reversal of the natural order. In both designs we see man giving birth.

17.   Inscription on a "Pencil Drawing of Nine Grotesque Heads" (E 667). The remark is typical of Blake's attitude toward "similars" or "monotony," but the drawing leads us to take a fresh look at the grotesque in his visionary portraits and phrenological heads.

18.   *Michelangelo's Theory of Art* (New York: New York Univ. Press, 1961), p. 217. Clements also observes, "Although he would be ill at ease to admit the affinity, his use of grotesque was merely the Gothic use . . . " (p. 216).

19.   *Michelangelo's Theory of Art,* pp. 36, 38. Blake and Michelangelo have two other important affinities in common. Both are very good illustrators of and have deep insight into the Old Testament. Their consciousness is essentially Hebraic rather than Greek despite their affinity for antiquity and their desire to restore the art of the ancients.

20.   Anthony Blunt, *Artistic Theory in Italy 1450–1600* (Oxford: Clarendon Press, 1940, rpt., 1968), pp. 140—41.

21. *Michelangelo's Theory of Art,* p. 212.

22. Quoted in *Michelangelo: A Self-Portrait,* p. 41.

23. Ibid., p. 36.

24. The fiery and tempestuous qualities to be found in Blake's work, even as late as the Job illustrations, are best defined in his terms as the spirit of Orc regenerated.

25. Quoted in *Michelangelo's Theory of Art,* p. 218.

26. Joshua Reynolds complains in *The Idler* of Michelangelo's excesses. Given Blake's comments on the *Discourses,* it takes little imagination to guess what his reaction would have been to Reynolds' criticism of Michelangelo's execution of his nudes. Blake's designs have often been described as overwhelming Young's verse.

27. Quoted in *Michelangelo: A Self-Portrait,* p. 34.

28. Georg Brandes, *Michelangelo,* trans. Heinz Norden (New York: Frederick Ungar [1963]), p. 274.

29. In *A Descriptive Catalogue* (E 540), Blake writes in a Michelangelesque tone, voicing in part one of Michelangelo's own prejudices: "The merit of a Picture is the same as the merit of a Drawing. The dawber dawbs his Drawings; he who draws his Drawings draws his Pictures. There is no difference between Rafael's Cartoons and his Frescos, or Pictures, except that the Frescos, or Pictures, are more finished."

Ozias Humphrey compares Blake's Last Judgment to Michelangelo's, "The Size of this drawing is but small not exceeding twenty Inches by fifteen or Sixteen (*I guess*) but then the grandeur of its conception, the Importance of its subject, and the sublimely multitudinous masses, & groups which it exhibits . . . In brief, It is one of the most interesting performances I ever saw; & is, in many respects superior to the last Judgment of Michael Angelo and to give due credit & effect to it, woud [*sic*] require a Tablet, not less than the Floor of Westminster Hall" (quoted in Bentley, *Blake Records,* p. 189). Such an opinion would have pleased Blake who was ready to decorate the Hall with portable frescos executed in "Watercolours, (that is in Fresco)."

30. Quoted in *Michelangelo's Theory of Art,* p. 252.

31. "l'aboutissant de toute la pensée gothique," quoted in *Michelangelo's Theory of Art,* p. 218.

"Wonderful Originals"
—Blake and Ancient Sculpture

Morton D. Paley

1

> The two Pictures of Nelson and Pitt are compositions of a
> mythological cast, similar to those Apotheoses of Persian, Hin-
> doo, and Egyptian Antiquity, which are still preserved on rude
> monuments, being copies from some stupendous originals now
> lost or perhaps buried till some happier age. The Artist having
> been taken in vision into the ancient republics, monarchies, and
> patriarchates of Asia, has seen those wonderful originals called in
> the Sacred Scriptures the Cherubim, which were sculptured and
> painted on walls of Temples, Towers, Cities, Palaces, and erected
> in the highly cultivated states of Egypt, Moab, Edom, Aram,
> among the Rivers of Paradise, being originals from which the
> Greeks and Hetrurians copied Hercules, Farnese, Venus of
> Medicis, Apollo Belvidere, and all the grand works of ancient art.
> They were executed in a very superior style to those justly ad-
> mired copies, being with their accompaniments terrific and
> grand in the highest degree. The Artist has endeavoured to emu-
> late the grandeur of those seen in his vision, and to apply it to
> modern Heroes, on a smaller scale. (E 521-22)

This statement in William Blake's *Descriptive Catalogue* reveals an
important and characteristic aspect of his mature theory of art. Earlier in his career he had, with virtually all of his contemporaries,
studied, copied, and adapted the sculptural forms so highly valued
in the age of neoclassicism. Now, in 1809, he expresses the view that
the Greek and Roman statues are but imperfect copies of more
ancient Eastern works. The visionary artist can, however, go back to
these "wonderful originals" themselves in order to produce his own

170

renditions of their archetypal forms, whether in marble, in paint, or copper, or in words. A further account is given in *Jerusalem:*

> All things acted on Earth are seen in the bright Sculptures of
> Los's Halls & every Age renews its powers from these Works
> With every pathetic story possible to happen from Hate or Way-
> ward Love & every sorrow & distress is carved here Every Affinity
> of Parents Marriages & Friendships are here In all their various
> combinations wrought with wondrous Art All that can happen to
> Man in his pilgrimage of seventy years Such is the Divine Written
> Law of Horeb & Sinai: And such the Holy Gospel of Mount
> Olivet & Calvary: (E 159)

The same sculptural forms which Blake envisages as having existed historically as the cherubim exist in an eternal present in the halls of Los, the Imagination, and all true artists render their works from these archetypes. This is an extraordinary weight of meaning for a nonsculptor to place upon sculpture, yet the meaning of sculpture to Blake and the extent and sources of his knowledge about it have not been discussed in detail up to now.[1]

The conceptual importance of ancient sculpture to Blake may easily be seen both in his writings and in his designs. In describing his Canterbury Pilgrims, Blake tells us that "every one is an Antique Statue." In painting his "Ancient Britons," he has been advised to take the Apollo Belvedere, Hercules Farnese, and Dancing Faun as his models, but "He knows that what he does is not inferior to the grandest Antiques."[2] As art is archetypal, it cannot be progressive. Each of the bright sculptures of Los's halls represents a permanent state to be captured by the artist according to the idiom of his particular period. "Lots Wife being Changed into Pillar of Salt alludes to the Mortal Body being renderd a Permanent Statue but not Changed or Transformed into Another Identity. . . ."[3] And so Blake renders her in his memorable title page to Night Five of Young's *Night Thoughts* (British Museum). In *Jerusalem* pl. 81, Cambel is portrayed as a Medici Venus, or *Venus Pudica,* in order to emphasize her false pretension to chastity. Albion in *Jerusalem* pl. 25, as well as the similar central figure in "The Blasphemer" (Tate Gallery), is an agonized version of the Belvedere Torso. In "The Escape from Doubting Castle" (Frick collection), in the *Pilgrim's Progress* series, the gateway is guarded by an inefficaciously drowsy Hercules Farnese.[4] In such instances Blake clearly intends the source to be recognized; his meaning is established in part by what he does with his "wonderful originals."

The statue, like other figures in Blake's works, is capable of a wide variety of meanings. It can be seen positively or negatively, depending on the perspective from which it is viewed and the context in which it is presented. At the negative pole, for example, is the Spectre of Urthona in Night IV of *The Four Zoas:*

> The Spectre rose in pain
> A shadow blue obscure & dismal. like a statue of lead
> Bent by its fall from a high tower the dolorous shadow rose (E 326)

Here the Spectre, representing the fallen imagination, is something like the human statue postulated by Condillac in his *Traité des Sensations* (1754): "He imagines the five senses bestowed one by one on the statue, and traces the resulting development of mind until a complete human consciousness has been evolved."[5] For Blake such an animated statue is a mere android, parodying human existence. Similarly negative are the sculptured ornaments of Urizen's Golden Hall, which invert the meaning of the temple ornaments Hiram made for Solomon:

> ... her Daughters oft upon
> A Golden Altar burnt perfumes with Art Celestial formd
> Foursquare sculpturd & sweetly Engraved to please their
> shadowy mother (*Four Zoas,* E 313)

To these sculptured images we may add another from Blake's *Notebook:*

> Twas the Greeks love of war
> Turnd Love into a Boy
> And Woman into a Statue of Stone
> And away fled every Joy (E 470)

This stone Venus is a comic analogue of Lot's wife, and all such images of the solidified body are symbols of life-in-death. When the death-principle is overthrown by the life-principle in "The Overthrow of Apollo and the Pagan Gods" (Huntington Library version) in the illustrations to Milton's "On the Morning of Christ's Nativity," Blake makes the central image an Apollo Belvedere.

At the opposite pole of meaning—and of course there may be

many intermediate meanings, as will be seen below—the sculptures of Los's halls can represent life, as in the parallel redemptive images of Dante illustration 80, "The Rock Sculptured with the Recovery of the Ark and the Annunciation" (Tate Gallery). The most powerful instance of this kind occurs in Blake's *Milton,* where Milton himself is the sculptor moulding his enemy Urizen into a human form:

> But Milton took of the red clay of Succoth, moulding it with care
> Between his palms; and filling up the furrows of many years
> Beginning at the feet of Urizen, and on the bones
> Creating new flesh on the Demon cold, and building him,
> As with new clay a Human form in the valley of Beth Peor.
>
> . . . .
>
> . . . Silent Milton stood before
> The darkend Urizen; as the sculptor stands before
> His forming image; he walks round it patient labouring.[6]

The same situation is represented in the full page design of plate 15, where Urizen-as-Jehovah clasps his tablets of Law as an athletic Milton reaches across the river Arnon to sculpt him into life. The sculptor's art can therefore be among the highest of human activities—". . . Painting and Sculpture as it exists in the remains of Antiquity and in the works of more modern genius, is Inspiration, and cannot be surpassed; it is perfect and eternal" (*Descriptive Catalogue,* E 535). There is much to suggest, too, that Blake thought of himself as an inspired sculptor and of his engraved plates with their inscribed "W. Blake inv[enit] & sculp[sit]" as bas-reliefs in copper replicating the originals seen in his visions. These ideas can best be understood after a consideration of what Blake knew about ancient sculpture.

2

Blake's interest in ancient sculpture began very early in his life, for we have the testimony of Benjamin Heath Malkin that Blake was given casts of the Venus de Medici, the gladiator, and Hercules (Farnese) among others, and that he drew after casts of antique statuary in Pars's drawing school.[7] After he was admitted as a student to the Royal Academy schools, Blake would have continued to do such copying after the antique, which was required of students before they could enter the life class. The objects used for these exercises were the Academy's extensive collection of plaster casts (some of which may be seen in Johann Zoffany's painting "The Academicians of the Royal Academy," 1771-72, Royal Collection). Copying would have been supplemented, according to Sir Joshua Reynolds' idea of painting as a liberal art, by study; and this would necessarily have included the study of engravings of ancient sculpture and of illustrated books on the subject. Through these activities Blake was to acquire a vocabulary of classical sculptural forms which he continued to draw upon throughout his life, even after he had rejected the aesthetic and moral values of classicism itself. By reconstructing Blake's knowledge of ancient sculpture we can better appreciate both the respects in which Blake was similar to his contemporaries and in what his uniqueness consists.

One of the works which almost certainly helped to acquaint Blake with ancient statuary was the *Paradigmata Graphices Variorum Artificium* of Jan De Bisschop (Amsterdam, 1671), referred to in Reynolds' fifteenth Discourse as "a book which is in every young Artist's hands—Bishop's Ancient Statues."[8] Among the seminal figures which are to be found among the 157 plates[9] of the *Paradigmata* are the Borghese faun (pls. 1-3), Hercules Farnese (pls. 8-12), Laocoön (pls. 16-17), the Torso (pls. 24-25), the Sleeping Nymph (pl. 35), a cowled Sibyl holding a scroll (pl. 44), Venus de Medici (pls. 47-50, 81), Marsyas (pl. 55), a son of Laocoön (pl. 56), and Leda and the Swan (pl. 83). (The *Paradigmata* may also have contributed to Blake's interest in Michelangelo, Raphael, and their followers, of whose works its last part contains many reproductions.[10]) For information in addition to illustrations (Bisschop provided no text), Blake could have gone to the well-known work of Bernard de Montfaucon. His grand series of five volumes on ancient sculpture, followed by a five-volume supplement, originally appeared in Paris as *"L'antiquité expliqué et representée en figures* (1719); it was translated into English by David Humphreys as *Antiquity Explained, and Represented in Sculptures* and published in London (1721-25) by Jacob Tonson and J. Watts.[11] "I have reduced into one body all Antiquity," Montfaucon triumphantly announced (p. v), but he refused to be drawn into the type of conjecture as to the origins of ancient sculpture that was to become so interesting to Blake. In particular, Jewish antiquities are excluded because, says Montfaucon, the Scriptures are obscure about them. "Other learned Men... have laboured to find a kind of Concordance between the Holy Scripture and Mythology; they pretend a great many passages of the Holy Scripture have been imitated by the Mythologists" (p. viii). This is precisely what Blake says "Jacob Bryant, and all antiquaries have proved."[12] "I think this literature mere conjecture," says Montfaucon (p. viii), but although for this reason *Antiquity Explained* could not satisfy Blake's curiosity about the Cherubim of Solomon's Temple, it could provide a treasury of images, with accompanying discussion, for Blake to use as he pleased. One of the most striking of these is plate 9, no. 13, representing Jupiter Pluvius (Plate 101). As described in the text (p. 28), this image from the Antonine Pillar "is the shape of an old Man with Wings and a long beard, with both his Arms extended but with his right Arm raised up a little higher than the other. The water runs down in a long stream from his Beard and Arms." This engraving seems to have influenced both Henry Fuseli, after whose design Blake engraved "The Fertilization of Egypt" for *The Economy of Vegetation* by Erasmus Darwin[13] and Blake, who uses such a conception frequently for his father-gods, as in *America* pl. 10 (Plate 2), *The Book of Urizen* pls. 1 and 12 among others, and the color printed drawing called "The House of Death" (Plate 102).

Among other suggestive images in Montfaucon is a chariot with winged serpents as wheels (Plate 103): "Ceres, upon the news of her daughter *Proserpine* being stole, mounts her Chariot drawn by Flying-Dragons... " (p. 49). This we may compare to the serpent-wheeled chariot of *Jerusalem* pl. 46 (Plate 104). The male figure bearing the child Bacchus (Vol. I, pl. 69, no. 6) is very similar to the adult carrying the child in the frontispiece to *Songs of Experience*. Mithras entwined by a serpent (Vol. I, pl. 96, nos. 1 & 2) presents a combination which occurs head-down in *The Book of Urizen* pl. 6, horizontally in "Satan Watching Adam and Eve," and vertically in details of the sixth design for *Comus* (Huntington Library version).[14] The winged discs of the Persians depicted in plate 55 of volume II are very similar to the one in *Jerusalem* pl. 37.[15] A striking prototype of the scaly armor with which Blake frequently clothes military oppressors, as in the separate plate "Our End is Come" and in *Europe* pl. 8 (Plate 106), may be found in plate 22 of volume IV (Plate 107), with the following explanation:

> The military Habit of the *Sarmatians* is the most extraordinary
> one we have yet seen. For it's so closely adjusted to their Body
> from the Neck to the very Sole of the Foot, that all the Motions of
> the Members and Muscles appear as plainly through it, as if the
> Body was naked. 'Tis also covered with Scales without the least
> Interval, even as low as the Hand, and down to the Sole of the
> Foot. (IV, 69–70)

It is further interesting that a few pages later we find a passage
which may well have prompted Blake's references to the "scythed
chariots of Britain" (*Jerusalem*, pls. 47, 56):

> The Greeks, as well as many other *Asiatick* nations, made use of
> Chariots with Scythes, as did also the *Gauls* and others. . . . These
> Chariots had sharp pointed Scythes at each Axis, so that when
> they rush'd upon the Enemy with full Career they might easily do
> a great deal of Mischief. . . . (VI, 75)

Such parallels both of design and of text strongly suggest that early
in his career Blake was impressed by Montfaucon's compilation of
ancient sculpture and that he continued to draw upon Montfaucon,
whether consciously or unconsciously, in later years.

Perhaps the best-known work on ancient sculpture originally
published in English in the eighteenth century was Joseph Spence's
Polymetis (1747), subtitled *An Enquiry concerning the Agreement Between
the Works of the Roman Poets, and the Remains of the Antient Artists.*
Spence confines his illustrated dialogue to Greek and Roman
sculpture, dismissing more exotic works such as the Egyptian—"I
should have been heartily vext to see a deity with a dog's or a hawk's
head upon its shoulders . . ." (p. 5). Within the confines of its subject
matter, however, *Polymetis* would have been useful to Blake.[16] In
addition to reproducing such standard figures of the neoclassical
pantheon as the Medici Venus (pl. V), Apollo Belvedere (pl. XI),
and Hercules Farnese (pl. XVI), Spence includes some specialized
subjects that were also to interest Blake. Plate I shows Jupiter holding a conventionalized thunderbolt of the type wielded in "The
Spiritual Form of Nelson Guiding Leviathan": Spence observes,
"This fulmen, in the hand of Jupiter, partook something of the
nature of an hieroglyph of old; and had different meanings, according to the different manners in which it was represented" (p. 50).
Plate XII shows a new-born infant held by a nurse while another

woman holds a robe open to receive it, calling to mind the situation of "Infant Sorrow" in *Songs of Experience* (Plate 12), where the infant is received by its father. Diana is depicted with three bodies in plate XIV, foreshadowing Blake's color printed drawing "Hecate" (1795): "This is very common among the antient figures of the goddess," writes Spence. "... Her distinguishing name, under this triple appearance, is Hecate, or Trivia" (p. 102). The infant Hercules strangling the two serpents, also the subject of a pencil drawing by Blake,[17] is represented in plate XVII. In such instances as these it is not so much a matter of assigning deliberately chosen sources as of recognizing that Blake internalized familiar images like these and transformed them in his art.

There are of course some other works on sculpture that would have been familiar to any art student of Blake's time. One of these is the seven-volume *Receuil d'Antiquité Egyptiennes, Etrusques, Greques, et Romaines* (Paris, 1752–57) of Anne Claude Phillippe de Tubières, Comte de Caylus. Of particular interest to us is the engraving of a statue of Jupiter as a giant eagle carrying off the naked boy Ganymede, to which we may compare Blake's rejected preliminary design (Rosenwald collection) for Hayley's ballad "The Eagle" in *Designs to a Series of Ballads* (1802), very similar in conception. The figure of a man writing with a quill pen in a book to the dictation of a sibylline cowled figure is very reminiscent of the false instruction scene of *America* pl. 16 and of *Night Thoughts* engraving 20,[18] and the gryphon in volume III, plate XXII, no. II has a strong resemblance to the one in Blake's "Beatrice Addressing Dante from the Car" (Tate Gallery). Very striking indeed is the serpent with a radiant halo (vol. V, pl. XXIII, no. V), which Caylus identifies as the serpent Agathadémon, worshipped with the phoenix at Heliopolis; compare the haloed Orc serpent of *Europe* pl. 13, for which no analogues or sources have previously been found. Animal-headed, and particularly bird-headed, human figures abound: an ibis-headed man with a long decurved beak (vol. III, pl. VI, no. I) and a man with the head of a sparrow-hawk (vol. IV, pl. V, nos. III and IV), among others. Such figures also occur in Montfaucon, as in the hawk-headed human figures identified as Osiris in *Antiquity Explained* (vol. II, pl. 39, nos. 10, 11). Such engravings may well have affected similar designs by Blake, most notably the bird-headed man of *Jerusalem* pl. 78 and the group of bird-headed creatures in *Comus* illustration 5, "The Lady Spellbound in the Chair" (Huntington Library version).

The Antiquities of Athens by James Stuart and Nicholas Revett should also be mentioned here, for although it is primarily a work on architecture, many of its plates include statuary. Furthermore, a considerable number of plates in volume I (1762) were engraved by James Basire, Blake's master in the 1770s, and these are particularly successful in conveying the mass and contour of sculpture.[19] (Blake himself was to execute four plates from volume III of the *Antiquities*, published in 1794; see below). Two of the Winds pictured in volume I, plate XIV (by Basire) and Plate XV (by Strange) are in positions resembling Satan's in "Satan Watching Adam and Eve."[20] In Chapter IV, devoted to the Choragic Monument of Lysicrates with its frieze of Bacchus and the Tyrrhenian Pirates, plate XVIII (by Basire) shows a bound pirate very much in the attitude of the bound Bromion of the frontispiece to *Visions of the Daughters of Albion* (Plate 61); he is described (p. 34) as "sitting on a Rock by the Sea-Side; Despair is in his Face; his arms are bound behind him by a Cord. . . ." In the same series, plate X, "Bacchus with his Tyger" (by C. Grignion), presents a Tyger as comic-grotesque as the one in Blake's famous, puzzling design; and plates XVI and XIX (by Basire), showing pirates turning into dolphins, seem to foreshadow some of Blake's renderings of transformations, such as Dante illustration 52, "Agnolo Brunelleschi Half Transformed into a Serpent" (Fogg Museum). Once more, such resemblances are noted not to suggest single sources for Blake's inspiration but rather to show how he built up a repertoire of sculptural images which he used freely in his poetry and art.

Among the works so far discussed, Blake could have found engravings of ancient statues and information about them but not the audacious speculation which his imagination also required. The most likely source of this last element is James Barry, whose powerful effect on Blake has not been discussed with respect to ideas about ancient sculpture.[21] Barry became Professor of Painting at the Royal Academy in 1782 and began his lectures there in 1784. The first of these is almost entirely devoted to the arts of antiquity, particularly sculpture. Like Blake in *A Descriptive Catalogue*, Barry alludes to the statuary of the ancient Near East, stressing its priority to that of the Greeks and Romans. He describes the palace of Semiramis as having walls on which "different animals were raised in bas-relief, and painted from the life . . . these figures were relieved and painted on the faces of the brick before they were well burned, and consequently must have been vitrified or enamelled."[22] A connection between Assyrian and Hebrew sculpture is also established: "That these works of sculpture in Assyria were not confined to temples and public places, we may be reasonably assured from the mention of the little images which Rachel stole away from her father's house. That the career of the arts in Assyria was also a very long one, we may learn from the golden statue, sixty cubits high, of Nebuchadnezzar, set up fourteen hundred years after the stealing of Laban's images" (p. 58n). Barry goes on to say that "The Assyrians, Egyptians, Phenicians, Persians, and the other oriental nations, had cultivated the arts long before the Greeks..." (p. 71).

Among other interesting parallels between Barry's ideas and those later expressed by Blake are the condemnation of stellar worship, the view of Nebuchadnezzar as representing humanity in its fallen state, the postulation of a flood which left remnants of antediluvian civilization behind, and the characterization of the Romans as a brutal, imperialistic culture. "Sabaism," says Barry, "... was already so reprobated in the Book of Job, and the other prophetical writings, with the odious appellation of the host of heaven" (p. 64)—a reference bringing to mind Urizen's starry hosts and the stars of plate 13 of the *Job* engravings as well as the defeated stars of "The Tyger." "The deification of Ouranos, Saturn, Jupiter, and other mortals," Barry says, "by the transfer and identifying of them with the heavens, the sun, and planets, was probably posterior to the catastrophe of the inundation which cut off communication with America..."[23]; while in his *America* Blake writes of "those vast shady hills between America & Albions shore; / Now barr'd out by the Atlantic sea..." (E 54). Nebuchadnezzar, memorably depicted by Blake as both tyrant and bestial man in the great color printed drawing of 1795, is singled out for some of Barry's most virulent rhetoric:

> When we reflect upon this horrid state of things, resulting from the gradual and accumulating corruptions of Sabaism or stellar worship, identified with those dead and living mortals, which had been thus superinduced on the primitive, traditional, pure theology, it affords a most dreadful exemplary spectacle of degraded (and in these matters impotent) human reason.... Nebuchadnezzar, Antiochus, and other such imperious tyrants, nursed and fed up with base adulation ... as inheritors and claimants of the same terrestial and celestial domination, were necessarily deter-

mined to uphold all this idol business, to immolate its opposers,
and to trample under the feet of their mercenary, pretorian,
janissary instruments, every right of equal common humanity,
mental and corporeal. (p. 66)

Furthermore, both Blake and Barry view the Romans as a nation of
oppressors, who, according to Barry, by their conquests diverted the
Etruscans from pursuing art "until this enormous mass of useless
destructive power was happily beaten to pieces by the barbarous
nations" (p. 82).

In comparing Barry and Blake we find not only a congruence of
details but a similar spirit underlying the interpretation of details —
Barry's libertarian fervor, his linking of subjects from antiquity with
modern political concerns (the first lecture ends with an attack upon
government subsidies to newspapers), and his use of such terms as
"mental" and "corporeal" are close to what we think of as characteristically "Blakean." In one respect, however, Blake goes further
than Barry: in regard to what Blake calls the "wonderful originals"
of Greek and Roman sculpture. Barry discusses the *priority* of the
statuary of the East and even devotes some words to Hebrew art.
The cherubim were "sculptured on the mercy-seat," and "the sacred
veil and the curtains, which surrounded the holy of holies, were also
ornamented with tapestry, or embroidered paintings of the same
figures of cherubims. . . . Afterwards, when the temple came to be
built, the cherubims were placed all round it, and the brass figures
of the lions, and the twelve oxen cast in the clayey soil near Jor-
dan . . ."p. 67). The leap Blake was to take consisted in postulating
that the sculpture of the Greeks and Romans was copied imperfectly
from the cherubim of Solomon's temple. This phase of his thought
did not begin, however, until after the turn of the century, and even
here, as we shall see later, he had some antecedents.

3

In his maturity as an artist, Blake continued to move in a milieu
in which ideas about ancient sculpture were very important, as manifested in writings such as William Hayley's *Essay on Sculpture* (1800),
in Flaxman's lectures on sculpture delivered from 1810 on, and in
numerous sculptural projects based on the antique. Elaborate books

reproducing classical sculpture continued to be published: Blake contributed to the engravings in the third volume of *Antiquities of Athens* (1794) and was among the subscribers to Charles Heathcote Tatham's *Etchings, Representing the Best Examples of Ancient Ornamental Architecture* (1799).[24] There were also important sculptural acquisitions in the early nineteenth century: a statue of Ceres, thought to be of the time of Phidias, was brought to Cambridge and was engraved by Blake after a drawing by Flaxman; the first shipment of Elgin Marbles arrived in London in 1804 and was displayed in 1807 ; the Towneley Collection was acquired by the British Museum in 1805 as was a collection of Egyptian sculpture which had been seized by the British after their defeat of the French at Alexandria.[25] At the same time, Blake's ideas about ancient sculpture were undergoing a crucial change, leading to polemical statements in the *Descriptive Catalogue* and elsewhere and to the great engraving and manifesto, *The Laocoön*.

Hayley's *Essay on Sculpture* can be taken as a collection of commonplaces widely accepted at the time; hence it has a claim, albeit a limited one, to our attention here. It consists of six epistles in heroic couplets with copious prose notes, is addressed to John Flaxman and embellished with three engravings by Blake: "Pericles" from the Towneley collection, "The Death of Demosthenes" after a drawing by Thomas Hayley, and "Thomas Hayley the Disciple of John Flaxman from a Medallion" after Flaxman. Although Blake could have found little or nothing that was new to him in the *Essay*, parts of it would have recalled his previous studies. Hayley, for example, quotes (p. 192) the same passage from Diodorus Siculus that Barry had drawn from in describing the palace of Semiramis with its gigantic statues of gods and its walls "upon which were pourtrayed in the bricks, even to the life, all sorts of living creatures." There are descriptions of the Laocoön, Gladiator, Hercules Farnese, Apollo Belvedere and Venus de Medici. Rome is viewed as an imperial vulgarizer, "a coarse gigantic glutton"; Virgil, says Hayley, "was their elegant but servile flatterer" (p. 91). "Virgil," Blake was to write, "in the Eneid Book VI. line 848 says Let others study Art: Rome has somewhat better to do, namely War & Dominion" (*On Virgil*, E 267). But Blake's condemnation, unlike Hayley's, includes the Greeks as well—"Rome & Greece swept Art into their maw & destroyd it."

Far more important than Hayley to Blake was the friend Blake addressed as "Dear Sculptor of Eternity."[26] John Flaxman had returned from seven years' residence in Italy in 1794 with sketch books (now principally in the Victoria and Albert Museum) full of drawings which were to furnish material not only for his art but also for his extensive writings and lectures on sculpture. Flaxman's communicative nature and the closeness of his relationship to Blake suggest that Blake would have been acquainted with what Flaxman thought about sculpture long before his Royal Academy lectures began in 1810; and since Flaxman's writings on the subject tend to repeat the same basic material, it seems reasonable to quote from them *en bloc* (while of course indicating the particular sources).

Perhaps the single most significant statement we can make about Flaxman here is that he had far more to say about Hebrew sculpture than any of the writers so far considered, both in his lectures and in his article on sculpture in Rees' *Cyclopaedia*[27] (the latter contains a section "Of Hebrew Sculpture" some 1700 words long). "In Egypt," according to Flaxman,

> the sculptures were hieroglyphical memorials of Divine and human knowledge: this was the earliest as it will always continue the most important element of this art, debased indeed according to the corruption of systems:—but in that nation which received the law with signs—wonders to enlighten a darkened world!—the Almighty directed the figures of Cherubim to guard the Ark of the Covenant. . . .[28]

Bezaleel and Aholiab are singled out by Flaxman as divinely inspired artists who were ordered in Exodus "to devise curious work in gold, in silver, and in brass" and who consequently produced for the tabernacle "the most admirable and lively decorations of angelic forms" (*Lectures,* pp. 52-3). Similarly, after Blake had rejected the art of Greece and Rome, he wrote verses in his *Notebook* setting the inspired against the profane:

> And if Bezaleel & Aholiab drew
> What the Finger of God pointed to their View
> Shall we suffer the Roman & Grecian Rods
> To compell us to worship them as Gods[29]

Also very similar to Blake in spirit is Flaxman's tendency to allegorize biblical statements, including those about sculpture—a similarity no doubt going back to the influence of Swedenborg's interpretation of the Bible on both artists. Flaxman calls the making of the golden calf "this dreadful attempt to annihilate inspired art at its birth," and he equates art and freedom in a particularly "Blakean" manner:

> And the necessity of such inspired sculptures and other inspired works of art is explained sufficiently in the deliverance of Israel from the idolatry of Egypt. . . . The Hebrew being born a slave, continued so under the Egyptian yoke, let his inspiration be what it would, he was compelled to work in making bricks and in iron-furnaces. Such was the deliverance of art and science from destruction, and the earth from returning to its primeval chaos. (Rees, "Sculpture").

"Israel deliverd from Egypt is Art deliverd from Nature & Imitation," says Blake in *The Laocoön* (E 272), adding a further dimension by including mimesis as a form of bondage.

A particular place in speculation about Hebrew sculpture is necessarily occupied by the adornments of Solomon's Temple. Flaxman writes:

> It contained the same cherubim that Moses had seen on the Mount; and they adorned and covered the whole temple within and without. Two in particular were placed in the holy of holies, of colossal dimensions: they covered the place of the ark with their wings; the height of each was ten cubits. A figure five yards high is capable of the greatest efforts at perfection in art, and this no doubt they had, being done by divine command, for purposes whose importance reaches to the end of time. (Rees, "Sculpture")

Blake, as we have seen, envisions these cherubim as the sources of ancient art; he also describes them as guarding the closed Western gate of Golgonooza (*Jerusalem*, pl. 13, E 155)—closed because the West is associated with Tharmas, Zoa of the body, and there can be no direct passage of the material body into the spiritual fourfold city of art. The cherubim can also in their positive sense represent mercy, having formed part of the mercy-seat, as in Albion's recollection of Jerusalem's "Cherubims of Tender-mercy / Stretching their Wings sublime over the Little-ones of Albion" (*Jerusalem*, pl. 24, E 168). The other temple ornaments also receive due attention from both Flaxman and Blake. Flaxman calls "the brazen sea of Solomon's temple, and its twelve oxen; the two pillars Jachin and Boaz" and other carved and cast temple ornaments "works inspired by God and wrought by his holy Spirit" (Rees, "Sculpture"). Blake describes his now lost painting "A Vision of the Last Judgment" as showing "Jesus seated between the two Pillars Jachin & Boaz" (E 545). These are of course the pillars cast in brass by Hiram (1 Kings), their capitals adorned with "nets of checker work, and wreaths of chain work" (6:17) with brass pomegranates and lilies on them. The brass sea and twelve oxen mentioned by Flaxman were cast for Solomon "in the clay ground between Succoth and Zarthan" (1 Kings 8:46): Blake's Milton therefore emulates Hiram when he "took of the red clay of Succoth, moulding it with care / Between his palms" in the passage already discussed. Thus the Old Testament sculptors and their divinely inspired works have a comparable importance to Blake and to Flaxman; Blake carries their symbolic meaning further, but it is also present in Flaxman's writings.

In addition to his discussion of Hebrew sculpture, Flaxman provides some interesting material about other ancient civilizations, including a striking description of the Palace of Carnac at Thebes. It contained "colossal statues" and was "approached by four paved roads, bordered on each side with figures of animals fifteen feet long—lions, sphinxes, rams, and lions with hawks' heads, nine hundred or more in number" (*Lectures*, p. 59). In *Jerusalem* the City of Golgonooza has four gates, each ornamented by sculpture:

> And the North Gate of Golgonooza toward Generation;
> Has four sculpturd Bulls terrible before the Gate of iron.
> And iron, the Bulls: and that which looks toward Ulro,
> Clay bak'd & enamel'd . . .

The Western Gate, as previously mentioned, is guarded by Cherubim; the Eastern Gate has "terrible & deadly" ornaments.

> The South, a golden Gate, has four Lions terrible, living!
> That toward Generation, four, of iron carv'd wondrous,
> That toward Ulro, four, clay bak'd, laborious workmanship
> That toward Eden, four; immortal gold, silver, brass & iron.[30]

The underlying models for this description are Ezekiel's vision of the restored Temple (especially in Chapter 41) and John's of the heavenly Jerusalem (Revelation 21),[31] but neither of these gives sculpture the weight and prominence that Blake does. Here we can see once more how Blake conflates and transforms his sources in order to create something uniquely his own, in this instance the vision of a City of Art guarded by gigantic sculptured forms.

So far our discussion has been limited to the Mediterranean world and Near East, but in Blake's time there was also a growing interest in the sculpture of the Far East and particularly in that of India. In his *Thoughts on Outline* (1796), to which Blake contributed eight engravings and other assistance, George Cumberland speculates that "It would not be very difficult to shew, that the Egyptians and the Greeks probably received their first germ of art from India; and that a striking similarity exists to this day, I could prove from monuments now in my possession."[32] The great pioneer of Indian studies was Sir William Jones, whose *Works* were published in six volumes, edited by his daughter, in 1799. Jones, who is quoted in *Thoughts on Outline,* actually does not go as far as to suggest the priority of Indian art and mythology, but rather, like some of the other writers we have considered, limits himself to parallels. He points out, for example, resemblances "between the popular worship of the old *Greeks* and *Italians* and that of the *Hindus*" and remarks on "a great similarity between their strange religions and that of *Egypt, China, Persia, Phrygia, Phoenice, Syria. . . .*" However, although Jones even finds "the Gothic system . . . not merely similar to those of *Greece* and *Italy,* but almost the same in another dress with an embroidery of images apparently *Asiatick*" (I, 228–30), he will have nothing to do with system-making. That is to say, he will not do precisely what Blake would wish to do and disclaims any intention of asserting "that such a God of *India* was *the* Jupiter of *Greece;* such *the Apollo,*" and he dismisses both the "refined allegories" of Bacon and the "poetical disguise of true history" (I, 232) of Newton. He does point out parallels such as that of Diana, "otherwise named Hecate, and often confounded with Proserpine" and Cálí, to whom human sacrifices were offered, and he asserts that "a connexion subsisted between the old idolatrous nations of *Egypt, India, Greece,* and *Italy,* long before they migrated to their several settlements, and consequently before the birth of Moses" (I, 270–71, 276). Among the plates illlustrating Jones's text is one engraving which may well have impressed Blake: the god Ganésa, possessing an elephant's head and human body. Blake drew a similar figure holding a little replica of itself, and this strange design (now in the Abbot Hall Art Gallery, Kendal) was later etched by William Bell Scott.[33]

A later but far more compendious work on India is Edward Moor's *The Hindu Pantheon,* published by Joseph Johnson in 1810. It contains 105 plates, many of them dated 1st January 1809. Moor goes further than Jones in declaring that "There can, I think, be but little doubt of the mythological legends of the *Hindus* being the source whence have been derived the fables and deities of *Greece* and *Italy,* and other heathen people of the West" (p. xi), though he rules out any further discussion of this as beyond his subject. *The Hindu Pantheon,* praised by Flaxman both in his lectures and in his encyclopedia article, gives a wealth of information, both pictorial and verbal, about Indian sculpture. On plates 44 and 45 are views of the elephant-headed Ganésa, while plates 10 and 105 portray the eagle-headed Garuda, of whom Moor writes:

> He is sometimes described in the manner that our poets and painters describe a griffin, or a cherub, and he is placed at the entrance of the passes leading to the *Hindu* garden of Eden, and then appears in the character of a destroying angel, in as far as he resists the approach of serpents, which in most systems of poetic mythology, appear to have been the beautiful, deceiving form that sin originally assumed. (p. 340)

To Blake this would surely have been reminiscent of the Covering Cherub, a symbol originally derived from Ezekiel 28:13, which Blake takes to represent the tyrannical Law which blocks man's way back to Paradise.[34] Very similar to the Garuda of Moor's plate 105 (Plate 105) are the winged, bird-headed riders of *Jerusalem* pl. 46 (Plate 104). Here Blake seems to have compounded elements from Montfaucon (the serpent-wheeled chariot, Plate 103), from engravings of Persepolis (the man-headed bulls[35]), and from Moor, thus drawing upon the sculpture of three ancient civilizations. Of course this is not to deny Blake's originality or inventiveness; it is rather to indicate the way in which his knowledge of ancient sculpture contributed to his inventiveness. Blake's most powerful conceptions frequently occurred in the form of eidetic images, and as Joseph Burke says, "An eidetic image . . . appeared to Blake, not merely as a kind of living sculpture, but in a shape suggested by antiquity."[36]

In the late eighteenth and early nineteenth centuries, as we have mentioned, important new publications about sculpture appeared and there were even more important new sculptural acquisitions. The third volume of *Antiquities of Athens* was published in 1794 and included four engravings by Blake after William Pars, depicting the battle of Lapiths and Centaurs from the frieze of the Temple of Theseus (pls. XXI–XXIV). Although these plates are far superior to those of the Parthenon metopes and frieze, poorly executed and anonymous, in volume II of the *Antiquities* (1787), they do not rise beyond the level of professional competence. As for the Elgin Marbles themselves, it would be pleasing to imagine that Blake was as moved by these magnificent works as Keats was to be a generation later, but it appears that after the arrival of the Marbles in England, Blake did not become an unequivocal admirer. According to Samuel Palmer, this was because of Blake's preference for "the purest art" by which Palmer seems in this instance to mean neoclassical idealization: "Thus he thought with Fuseli and Flaxman that the Elgin Theseus, however full of antique savour, could not, as ideal form, rank with the very finest relics of antiquity."[37] Flaxman, however, in his *Lectures* urges his students to study the Elgin Marbles and calls the horses in the frieze "the most precious examples of Grecian power in the sculpture of animals" (p. 101); and both Flaxman and Canova were to recommend the acquisition of the Elgin Marbles by the British Museum. Blake's failure to respond to them more enthusiastically is a reminder of how thoroughly eighteenth-century his training was. Blake, who owned Henry Fuseli's translation of Winckelmann's *Reflections on the Painting and Sculpture of the Greeks* (1765), would no doubt have agreed with Winckelmann that "The last and most eminent characteristic of Greek works is a noble simplicity and calm grandeur in gesture and expression."[38] Flaxman and Canova, educated according to the same ideal, overcame its limitations with respect to the Elgin Marbles; Blake, it appears, did not. Perhaps the explanation for this lies in part in the difference between an artist's interest in another medium, however deep, and actual practice in that medium.

The period under discussion was also a particularly fertile one for British sculpture. In addition to the work of Flaxman, mention should be made of the achievement of Thomas Banks, whose name is joined to those of Stothard and Blake in an anonymous obituary of Flaxman, published in 1828:

> The works of the two first-mentioned artists together with Mr. Flaxman's own, partake, though in different degrees, of the same character; which appears to be founded on the style of the very

eminent English sculptor, Banks, whose basso-relievos of "Thetis and Achilles," and "Caractacus before Claudius" will furnish, to those who examine them, sufficient proofs of the validity of this supposition.[39]

When Banks died, Blake wrote to Hayley on 25 April 1805: "Banks the Sculptor is Gone to his Eternal Home. I have heard that Flaxman means to give a Lecture on Sculpture at the Royal Academy on the Occasion of Banks's Death" (*Letters*, p. 116). In this address Flaxman remarked that "The basso-relievo of Caractacus before Claudius, is composed on the principle of those on the ancient sarcophagi, of which many are to be seen in Rome," and he asserted that before Banks only Nollekens had formed his taste on the antique.[40] After 1798 Banks was one of the British sculptors working on monuments commemorating naval heroes of the war against France. "The style," he wrote of his monument to Captain Burges in St. Paul's, "... is chiefly conformable to that of the antique."[41] Blake's attitude towards such projects must necessarily have been equivocal. On the one hand, they employed contemporary artists, some of whom he admired, in publicly sponsored works—something which Blake himself urges in his prose writings. On the other hand, these productions honored "War & its horrors & its Heroic Villains" (Annotations to Bacon, E 612); furthermore, patronage was limited to sculpture, and Blake understandably preferred his own art:

> The Painters of England are unemploy'd in Public Works. while the Sculptors have continual & superabundant employment... While Painting is excluded   Painting the Principal Art has no place among our almost only public works. Yet it is more adapted to solemn ornament that *dead* marble can be as it is capable of being Placed in any heighth & indeed would make a Noble finish Placed above the great Public Monuments in Westminster S^t. Pauls & other Cathedrals. (*Public Address*, E 570)

These comments nevertheless pay a kind of tribute to sculpture, proposing as they do, and as Blake also does in the *Descriptive Catalogue*, to create painted monuments akin but superior to statues:

> Those wonderful originals seen in my visions, were some of them one hundred feet in height; some were painted as pictures, and some carved as basso relievos, and some as groups of statues, all

containing mythological and recondite meaning, where more is meant than meets the eye. The Artist wishes it was now the fashion to make such monuments, and then he should not doubt of having a national commission to execute these two Pictures . . . in high finished fresco . . . (E 522)

Something of Blake's disquietude about the heroic subject matter is conveyed by his reference to recondite meaning, which is certainly an apt description of the symbolism of "The Spiritual Form of Nelson Guiding Leviathan" and its companion painting "The Spiritual Form of Pitt Guiding Behemoth."[42]

In addition to the various projects in honor of individual naval heroes, there was a plan for a National Naval Monument announced in 1798. Drawings were submitted in 1799 and an exhibition of them was held by William Bowyer. The monument was to be two hundred feet high, and "a chaste and classical simplicity in its embellishments, as well as in its general form" were among the desiderata.[43] Although no such monument was executed at the time, at least two sets of designs were published: *A Letter to the Committee for Raising the Naval Pillar, or Monument* by John Flaxman (1799) and *Three Designs for the National Monument* by Charles Heathcote Tatham (1802). Blake subscribed to Tatham's book of etchings and engraved the plates for Flaxman's *Letter*. There are three engravings: a frontispiece showing Flaxman's projected statue of Britannia Triumphant, six outline designs of various types of monuments, and "A View of Greenwich Hospital with the Statue of Britannia on the Hill." Flaxman's text adduces numerous examples in antiquity for such a monument, dwelling upon their colossal size and on the superiority of the human figure to merely architectural monuments. His own Britannia Truimphant was "intended to last as long as the Trajan Column, the Ampitheatres, or the Pyramids of Egypt . . . " (*Letter*, p. 11). A few years later, Flaxman published an account of his monument to Nelson in St. Paul's cathedral, also mentioning two statues of Pitt, one destined for Glasgow and the other for India. Joseph Nollekens was at the same time executing a statue of Pitt for the Senate-House in Cambridge, and Parliament voted funds for yet another monument to Pitt to be placed in Westminster Abbey.[44] During this same period, Blake was rendering satirical spiritual portraits of these "heroes" and associating the Royal Navy, in his long poems, with the Druid Oaks of Albion. He was also vehemently repudiating the ideals of classical art which he had previously shared with Banks, Flaxman, and other contemporaries.

4

As late as 2 July 1800, we find Blake writing to George Cumberland: "I have to congratulate you on your plan for a National Gallery being put into Execution. All your wishes shall in due time be fulfilled; the immense flood of Grecian light & glory which is coming on Europe will more than realize our warmest wishes." In the same letter Flaxman is praised as "more & more A Grecian," and the hope is expressed that the inhabitants of London are entering into "an Emulation of Grecian manners" (*Letters*, pp. 36-7). Within a few years Blake's attitude toward Greek art had changed radically. He now linked it with the art of the Romans, which Hayley and Flaxman also condemned, but in contrast to that of the Greeks rather than together with it. Blake's *Milton* begins with the declaration that "The Stolen and Perverted Writings of Homer & Ovid: of Plato & Cicero. which all men ought to contemn: are set up by artifice against the Sublime of the Bible. . . . Shakespeare & Milton were both curbd by the general malady & infection from the silly Greek & Latin slaves of the Sword" (E 94). This reversal appears to have been one of the results of the conversionary experiences Blake had at Felpham, and it was reinforced by a further illumination after visiting the Truchsessian Gallery in London in 1804.[45] Nevertheless, Blake continued to draw upon classical sources in his own work, while also going to Persian, Indian, and Egyptian art for material. Concomittantly he developed a theory in which classical art is viewed as deriving from more ancient originals, so that the Greek statues could be considered alternatively to be "justly admired copies" or debased imitations. This ambiguity attains its definitive expression in *The Laocoön,* in itself—if we are to follow Blake in this—a copy of a copy, yet at the same time an attempt to go back to the presumed archaic source of its subject.

The genesis of *The Laocoön* lay in a commercial project. In 1815 and 1816 Blake was engaged in drawing and engraving plates for Rees's *Cyclopaedia,* four of which illustrate Flaxman's essay on Sculpture. Three of the plates are devoted to classical sculpture, while Plate IV includes Hindu, Persian, and Egyptian examples (see

Plates 108–11). It was inevitable that the Laocoön be included, especially as Flaxman's article refers to it as "a work to be preferred before all both of painting and statuary." In 1815 Blake went to the Royal Academy to make a pencil drawing after the plaster cast of the Laocoön group; he completed a stipple engraving of the Laocoön in October of that year, and it was published in volume IV of the plates of *The Cyclopaedia* in 1820.[46] Evidently this planted the seed that germinated as Blake's own *Laocoön,* conjecturally dated by Keynes as *c.* 1820.[47] Executed in Blake's mature, monumental style, it is at once a great work of art in its own right and, surrounded by aphorisms, a manifesto (Plate 112).

The Laocoön has a fair claim to being Blake's ultimate statement about the nature of art, and it is this aspect of it that concerns us here.[48] Blake sees the statue as essentially a mistaken reading of a true story. The Rhodian sculptors thought they were depicting an episode from *The Aeneid*—but "The Gods of Priam are the Cherubim of Moses & Solomon The Hosts of Heaven." The true title of the work is rendered by Blake as "יה & his two Sons Satan & Adam as they were copied from the Cherubim of Solomons Temple by three Rhodians & applied to Natural Fact or History of Ilium." So in this true version, the central figure is given the names "The Angel of the Divine Presence," *Angel of Jehovah* in Hebrew, and *Serpent-holder* in Greek; "Good" is to his left and "Evil" to his right. The Greeks could not understand the symbolism, mistaking it for an episode in a war between empires. Actually, or at least in its Blakean meaning, it represents the demiurge caught in his own material creation and his "Sons"—Adam the natural man and Satan the separated will—caught as well. "Adam is only the Natural Man & not the Soul or Imagination," while Satan imputes sin to "all the Loves & Graces of Eternity." But this closed world of "Generation & Death" shows, by negation, a way out: the true artist must turn his back on this. He must reject the examples of Greece and Rome, "States in which all Visionary Men are accounted Mad Men," and pursue "Hebrew Art." In so doing he will, like Blake, wage "Spiritual War"— "Israel deliverd from Egypt is Art deliverd from Nature & Imitation." *The Laocoön* is, then, a copy not of a Greek statue but of one of the "wonderful originals" of Blake's vision. More than that, it is not merely a copy but an original in its own right. Since the arts are not progressive, it has, according to Blake's argument, a status equal to that of the Cherubim, though its scale is smaller. Considered as a copper plate rather than as a print, it can even be thought of as sculpture.

The conceptions behind *The Laocoön* are characteristic of Blake's later thought, and in his postulation of "wonderful originals" he goes far beyond the speculations of Barry and of Flaxman. Even here, however, there are some antecedents. Sir Anthony Blunt has persuasively argued that Blake was familiar with the theory that the principles of architecture embodied in Solomon's temple were dictated by God to the Jews and afterwards carried by them to other nations, as maintained by Philibert de l'Orme, by the Jesuits Pradus and Villapandus in their commentary on Ezekiel (1596–1605), and by John Wood of Bath in *The Origins of Building; or the Plagiarism of the Heathen Detected* (1741). This theory, says Professor Blunt, "was widely upheld, but Blake seems to have been alone in extending it yet further to include sculpture."[49] Yet even here there is at least one forerunner—John Evelyn,[50] whose *Sculptura,* first published in 1662, asserts that the arts of sculpture, engraving, and writing were identical in their inception. According to Evelyn, there were antediluvian sculptures in stone and brick at Joppa, "containing (as some depose) the sidereal and celestial sciences."[51] Long before Moses, Zoroaster engraved the liberal arts on seven columns of brass and seven of brick, and Mercurius Trismegistus "engraved his secret and mysterious things in stone...."[52] Then "in Moses we have the tables of stone, engraven by the finger of GOD himself" (p. 26). Evelyn finds that in the words of Job "O that my words were printed in a book, that they were graven with an iron pen and lead in the rock for ever!" allusion is made to "almost all the sorts of antient writing and engraving; books, plates, stone, and stile."[53] These early sculptor-engravers are suggestive equally of Blake's Los, the inspired artist and worker in metals, and of his tyrannical Urizen, copying in his Book of brass.

The underlying unity of sculpture and engraving is also suggested by etymology: Flaxman at the beginning of his *Cyclopaedia* article derives *sculpture* from a Latin root which means both—"the verb *sculpo, I carve* or *engrave,* which is the same as the Greek γλυφω: therefore basso-relievo was called *anaglyphic* in that language, which word was also understood for carved representation in general." Evelyn tends to use words associated with sculpture and with engraving interchangeably, as when he says the commandment against graven images attests to the antiquity of sculpture or that the pe-

nates of Laban and idols of Terah are examples of engraving. Bezaleel and Aholiab, according to Evelyn, possessed "a spiritual talent" which led them to make "intaglios to adorn the high priest's
pectoral"; and Moses was the inventor of sculpture, "since whoever
was the inventor of *letters* was also doubtless the father of
SCULPTURE." After Moses, the art was pursued by the Greeks:
"Homer tells us of the engraving in the shield of Achilles."[54] Flaxman's superb rendition of the Shield in relief, one example of which
is in the Huntington Art Gallery, again indicates that he too viewed
these arts as closely related.

In discussing Blake's theory and practice in the light of traditions about ancient sculpture, we do not at all detract from his
uniqueness as an artist; nor do we violate Blake's own view of art.
"The difference between a bad Artist & a Good One," Blake wrote in
his Annotations to Reynolds, "Is the Bad Artist Seems to Copy a
Great Deal: The Good one Really does Copy a Great deal" (E 634).
Blake really did copy a great deal. The material he copied often
originated in other works of art but was assimilated by his own mind
and thoroughly recast, so that Blake could truly say, no matter how
important or how numerous his "sources," that he copied Imagination. We have seen that there are many points of congruency between Blake and certain contemporaries and predecessors, all of
whom shared an interest in ancient sculpture, but it was for Blake to
achieve works like *The Laocoön*—in which the written word and the
engraved design combine with the "wonderful originals" of his own
vision.

NOTES

1. Stephen A. Larrabee provides an introduction to the subject in
English Bards and Grecian Marbles (New York: Columbia Univ. Press, 1943),
pp. 99–119, but much of his discussion is given over to Blake's general ideas
about art.

2. *Descriptive Catalogue*, E 527, 534.

3. *A Vision of the Last Judgment*, E 546.

4. As pointed out by Larrabee, p. 100.

5. Quoted by Alfred Cobban, *Edmund Burke and the Revolt Against the
Eighteenth Century* (London: Allen & Unwin, 1929), p. 19.

6. Pl. 19, E 111; pl. 20, E 113. For discussions of the Biblical sym-

bolism here see S. Foster Damon, *William Blake: His Philosophy and Symbols* (London: Constable, 1924), pp. 414–15.

7. See *Blake Records*, ed. G.E. Bentley, Jr. (Oxford: Clarendon Press, 1969), p. 422.

8. *The Works of Sir Joshua Reynolds, Knt.* (London, 1797), I, 327. The tenth discourse, entirely devoted to sculpture, was delivered on Dec. 11, 1780 (I, 199–218).

9. Reynolds' own copy, later the property of Robert Balmanno, is in the New York Public Library; this has been examined in conjunction with another copy, formerly George Romney's, also in the New York Public Library.

10. Among these are the Michelangelo "Moses"; an aged sibyl with a book on her lap, drawn by Salviati after Michelangelo and engraved by Bisschop; Michelangelo's "Night"; figures of Cupid and Psyche after Giulio Romano; and a Madonna and Child after Francesco Parmigianino.

11. The influence on Blake of Cupid and Psyche figures from this work has been suggested by Irene H. Chayes in "The Presence of Cupid and Psyche," *Blake's Visionary Forms Dramatic*, eds. D.V. Erdman and J.E. Grant (Princeton: Princeton Univ. Press, 1970), pp. 221–24.

12. *Descriptive Catalogue*, E 434. According to Bryant, for example, Moses learned hieroglyphics in Egypt from a people called Hellenes, wrongly confused with the later Greeks: "But these writings were in reality sculptures of great antiquity: and the language was Cuthite, styled by Manethon the sacred language of Egypt" (*A New System, or an Analysis of Ancient Mythology*, London, 1776, III, 157, 158). On the influence of Bryant and other "speculative mythologists," see Edward B. Hungerford, *Shores of Darkness* (New York: Columbia Univ. Press, 1941), and Ruthven Todd, *Tracks in the Snow* (London: Gray Walls Press, 1946).

13. *The Economy of Vegetation* (Part I of *The Botanic Garden*), London, 1791, facing p. 127.

14. "Comus, with the Lady Spellbound in a Chair."

15. For an excellent discussion of Blake's use of Persian imagery, see Mary V. Jackson, "Blake and Zoroastrianism," *Blake: An Illustrated Quarterly*, 11 (1977), 72–85.

16. On the possible use of Cupid and Psyche images from Spence, see Chayes, pp. 221, 224.

17. "The Infant Hercules Throttling the Serpents" (Lessing J. Rosenwald collection), reproduced in *Pencil Drawings*, ed. Geoffrey Keynes (London: Nonesuch Press, 2nd ser., 1956), no. 5.

18. Edward Young, *The Complaint, and the Consolation, or, Night Thoughts* (London: R. Edwards, 1797), p. 35.

19. Margaret Whinney observes: "The use of engravings probably led also to an increased interest in contour, independently of the fact that

its value had been praised by Winckelmann; for tracings are known to have been made from Stuart's *Athens* by Flaxman . . ."—*Sculpture in Britain, 1530 to 1830* (Middlesex: Penguin Books, 1964), p. 155. In 1796 Flaxman gave these tracings to his pupil Thomas Alphonso Hayley.

20.   Boston Museum of Fine Arts. Robert N. Essick compares plate XIX in the same group of Winds to "Elohim Creating Adam"; see C.H. Collins Baker, "The Sources of Blake's Pictorial Expression," in *The Visionary Hand,* ed. Essick (Los Angeles: Hennessey and Ingalls, 1973), p. 126.

21.   On Blake and Barry, see Mona Wilson, *The Life of William Blake,* ed. Geoffrey Keynes (London: Oxford Univ. Press, 1971), pp. 48–49; David V. Erdman, *Blake: Prophet Against Empire* (Princeton: Princeton Univ. Press, 2nd ed., 1969), pp. 38–42; and David Bindman, *Blake As an Artist* (Oxford: Phaidon Press, 1977), p. 36.

22.   *Lectures on Painting by the Royal Academicians,* ed. Ralph N. Wornum (London: Henry G. Bohn, 1848), p. 57. Barry's lectures were published in 1809, three years after his death.

23.   P. 65. Also see p. 73: ". . . When the time, the establishments, the knowledge, original beginnings, and progressional practice which must necessarily have preceded the state in which we have found the art in Egypt, Chaldea, and the other oriental nations, be freely considered, it will be difficult to reconcile this aggregate of things with the duration and circumstances of any known people existing in that period of time between Abraham and Noah. To me these broken, unconnected knowledges seem to carry the evident marks of being really the wrecks and vestiges which might have been preserved after such a general catastrophe as the Deluge; or, rather, a deluge sufficiently universal to have destroyed those countries which could have furnished us with the clues."

24.   Tatham was the father of Blake's future (and possibly self-appointed) executor, Frederick Tatham. The elder Tatham owned a copy of *America,* inscribed to him by Blake in 1799 (see Wilson, p. 349).

25.   See Prince Hoare, *Academic Correspondence* (1804), *Academic Annals* (1804–05), and *Academic Annals* (1809); William St. Clair, *Lord Elgin and the Marbles* (London: Oxford Univ. Press, 1967), p. 150. The installation of the newly acquired ancient collections was superintended by Henry Fuseli and Richard Westmacott and described by the latter in *Account of the Arrangement of the Collections of Antique Sculpture Lately Placed in the British Museum* (Nov. 19, 1809).

26.   21 Sept. 1800, *The Letters of William Blake,* ed. Geoffrey Keynes (London: Rupert Hart-Davis, 2nd ed., 1968), p. 41.

27.   "Sculpture," in *The Cyclopaedia; or, Universal Dictionary of Arts, Science, and Literature* by Abraham Rees (London: Longman, Hurst, Rees, Orme and Brown, 1819), XXXII, not paginated.

28. *Lectures on Sculpture* (London: Bohn, 2nd ed., 1838), p. 30.

29. "If it is True What the Prophets write," E 492. Note that Flaxman too condemns Roman (but not, of course, Greek) sculpture: "They breathe the spirit of the people they commemorate—war, conquest, and universal dominion!" (*Lectures,* p. 144).

30. Pls. 12, 13; E 155. For a useful schematic representation, see S. Foster Damon, *A Blake Dictionary* (Providence, R.I.: Brown Univ. Press, 1965), p. 163.

31. See Damon, *William Blake: His Philosophy and Symbols,* pp. 440–41.

32. P. 29n. "A statue," says Cumberland, "is *all* Outline" (p. 9).

33. *William Blake: Etchings from His Works* (London: Chatto and Windus, 1878), plate III.

34. See Damon, *William Blake: His Philosophy and Symbols,* p. 408; Northrop Frye, *Fearful Symmetry* (Princeton: Princeton Univ. Press, 1947), p. 209; Morton D. Paley, *Energy and the Imagination* (Oxford: Clarendon Press, 1970), pp. 166–67.

35. See Jackson, op. cit.

36. "The Eidetic and the Borrowed Image," in *The Visionary Hand,* ed. Essick, pp. 253–302. I was unaware of this important essay (first published in *In Honour of Daryl Lindsay: Essays and Studies,* eds. F. Philipp and J. Stewart [Melbourne: Oxford Univ. Press, 1964], pp. 110–27) at the time of writing my own discussion of Blake's eidetic imagery in *Energy and the Imagination,* and therefore I would especially like to note its very great interest here. Some specific sculptural sources indicated by Burke are the Capitoline she-wolf for Dante illustration 1, "Dante Running from the Three Beasts" (Melbourne); Durga from *The Hindu Pantheon* for Dante illustration 69, "Lucifer" (Melbourne); and a lion from the Towneley collection for the *Pilgrim's Progress* illustration "Christian Passes the Lions" (Frick collection).

37. See Alexander Gilchrist, *Life of William Blake,* ed. R. Todd (London: J.M. Dent, 1942), p. 302.

38. P. 30. This book was owned by Blake and was obviously of considerable importance to him. Lessing's *Laocoön,* on the other hand, does not seem to have been known by Blake at all, though it could have been through reports and fragmentary translations. As its concerns seem to me remote from Blake's, I have not included it in this discussion.

39. Rpt. in *Blake Records,* p. 362, from *The Annual Biography and Obituary for the Year 1828,* 12 (1828), 21.

40. *Lectures,* p. 291. On Banks, see Whinney, op. cit.; on Banks's possible influence on Blake, see Bindman, *Blake As an Artist.*

41. *Academic Correspondence* (1804), ed. Prince Hoare, pp. 22–23.

42. See *Energy and the Imagination,* pp. 180–99.

43. See C.H. Tatham, *Three Designs for the National Monument* (1802), pp. 5–6.

44. See Prince Hoare, *Academic Annals* (1809), pp. 34–37; Flaxman's letter is dated 10 Oct. 1808.

45. See M.D. Paley, "The Truchsessian Gallery Revisited," *Studies in Romanticism*, 16 (1977), 165–77.

46. For reproductions of all Blake's versions of the Laocoön and accompanying discussion, see Geoffrey Keynes, *William Blake's Laocoön, a Last Testament* (Paris: Trianon Press, 1976).

47. *Blake's Laocoön*, p. 56.

48. For further discussion of the plate, see Keynes, pp. 28–30; and Irene Tayler, "Blake's Laocoön," *Blake Newsletter*, 10 (1976–77), 72–81.

49. *The Art of William Blake* (New York: Columbia Univ. Press, 1959), p. 18.

50. I am indebted to Dr. David Bindman for this suggestion, which appears in the Introduction to his *Complete Graphic Works of William Blake* (forthcoming from Thames and Hudson).

51. *Sculptura; or, the History and Art of Chalcography, and Engraving in Copper*, 2nd ed. (London: J. Payne, 1755), p. 24.

52. Pp. 25, 26. Evelyn quotes Pico della Mirandola as speaking of books in the Chaldaic tongue "on plates of different metals" and saying that these were "maimed and miserably corrupted" by the Greeks.

53. P. 25. "Stile" signifies the writing or engraving instrument.

54. Pp. 29, 30–31. Note that in the *Four Zoas* passage (E 313), quoted above, the Altar in Urizen's Golden Hall is both "Foursquare sculpturd & sweetly Engraved."

IV
CONTEMPORARIES

To recognize the fact that other artists of Blake's time shared his interests and images is to diminish his isolation, not his value. The concern with context and process, central to all the essays in this volume, finally carries us beyond any one sensibility to the community of artists that helped form it. In the concluding prophecy of *Jerusalem*, Blake asks no less of his students: to identify minutely each individual, yet to see each as a component of a dynamic unity.

Romney and Blake: Gifts of Grace and Terror

Jean H. Hagstrum

H E N R Y Fuseli gave to the Burkean sublime of grandeur and terror an insistently Michelangelesque idiom, to which he added the
accent of the demonic grotesque. That grotesque he adapted out of
the Italian mannerists, particularly Pellegrino Tibaldi. Fuseli's pictorial language possessed such power and originality that it left a lifelong impression on those who came within his orbit in Rome. That
circle included George Romney, who arrived in the Eternal City in
1773 and who soon absorbed the new idiom and used it in hundreds
of his private drawings, into which the fashionable society
painter—who had divided and was to continue on his return to
divide London with Reynolds[1]—poured the neurotic and turbulent
agitation of a mind that a few years before his death became alien-
ated. It is an eloquent fact that that defender of the Establishment,
Edward Edwards, who censured Barry, should also have censured
Romney, when he strayed from his lucrative métier. He says that
Romney "made some attempt in historical painting, but his compositions in that line are conducted too much upon those eccentric
principles which have lately been displayed in painting as well as
poetry."[2] In our own day, which is of course acquainted with the
fashionable portraits and the seemingly endless variations on the
face of Emma Hart, the layman has forgotten the Romney of
Burke's terrible sublime. But Hayley knew of it, referring to "those
excesses of impetuous and undisciplined imagination"[3] that needed
guidance—a guidance that the hermit of Felpham tried to impose
on the posthumous reputation of his painter-friend by eliminating
from the biography some of the most interesting work that Flaxman
and Blake urged him to include. For Romney, Italy must have been,
after the fashionable purlieus of London, a redemptive release,

however intoxicating to a neurotic imagination. Here he came under the spell of Fuseli; here he studied the paintings of Giotto and Cimabue; here he met Wright of Derby and began, like Fuseli, to illustrate Gray's sublime poetry. Richard Paine Knight also became an acquaintance, in 1777 writing Romney a letter on emotion and sublimity in painting. All these stimuli sent his spirits into a ferment that was to continue when he came into the Hayley circle in 1777, making it impossible for that ineffable poet—avant garde in taste but cold and clammy in spirit—to dampen the painter's aroused spirit. From now on Romney seized subjects from Milton, the Greek dramatists, and the more violent episodes of Greco-Roman mythology. He delighted in darkness, threat, mystery, the weird, and the supernatural. Violence, battles, the storming of cities attracted his always facile pencil, and the gentle tutelage of Cowper sensitized him to the great humanitarian movements of the day, notably that of the prison reformer Howard. Howard's reports on conditions in English and Continental jails led Romney to portray in many versions mysterious and suffering people lurking in dark and gloomy dungeons—privately preserved records of a *sensibilité* touched by terror, sublimity, and humanity.[4]

One of the most notable of Romney's sublime drawings, "The Spirit of God Moving On the Face of the Waters," inspired by *Paradise Lost* and representing God the Father, is well known and has been seen as a direct influence on Blake's figure of Urizen, who with extended arms appears as the antagonist in *America* (Plate 2) and as the cause of the misery in the portrayal of the hideous "Lazar House" (Plate 102). The boldness of Romney's imagination may be gauged from the fact that this representation of God seems to have been considered impious by his son John, who entitled it "Jupiter Pluvius."[5] Like Barry, Mortimer, and Fuseli, Romney also absorbed Shakespeare and transformed him into a version of the Burkean sublime. His fine head of Edgar, the youthful face unshaven in its profile, shows depths of suffering in the open mouth, the eyes, and the slightly flared nostrils. Bolingbroke from *Henry VI* is mad and haunted by a palpable fiend, and in "Miranda, Prospero, and Caliban" Romney chooses to make the stormy sea and the wrecked ship evoke awesome fright in the delicate girl, not the tender concern upon which Shakespeare dwells. Like other members of the "sublime" school, Romney found the head of Lear irresistible. (Many studies and one powerful pen and ink sketch may have preceded the painting now at Dallam.) King Lear in the storm raises sad and suffering eyes as his beard and hair are blown to the right.[6]

Romney's powerful and, if we judge by the fashionable portraits, untypical renditions of the terrible sublime can be further illustrated by drawings from the Walker collection in Liverpool. In "The Birth of Shakespeare" (Plate 113), a drawing inspired by Gray's *Progress of Poesie* in which the infant Shakespeare is attended by Nature, by Comedy, by Tragedy, we can allow the figures of Comedy and Nature and of the child himself to stand without comment since they are representations of the delicacy we shall discuss later on. But Tragedy strikingly anticipates the demonic in Blake. A sinister figure with a hood, mantle, and a smothering blanket, she foretells the "mother of my mortal part" about whom Blake sings with such fear and awe, and she summons from the vasty deep of Blake's fear of female dominance the figure on plate three of *Jerusalem,* who sits like a cowled sibyl judging mankind, disposing of it to the right and to the left. The expression in Romney's figure is one of heavy disappointment as the lidded eyes look down and as the whole pose tends to be leaden and earthbound.

In "Atossa's Dream"[7] the wife of Darius sees her handsome son prostrate on the ground in ignominious defeat. Her husband, Xerxes' father, appears dim in the dark clouds above, emerging from deep black recesses, a mantled ghost, who spreads his arms in the manner of Urizen. The two women to the left express in their bodily positions, their arm and hand gestures, and their faces the terror that the scene is intended to invoke.

Another black-chalk drawing from Liverpool, inspired by a recent translation of Aeschylus and entitled "The Ghost of Darius" (Plate 114), contains an even more sinister spirit, one closer to the human and therefore more palpable and menacing. The real world represented by the grieving Atossa to the right-hand is separated from the supernatural world, as so often in Blake, by a cloud. Beside the anticipation in the figure of Darius of many Urizens with arms stretched out, the crouched and kneeling figures, which appear again and again in Blake, are anticipated by the three Persian elders who had prayed for the appearance of Darius and who now bend their backs in holy fear, their hands clasped together. A close analog is a central *Job* illustration, when God speaks to Job from the whirlwind and sends Job's friends and counsellors into a prostration of terror.

These—and many other illustrations could be given—must be allowed to stand for Romney's expressions of the sublimity of terror. The drawings in black chalk given by Romney's son John to the Liverpool institution and now in the Walker Art Gallery are among the most striking anticipations of Blake in existence, equal in relevant power to the better known influences from Fuseli and in some ways more central because they lack the angular and perverse neuroticism of the Swiss painter's achievement. No one would say that the drawings of Romney that expressed his hidden and private nature rank in quality with the Michelangelos, Raphaels, Giulios, and Tibaldis that also influenced Blake. But they are closer to Blake in time, hence they possess a kind of *Zeitgeist* authority that the remoter pieces lack. They also have on them the impress of personal suffering and thwarted choice. Romney, a brilliantly successful painter in daily contact with the fashionable world, perhaps experienced conflicts which even Blake, himself a sufferer, did not and could not know, but which may have leapt like an arc of fiery inspiration from Romney's sheet to the poet's spirit.

When William Hayley wrote that the cartoons of Romney "were examples of the sublime and terrible, at that time perfectly new in English art,"[8] he told only part of the story, the part that we have just discussed under the heading of the Burkean sublime and the grotesque of Fuseli. The story remains incomplete without consideration of another Burkean quality, the antithetical one of beauty. Supported by the enormous pioneering prestige of Raphael and by the more graceful examples of Correggio and Guido Reni, beauty was one of the dominant strains in the eighteenth century, one that could be lightened into grace and deepened—the word may seem too strong but the development was profound and complex—*deepened* into delicacy. Both grace and delicacy are alike applicable to Romney and Blake. *Grace* was conceived of as beauty in motion. One of the inescapable characteristics of the art of Blake is that light and beautiful forms are everywhere set into appropriate movement. And the word *delicate,* with all its old and its changing nuances, throws a revealing light on Blake and on the private world of Romney.

When he was in Rome with Fuseli, Romney did more than investigate Michelangelo and mannerists like Tibaldi and absorb the neurotically grotesque and demonic idiom that characterized the circle we have already discussed. In a dramatic monologue by Tennyson entitled "Romney's Remorse" (the artist had deserted his wife almost at the beginning of his highly successful career and did not return to her until shortly before his death) the title character says that in Europe he "stood / Before the great Madonna-masterpieces / Of ancient art in Paris, or in Rome." Ignoring Tennyson's Victorian censure of Romney's marital behavior, we must agree that the artist did respond during his Italian stay to the delicacies of Raphael, Correggio, and other members of that school. But living in the latter part of the eighteenth century, Romney inherited a *complex* conception of delicacy, one to which the whole course of English literature and English sensibility had made its contribution and one with which his exposure to fashionable life and to successful portraiture and even to a bland but still avant-garde intellectual like Hayley would have acquainted him. Romney does not simply take over "the grace beyond the reach of art" of Pope, who had admired the "graceful" painters, especially the famous "air" of Guido. In the novels of Richardson and Rousseau, and even in the "Gothic" situations of Mrs. Radcliffe, he could have encountered one of the newer obsessive concerns of the age, the threat to virginal delicacy in physically or psychologically dangerous and unknown environments. And in fact what some of the drawings in Liverpool and elsewhere demonstrate beyond any cavil is that the painter, like many literary predecessors, has associated delicacy and mystery, grace and the threat to innocence. He has presented innocence trembling on the edge of experience or entering it or triumphing over it or withdrawing from it. Greek-like, delicate, virginal maidens in danger, sometimes of abhorrent sexual assault but sometimes of half-desired and fully sanctioned sexual experience, are given powerful iconic expression in the private and hidden art of Romney.

Threatened innocence is also a great Blakean theme, and in Romney Blake might have observed visual forms that expressed it successfully and suggestively. Romney's free-flowing line, gathering drapery into graceful folds, outlining the human body and partly exposing it, can be illustrated in innumerable drawings. The "Cassandra," the "Study for the Viscountess Bulkley as Hebe," and several figure studies possess all those qualities of graceful motion and also facial expressions of distress, pity, freshness, naiveté, wonder, and beauty—those Miranda-like qualities that made Shakespeare's heroine a favorite in the period—qualities that recall Botticelli and other "Pre-Raphaelites." In his "Captive or Dejected Woman," a pen and ink drawing now at Yale, the profile is delicately Grecian and the flow of body and drapery is extremely graceful, the figure reminding us of Blakean virgins standing on the edge of experience.[9] Romney's use of the King Lear motifs reminds one less of the terrible sublime than of Blake's *Songs of Innocence and of Experience.* Consider the death of Cordelia (Plate 115), in which the dead daughter lies on a flat bed surrounded by six mourning figures—an example of one of the powerful pre-Romantic themes, the lamentation over a dead body, a secularized version of the sacred lamentation over the body of Christ removed from the cross. Cordelia's posture is that of a mortuary figure and anticipates the title page to the *Songs of Experience.*

Romney illustrated the story of Orpheus and Eurydice in at least three black chalk drawings, all of them anticipating *The Book of Thel.* The first[10] shows Eurydice fleeing from Aristaeus, the son of Apollo and the father of Actaeon, who fell in love with the wife of Orpheus and pursued her. Here Eurydice is presented as crossing a stream on a plank, not seeing the water snake which is ready to administer the fatal bite. Resembling that of *Thel* and *Tiriel,* the landscape is mysterious and misty. The young lady is delicately beautiful but frightened, her hands spread in horror, her gown gauzy, her feet bare, her filleted hair flowing backwards. In the second of these drawings (Plate 116), Orpheus, youthful, Grecian, and handsome, embraces his wife and attempts to hold her back from the forces that inexorably bear her away. The two figures in the sky that point towards Hades suggest the forward motion of Blake's sightless couriers of the air in his color-printed drawing entitled "Pity" (Plate 45), and the swirls and vortexes in the atmosphere remind one of the two nudes and the arcs that they describe in the grain on the twelfth plate of *Europe.* In the last of the drawings (Plate 117), Orpheus loses Eurydice, who, like Thel, shrinks back to the place of her origins, already a wraith as she vainly reaches out her arms, impelled by the fates to the misty region and pathetically withdrawing from her loving husband's arms, which are held out to receive her. From Blake's earliest relief engravings where the child reaches out toward a bird or a mother toward a child (Plate 12) through too many of his designs to specify, the stretching of arms that almost touch and that strive to end separation and restore harmony is a characteristic Blakean signature. It is profoundly anticipated by Romney in this series.

It has been noted by more than one scholar that traces of the Cupid and Psyche legend from Apuleius appear in Blake's *The Book of Thel.*[11] It has not, so far as I am aware, been suggested that the *visual* antecedents of the main character may lie in Romney's black chalk drawings now in Liverpool. If in fact Romney's series did kindle Blake's imagination (they were created around 1776), it was perhaps because they represented a highly original response to the famous legend, which had been illustrated innumerable times in more than one epoch and which was obsessive among the pre-Romantics. Romney breaks sharply with the erotic-uxorial treatment of the theme, of which the best early example is Giulio Romano's "Sala di Psyche" in Mantua. Nor does Romney share the drive toward unisexuality, in which both Cupid and Psyche are mirror images of one another, a vision of androgynous love best exemplified by Canova's and Thorvaldsen's renditions in marble.[12] Romney instead concentrates on the great eighteenth-century literary theme already alluded to, that of innocence and danger, that of delicacy threatened by hostile natural, social, or supernatural forces. In all of them Psyche is a modest, gauzily-dressed, Grecian girl—like the classical shepherdess, Thel—caught in a misty and mysterious landscape which produces a look of passive wonder or sad acceptance or kneeling submission and supplication. Seven drawings survive. (One is missing and may have treated the nuptials of Cupid and Psyche; if so, that joyful scene would have been out of harmony with the remaining works in the series.) A clearly-drawn girl, modestly attired, has just arrived in a supernatural landscape of gray, misty uncertainty, where the issue of her safety and success is obviously in doubt. In one scene (Plate 118) a worried Cupid leans over Psyche, who has escaped from the palace and who modestly covers one breast as she bows her head. Back of the lovely girl lies a black cave, and threatening clouds and swirls of mist suggest danger. In another scene (Plate 119) Psyche supplicates Juno, kneeling, very much in the posture of the lily in *The Book of Thel,* while the veiled statue of the goddess reminds one of Blake's representations of classical marbles. But perhaps the most striking anticipation of all is "Psyche by the River Styx" (Plate 120). The figure of Psyche, seen in profile, suggests strongly the somewhat more static and placid Thel from the title page, who is also seen in profile contemplating an object of curiosity. But the real equivalent in Blake of Romney's scene is the final page of poetic text in *The Book of Thel,* where the virgin contemplates her own grave plot (that is, future sexual experience) and flees away from it with a shriek. In Romney Psyche stands before a black hole, from which a wind blows her hair and mantle—a somber but haunting portrayal of innocence trembling on the edge of the unknown. The issue may be said to be in doubt. In Blake the shriek and the flight show that it is not.

It was earlier said that what may have given Romney's private vision of threatened innocence its exemplary and even mythical force is that it recalled an important tradition which the eighteenth century brilliantly and charismatically exploited, both in sentimental and Gothic fictions. And it was also suggested that Romney, by translating that obsessive literary theme into visual expression, may have made a profound impact on the imagination of Blake, whose central problem was to bring the psychological, moral, religious, and esthetic concerns of his age into visual and verbal ideogram. Outside the series in Liverpool, in a drawing (Plate 121) that is only in the sketch stage and is now at the Fitzwilliam, Cambridge, Romney once more—and in a sharply focused way—exemplifies this theme. Psyche does not here so much contemplate the Styx as Charon. Nude, angry, his *membrum virile* visible, the rower is faced by Psyche, who sits in the prow of the boat looking toward him. Her back is nude, she seems to be covering her breasts, she looks chaste and prim and confident in these fearful surroundings on the way to the underworld. Blake has nowhere exactly duplicated this design, but his visions of women entering experience here find concentrated visual anticipation. The calm and unruffled fortitude of Charon's delicate and graceful passenger is, however, sophisticated into greater drama and variety by the Blake who created Thel, Ona, Oothoon, and Vala.

If, as I believe, a linear and thematic stamp from Romney is visible on Blake's works from the early *Tiriel* to the very late Dante illustrations, we should ask if biographical evidence supports what the eye discovers. Romney appears to have admired Blake, bestowing extravagant praise on "A Breach in a City Wall."[13] A story has persisted that during the difficult 1790s Romney and Blake were friends, and that the older artist gave to the younger the vine and fig tree which so much pleased the poet in his garden at Lambeth. There is abundant evidence that the admiration evinced by Romney was usually reciprocated by Blake. The only criticism of Romney that has survived comes from the year 1810, a time when Blake expressed profound disagreement with Romney about line and drawing and when he felt very close to his mentor Albrecht Dürer, believing that Heath, Stothard, and even such a good friend as Flaxman had underrated line and had seemed to fall into the heresy that linear drawings spoiled an engraving—a position that Blake regarded as a gratuitous absurdity and a personal insult. But during the still formative years 1803 to 1804 Blake heaped praises upon the drawings and even the paintings of Romney. He called "the Mrs. Siddons," a half-length portrait, "very fine," "in his best style." He called a figure of Hecate "a very sublime drawing." The "Pliny in the Eruption of Vesuvius" was "very clever and indeed . . . sublime." "The Shipwreck" (one of the two Romney drawings engraved by Blake that Hayley finally used in the biography) was a "beautiful performance." The "Lear and Cordelia" he regarded as "an incomparable production," "exquisite for expression" "most pathetic"— "the heads of Lear and Cordelia can never be surpassed and other attendants are admirable." And after that quasi-mystical experience at the Truchsessian Gallery Blake paid tribute to Romney, "whose spiritual aid has not a little conduced to my restoration to the light of art." (That aid must have been posthumous for when Blake wrote those lines Romney had been dead for two years.) One could perhaps take a cynical attitude and believe that because Blake was very much in need of work, because Hayley admired Romney and was now doing his biography, and because Romney's work tended to be tonal in effect, full of depth in light and shadows—that for all these reasons Blake was hypocritical in praising an artist whom he really regarded as an enemy to the linearity of his engraving style. But such a cynical view does not fit what we know of Blake's character or what we have seen of the strikingly powerful anticipations of Blake's style and iconography in the chalk drawings of the older artist.[14]

And yet the question still remains: did Blake in the late 1780s and early 1790s, when he began his work of composite art, with *Tiriel, Thel,* and the *Songs of Innocence*—did he at that early date know Romney's drawings, which were then concealed from the public eye and which even today are not widely known or studied? The strong likelihood is that he did. Flaxman, a friend of Blake, was also a friend of Romney, and knew his work intimately. In a letter to Hayley, which should perhaps be dated 1784, shortly after the friendship between the two men was formed in 1783, Flaxman wrote as follows: "I have before mentioned that Mr. Romney thinks [Blake's] historical drawings rank with those of Michelangelo." It seems extremely unlikely that work by Romney so close to the spirit of Blake would have been kept from a potential disciple, particularly when both had a common friend who admired the traits that the two shared. Some years later, in 1804, Flaxman wrote to Hayley about Romney's cartoons, which he was anxious for Blake to engrave "in a bold manner" that would suit the drawings and that would also be congenial to Blake. These drawings, he said, expressed the "painter's noblest sentiments and grandest thoughts." Flaxman had been highly perceptive, sensing a deep affinity between Blake and Romney and hoping that Hayley would observe the same. But Hayley surprised Flaxman by not seeming to remember "the whole catalogue of [Romney's] Chalk Cartoons as I think it was Your opinion in common with other Sufficient judges that they were the noblest of his studies." Then Flaxman goes on to mention some of the titles we have already encountered, including the one of the shipwreck, which Blake did finally engrave and which was published in Hayley's *Life of Romney*.[15]

The entire exchange between Hayley and Flaxman in January, 1804, is fascinating. The correspondence shows that Romney's cartoons had long been admired, so long that Hayley had seemed to have forgotten them. (Or were they too powerful for him, making him shy away from their reproduction in his bland life of the artist?) Flaxman believed these were Romney's best works and also believed that Blake would be their proper engraver because of the similarity of spirit that he seems to have discerned between the two. If we may take our cue from Flaxman, no mean critic and a friend of both artists, we can make the not at all unreasonable assumption that the work which strikes us today as being so unmistakable an anticipation of Blake was in fact known and admired by the younger painter. We lack external substantiation that the hidden Romney of both the sublime and delicate drawings was seen by Blake's eyes; but the evidence of the style alone appears sufficient to make a direct influence likely.

Scholarship has only begun to open an insufficiently explored chapter in the story of Blake's relations to English art. Hundreds of Romney drawings have not been dated, the themes and subjects of many have not been identified, and little is known about their accessibility to Blake or to anyone else. Perhaps not all or even most of them are classifiable under the categories we have used, the terrible sublime and the beauty of graceful delicacy. Drawings of these types often anticipate Blake in visual vocabulary—in gesture, posture, expression, attitude, grouping of figures. But such details are less important than the fusion of icon and form—the union of theme and manner—that suggests we are here in the foothills of Blake's visual landscape and psychological iconography. If Romney gave to Blake an opportunity to see in his developing years Urizenic terror as a visualizable personal and cosmic force threatening man's aspirations and young Innocence as a gracious personification confronting unknown and mysterious Experience, then we have a major intellectual and artistic gift which ought to be studied with the full resources of modern scholarship and criticism.

Did Blake's other contemporaries and friends—Fuseli, Flaxman, Barry, Mortimer—contribute gifts of equal importance? That iconic motifs, pictorial arrangements, figures, and scenes came to the poet-painter from these other "prophetic" and imaginatively avant-garde artists has been demonstrated beyond cavil. Did they also contribute ideas as weighty as those we have encountered in the Romney nexus? Fuseli doubtless did; such contributions by others need still to be investigated. Perhaps only after detailed comparative analyses have been made and only after the Romney archive has been fully opened and studied will we know whether that fashionable portraitist deserves the very special place Blake seems to have accorded him by calling his work "a spiritual aid" which, like the overpowering experience at the Truchsessian Gallery, helped induce a "restoration to the light of art."

NOTES

1. "Reynolds and Romney divide the town, I am of the Romney faction." Lord Chancellor Thurlow, quoted in John Romney, *Memoirs of the Life and Works of George Romney* (London, 1830), p. 171.

2. *Anecdotes of Painting* (London, 1808), p. 278.

3. William Hayley, *Life of Romney* (London, 1809), pp. 72–73.

4. See entry "George Romney" in Frederick Cummings and Allen Staley, *Romantic Art in Britain Paintings and Drawings 1760–1860* (Detroit and Philadelphia: Institute of Arts and Museum of Art, 1968) pp. 73–80.

5. Ann Crookshank, "The Drawings of George Romney," *Burlington*

Magazine, 99 (Feb., 1957), Fig. 18 and pp. 42–48 esp. p. 46; Anthony Blunt, *The Art of William Blake* (New York: Columbia Univ. Press, 1959), Plate 21c. Of this wash drawing, now in the Fitzwilliam Museum, Cambridge, Blunt says: "Never did Romney come so close . . . to the spirit of Blake . . . " (p. 42).

6. The head of Edgar and the figure of Bolingbroke are reproduced in Robert R. Wark, *The Drawings of Romney* (Alhambra, Calif.: Borden Pub. Co., 1970). These also appear, along with "Miranda . . . ," as Figs. 2, 8, and 9 in Ellen Sharp, "Drawings by George Romney at Yale," *Antiques* 86 (Nov., 1964), 598–603. Studies of the head of Lear are in the collection of the Kendal Borough Council.

7. A black chalk drawing, now at the Walker Art Gallery, Liverpool, fully described but not reproduced in the catalogue, *Early English Drawings and Watercolours* (Liverpool: Walker Art Gallery, 1968), item no. 4040.

8. *Life of Romney,* p. 309. Hayley says that some of Romney's cartoons had perished.

9. All the works referred to in this paragraph are reproduced in Wark.

10. *Early English Drawings* (at Walker, Liverpool), item no. 4029. Not reproduced but described. Studies for these finished drawings are preserved at the Fitzwilliam Museum, Cambridge. Thurlow, who sat to Romney for his portrait, translated the Orpheus and Eurydice passage from Virgil, highlighting the pathos and drama of the scenes and interpolating advice to the painter. See John Romney, *Memoirs,* pp. 168–72, where the Lord Chancellor's highly emotional translation is printed.

11. Kathleen Raine, "Blake's Cupid and Psyche," Chap. 7 of *Blake and Tradition* (Princeton: Princeton Univ. Press, 1968), I, 180–203; Irene H. Chayes, "The Presence of Cupid and Psyche" in David V. Erdman and John E. Grant, eds., *Blake's Visionary Forms Dramatic* (Princeton: Princeton Univ. Press, 1970), pp. 214–43.

12. See my forthcoming article on Eros and Psyche in *Critical Inquiry.*

13. Archibald G. B. Russell, *The Letters of William Blake* (London: Methuen, 1906), p. xxi. Russell finds that "Har and Heva Bathing" bears a "visible mark" of Romney's style in the figures, the light effects, and the forest background (pp. xxii–xxiii).

14. The quotations and references of this paragraph are drawn from *The Letters of William Blake,* ed. Geoffrey Keynes (London: Rupert Hart-Davis, 1968), pp. 63, 88–9, 91–3, 96–7, 101–102, 107, 111–12. The attitudes of 1810 come from the *Notebook* ("Public Address"), E 560–62.

15. Flaxman's letters are quoted from G. E. Bentley, Jr., *Blake Records* (Oxford: Clarendon Press, 1969), pp. 27 and n.3, 137–39, 152, 153. See also *Blake Records,* p. 627.

A Jewel in an Ethiop's Ear

The Book of Enoch as Inspiration for
William Blake, John Flaxman,
Thomas Moore, and Richard Westall

G. E. Bentley, Jr.

Enoch walked with God; and he
was not, for God took him
—Genesis 5:24

T H E apocryphal Book of Enoch was first published in a modern
European language in 1821 after centuries of obscurity and a history in its own way as wonderful as the tales which it relates. Despite
the fact that it was venerated by the very early Christians and
exerted a major influence on the New Testament, it seems to have
attracted the attention of few thinking contemporaries when it was
first published in 1821, and even the theologians showed little interest in it for a time.

However, within a very few years its divine eroticism had attracted the attention of five major artists and poets. Almost immediately, Byron's friend the popular poet Thomas Moore wrote a
novel entitled *The Epicurean* in which appeared an episode called *The
Loves of the Angels* (separately published in 1823) which derives from
The Book of Enoch. Moore's *Loves of the Angels* (1823) was illustrated
by one of the most prolific and successful artists of the time, Richard
Westall. Byron's own *Heaven and Earth* (1823) derives from The
Book of Enoch.[1] John Flaxman, Blake's intimate friend and the

This paper, in a much briefer oral version, was read at the Santa Barbara
Conference by my generous friend Professor Morton Paley because my teaching
responsibilities at the University of Poona in India unfortunately made it impossible
for me to be present at the Conference. I am very grateful to Professor Paley for
this last in a long series of kindnesses to me.

213

greatest English sculptor of his age, made a series of unpublished drawings for it before he died in 1826. And William Blake made a number of powerful and enigmatic designs for it before his death in 1827. This artistic response is important in itself, has scarcely been remarked upon before,[2] and is especially intriguing in view of the general apathy which seems to have greeted the appearance of the book. These works, their source, and what they have in common deserve to be better known.

The present essay is divided into three parts: I. The History of The Book of Enoch; II. A Summary of the Most Influential Part of The Book of Enoch; and III. An Account of the Works by Moore, Westall, Flaxman, and Blake Based on The Book of Enoch, together with reproductions of the chief designs.

I. THE HISTORY OF THE BOOK OF ENOCH

The Book of Enoch was apparently written in Hebrew or Aramaic[3] in the First Century before Christ[4] by a Jew who lived a little north of the Black Sea.[5] It was written at a time when belief in contemporary miracles and prophecies was waning and when religious legalism was waxing. Consequently, in order to gain credence for the book, it was attributed by its author(s) to the Prophet Enoch, who was in the seventh generation from Adam (Jude 14) and who was translated to heaven at the age of 365 in 3017 B.C. according to the chronology of Archbishop Ussher: "Enoch walked with God; and he was not, for God took him" (Genesis 5:24; "Enoch was translated that he might not see death," Hebrews 11:5).

For several centuries, The Book of Enoch was evidently accepted as a genuine prophecy, being well known to early Jews and Christians; according to one authority, "The influence of 1 Enoch on the New Testament has been greater than that of all the other apocryphal and pseudo-epigraphical books taken together."[6] It was quoted in Jude 14–15 and referred to elsewhere in the New Testament, but there are few references to it after the second century A.D. Both Enoch and Jude were excluded from the biblical canon by the Council of Nicaea in 325 A.D. (Jude because it quoted Enoch), but Jude was reinstated at the Council of Trent (1545–63).[7] By the time of Jerome in the fourth century A.D., The Book of Enoch was taken to be apocryphal, and there are only occasional references to it thereafter. No early copy survives in Hebrew or Aramaic, and only chapters 1–32:6 survive in Greek.[8] It was mentioned in Origen, *Contra Celsam*, lib 5, and in Tertullian, *de Idolol.*, c. 4; chapter 7:1 to chapter 10:15 was given in parallel Greek and Latin texts by Georgius Syncellus, *Chronographia* (printed in J. J. Scaliger, *Thesaurus Temporum*, 1606) and reprinted by J. H. Fabricius, *Codex Pseudoepigraphis Veteris Testementi* (1703), 179–198 (reprinted in Laurence, *The Book of Enoch* [1838], pp. 203–212), who names some twenty places where Enoch is cited or quoted (according to Laurence, p. iv); and it is cited in the Cabala. But in Europe generally it disappeared so completely that its very existence was doubted: "Enoch . . . was not, for God took him."

From a very early date, the Church of Ethiopia adopted The Book of Enoch (*Metsahaf Henoc*) as a canonical book of the Bible, and in Ethiopic translations it appeared between 2 Kings and Job—at least it did in the copy of James Bruce. The Ethiopian Christians and Jews believed it "to be an antediluvian monument" obtained in pagan times even before the books of Moses (Laurence [1838], p. viii). The only known complete copies today are in Ethiopic, and some twenty-nine copies are known, all rather late ones, and all notably corrupt[9]—not surprisingly, considering their history of translation from Hebrew to Greek to Ethiopic. According to Bruce, "It is the most classical book of the Abyssinians," being "written in the pure Ethiopic Language, or Feez" (Laurence [1838] p. xi). But during many centuries, while The Book of Enoch was revered by the Ethiopians, it was virtually forgotten in Europe.

It was occasionally talked of, however, and Louis XIV's great minister Colbert tried vainly to get a copy for the king. His first emissary was refused permission to enter Abyssinia, and the second was assassinated at Sennaar[10] in Nubia (Laurence [1838], p. ix). In the seventeenth century, Peiresc obtained what he thought was a copy, but when Ludolph examined this in 1683 it was found to be a work entirely distinct from The Book of Enoch.[11] Consequently, for a time it was believed that even the pseudo-Enoch was a mere rumor.

There were a few who were concerned with the known fragments,[12] but it was not until the formidable Scots explorer James Bruce reached Ethiopia in his triumphant but vain search for the sources of the Nile in 1768–1773 that The Book of Enoch was seen whole by a modern European who recorded the fact. While struggling with incredible difficulties,[13] Bruce discovered that the Ethiopians preserved The Book of Enoch in their Bible, and in great excitement he obtained three beautiful copies to bring home with him: "I think it is the most curious and most rare thing I brought from my travels." One copy he left in Paris for the Library of Louis XV, one copy he gave to the Bodleian Library in Oxford, and one copy he kept for himself. And once again the great silence set in, though Bruce had certainly brought to light one of the most influential prophetic books of the time of Christ.

Bruce himself described the work in his *Travels to Discover the Source of the Nile* (1790), I, 497–500; he translated chapters 1–18 in manuscript, and his editor E. Murray summarized its contents in the octavo edition of Bruce's *Travels* (1805), II, 424–426.[14] Dr. Woide made an incorrect transcript of the Paris copy Bruce had given to the King[15] and translated a few detached passages (not all of it, as Bruce said) into Latin, according to Laurence (1821), p. vii. M. Silvestre de Sacy published a Latin translation of chapters 1–3, 6–16, 22–23 in the *Magazin Encyclopédique*, I (1800), 382, and this was reprinted by Laurence (1821), 169–180. Bruce's copy of the Ethiopic Psalter containing The Book of Enoch is referred to in [William Beloe], *The Sexagenerian* (London, 1818), II, 47. But these references are all partial and somewhat obscure. While a reader of Latin or Greek could have had access before 1820 to the most exciting and influential part of The Book of Enoch, the account of the seduction of the daughters of men by the angels of God, it is exceedingly unlikely that any of the artists and poets with whom we are concerned in fact did so.

The first translation of The Book of Enoch into a modern European language was made by the Reverend Professor (later Archbishop) Richard Laurence: *The Book of Enoch The Prophet: An Apocryphal Production, Supposed to Have Been Lost for Ages; But Discovered at the Close of the Last Century in Abyssinia; now First Translated from An Ethiopic MS. in the Bodleian Library* (Oxford: At the University Press for the Author: Sold by J. Parker [Oxford]; and by Messrs. Rivington, London, 1821).[16] Laurence's book consists of a "Preliminary Dissertation" about the history of the book (pp. iii–xlviii), his translation into English of The Book of Enoch (pp. 1–168), Silvestre de Sacy's Latin translation of 1800 (pp. 169–180), and notes on Laurence's translation (pp. 181–214). It was published so quietly that it was scarcely noticed by Laurence's contemporaries; I have only encountered one review before 1829.[17] Even eight years after its publication, *The Christian Observer* could say that "the work does not appear to have excited much attention among biblical scholars" (p. 419). What attention there was was exhibited chiefly in J. M. Butt, *The Genuineness of the Book of Enoch Investigated* (1827) ("neither convincing nor scholar-like," according to *The Christian Observer*, p. 423), and in John Oxlee, *Three Letters to the Lord Archbishop of Cashel, on the Recent Apocryphal Publications of his Grace &c. &c.* (1827), esp. pp. 107–119 (defending the genuineness of The Book of Enoch), and these two plus Laurence's translation were vigorously attacked in an anonymous review in *The Christian Observer*, 29 (July-August 1829), 417–426, 496–503. The crux of the argument against its authenticity, according to *The Christian Observer*, was that a) Jude would only have quoted a *book* if it had been inspired; b) if Enoch's *book* had been inspired, God would not have permitted it to be lost; c) therefore Jude was not quoting from the *book* of Enoch (he was quoting an oral tradition), and the *book* we have must postdate Jude—it is by a Christian Jew writing about 140 A.D.[18] This argument today seems neither convincing nor scholarlike. According to the same account, "By far the greater number of [*unnamed*] biblical critics gives up the point of inspiration, and even of the authenticity, of the Book of Enoch," and *The Christian Observer*'s anonymous author was so alarmed by "the absurdity of its legends, and the grossness, and even obscenity, of some of its descriptions" that "We may ... perhaps regret, that this translation was not made in a language [*i.e., Latin*] accessible only to scholars" (pp. 425, 501, 502). Perhaps the most effective rejoinder to this complaint had already been made by Laurence: The Book of Enoch can "only be deemed injurious, when pressed into the service of vice and infidelity" (1821, p. xlvii).

II. A SUMMARY OF THE MOST INFLUENTIAL PART
OF THE BOOK OF ENOCH

Laurence recognized that "different parts of the book itself may have been composed at different periods ... they may have been different tracts, as well as tracts composed by different authors" (1838, p. lviii). The oldest of these separate parts is The Book of Noah, which forms the basis of Enoch chapters 6–11, 54:7–55:2, 60, 65–69:25, 106–107 (according to the R. H. Charles translation [1912], p. xi), and which is also partially preserved in Jubilees. In

1836, the Rev. E. Murray classed the parts of The Book of Enoch as:

1 The Ancient Book
2 The Prophecy
3 The second Ancient Book
4 The first Book of Watchers
5 The second Book of Watchers
6 The first Book of Secrets, or Vision of Wisdom
7 The second Book of Secrets, or Vision of Wisdom
8 The Vision of Noah, or History
9 The second Book of the Vision of Noah
10 The Book of Astronomy

With most of these books we need have little concern; some are exceedingly obscure, and I find only glancing allusions to them in the poets and artists with whom we are concerned. The most influential parts of The Book of Enoch were chapters 7–16, which constitute mostly what Murray called The first and second Books of Watchers. Since these texts survived in Greek and were translated into Latin, a classical scholar might have been familiar with them, but it is very likely that all four of the English artists and authors derived their inspiration from the 1821 Laurence translation.

These early chapters are based on a very early myth, perhaps a Persian one, about the corruption of the earth by demons before the coming of Zoroaster (according to Charles [1912], p. 14). The immediate source is Genesis 6:1–4:

> And it came to pass, when men began to multiply on the face of the earth, and daughters were born unto them, That the sons of God saw the daughters of men, and that they were fair; and they took them wives of all which they chose. And the Lord said, My spirit shall not always strive with man, for that he also is flesh: yet his days shall be an hundred and twenty years. There were giants in the earth in those days: and also after that, when the sons of God came in unto the daughters of men, and they bare children to them, the same became mighty men which were of old, men of renown.

The account in The Book of Enoch is essentially an amplification of this passage.

In Enoch, after "the sons of men had multiplied in those days, . . . daughters [*were*] born to them elegant and beautiful." Two hundred Watchers of heaven (i.e., angels) beheld them, they became enamoured of them, saying to each other; Come, let us select for ourselves wives from the progeny of men, and let us beget children.

(7:1–2)

In order to keep the Watchers to their purpose, and to spread the guilt, Samyaza, the chief Prefect,[19] persuades them all to bind "themselves by mutual execrations . . . [*on*] the top of mount Armon [*Hermon*]" (7:7).

> Then they took wives, each choosing for himself; when they began to approach, and with whom they co-habited, teaching them sorcery,[20] incantations, and the dividing of roots and trees [*as well as astronomy,*[21] *the making of*] swords, knives, shields, breastplates, . . . mirrors . . . bracelets and ornaments, the use of paint, the beautifying of the eyebrows, *the use of* stones . . . and of all sorts of dyes, so that the world became altered.
>
> (7:10, 9:5, 8:1)

The women bore to them giants three hundred cubits high (about five hundred feet tall), who "devoured all *which* the [*agricultural*] labour of men produced; until it became impossible to feed them," so that the giants became carnivores, eating the flesh of "birds, beasts, reptiles, and fishes" and "drink[*ing*] their blood" (7:11–14). Then "Impiety increased;[22] fornication multiplied; and they transgressed and corrupted all their ways. . . . Men, being destroyed, cried out; and their voice reached to heaven" (8:2, 8:9). They were heard by "Michael and Gabriel, Raphael, Suryal, and Uriel," who reported "to their Lord, the King" that Azazyel "has taught every species of iniquity upon earth, and has disclosed to the world all the secret things which are done in the heavens" (9:1, 3, 5).

Consequently God sent Arsayalalyur to Enoch to

> explain to him the consummation which is about to take place; for all the earth shall perish; the waters of a deluge shall come over the whole earth,[23] and all things which are in it shall be destroyed
>
> (10:4)

except for Noah. God sent Raphael to

> Bind Azazyel[24] hand and foot; cast him into darkness; and opening the desert which is in Dudael, cast him in there. Throw upon him hurled and pointed stones . . . cover his face, that he may not

see the light. And in the great day of judgment let him be cast into the fire. Vivify the earth, which the angels have corrupted; and announce life to it, that I may revive it.

(10:6–10)

God sent Gabriel

to the biters, to the reprobates, to the children of fornication; and destroy the children of fornication, the offspring of the Watchers, from among men; bring them forth, and excite them against one another. Let them perish by *mutual* slaughter.

(10:13)

God sent Michael "to Samyaza, and to the others who are with him" to announce their crimes to them, to let them witness the perdition of their beloved sons, and then to

bind them for seventy generations underneath the earth, even to the day of judgment.... Destroy all the souls addicted to dalliance, and the offspring of the Watchers, for they have tyrannized over mankind.... [*Then*] Let every evil work be destroyed; The plant of righteousness and of rectitude appear, and its produce become a blessing [*in a time of peace*].... Then shall all the children of men be righteous, and all nations shall pay me divine honours, and bless me; all shall adore me.

(10:15, 18, 20–21, 26)

Enoch delivers the messages to the delinquent Watchers and is persuaded by them to present their prayer for mercy to God:

Then I wrote a memorial of their prayer and supplication, for their spirits, for every thing which they had done, and for the subject of their entreaty, that they might obtain remission and rest.

(13:7)

But Enoch has a vision, which he reports to the Watchers, "that what you request will not be granted you as long as the world endures" (14:2), and God confirms this to Enoch:

Go, say to the Watchers of heaven, who have sent thee to pray for them; you ought to pray for men, and not men for you. Wherefore have you forsaken the lofty and holy heaven, which endures for ever, and have lain with women.... You being spiritual, holy, and possessing a life which is eternal, have polluted yourselves with women; have begotten in carnal blood; have lusted in the blood of men; and have done as those *who are* flesh and blood do. These however die and perish. Therefore have I given to them wives, that they might co-habit with them; that sons might be born of them; and that this might be transacted upon earth. But you from the beginning were made spiritual, possessing a life which is eternal, and not subject to death forever. Therefore I made not wives for you, because being spiritual, your dwelling is in heaven. Now the giants, who have been born of spirit and of flesh, shall be called upon earth evil spirits, and on earth shall be their habitation. Evil spirits shall proceed from their flesh.... The spirits of the giants *shall be like* clouds, which shall oppress, corrupt, fall, contend, and bruise upon earth.

(15:1–9)

III. AN ACCOUNT OF THE WORKS BY MOORE, WESTALL, FLAXMAN, AND BLAKE BASED ON THE BOOK OF ENOCH

Thomas Moore and Richard Westall

About 1821[25] Thomas Moore began a novel (his only novel), *The Epicurean,* in which Alciphron,[26] the young leader of the Athenian Epicureans, comes to Egypt about 257 A.D. in search of knowledge and there falls in love with a young Christian follower of Origen. Alciphron follows her up the Nile and converts to Christianity, at first hypocritically and then, on witnessing her martyrdom, sincerely. In a note, Moore explained: "In the original construction of this work, there was an episode introduced here (which I have since published in another form), illustrating the doctrine of the fall of the soul by the Oriental Fable of the Loves of the Angels."[27] *The Loves of the Angels* (1823) was omitted from *The Epicurean* (1827) and published separately in 1823 because "I found that my friend Lord Byron had, by an accidental coincidence, chosen the same subject for a Drama [*HEAVEN AND EARTH(1823)*]; and, as I could not but feel the disadvantage of coming after so formidable a rival, I thought it best to publish my humble sketch immediately."[28] *The Loves of the Angels* proved immediately popular; there were editions in English (1823 [five, plus two pirated editions in Paris and one in Philadelphia], 1824, 1826, 1844, 1873), in French (1823 [two versions]), Dutch (1835), Spanish (1843), and Italian (1873).

On the title page is a quotation from The Book of Enoch, 7:2:

> It happened, after the sons of men had multiplied in those days, that daughters were born to them elegant and beautiful; and when the Angels, the sons of heaven, beheld them, they became enamoured of them.

Recognizing that his reputation for easy sentiment if not for lasciviousness in conjunction with such a title and motto might shock the pious, Moore hastened to explain that the phrase "Angels of God" in Genesis 1:2 upon which The Book of Enoch is based is a mistranslation in the Septuagint and elsewhere of what should read "the Sons of God" or even "the sons of the nobles."[29] According to this version, the meaning is merely that the orthodox sons of Seth married the heterodox daughters of Cain. However, Moore goes on ingenuously, the misconception "may suit the imagination of the poet" (p. 127), and his poem tells the stories of angels enamored of beautiful women. In fact, though Moore has many learned notes[30] seriously citing equally preposterous opinions of the Church Fathers, their modern commentators, the Cabala, and "this absurd production" The Book of Enoch (p. 125), his stories are based on little more than a connection of immortal angels with mortal women.

Essentially, *The Loves of the Angels* tells the stories of three angels who fall from heaven through their love for the daughters of men. When Richard Westall came to make four octavo-size illustrations for the poem,[31] he made one design for each of the stories, at pp. 6, 33, 104, and a fourth to serve as a title page also illustrating the Third Angel's story. Generally his designs are chaste and literal depictions of the scenes described in the poem. In the First Angel's Story, the angel sees a beautiful girl in the water and falls in love with her beauty.[32] She loves him chastely as an angel "not as man" (Fourth Edition, p. 11), and when he avows his love she shows

a sorrow, calm as deep,
A mournfulness that could not weep
...   to think
That angel natures ...
Should fall thus headlong from the height
Of such pure glory into sin

(p. 13)

When they meet in a "bower" (p. 18), he begs:

> "Nay, shrink not so—a look—a word—
>   "Give them but kindly and I fly;
> "Already, see my plumes have stirr'd,
>   "And tremble for their home on high.
> "Thus be our parting—cheek to cheek—
>   "One minute's lapse will be forgiven,
> "And thou, the next, shalt hear me speak
>   "The spell that plumes my wings for heaven!"

(p. 22)

This is the scene which Westall illustrates (Plate 122): The angel, with his halo still bright and his wings rising, gestures toward the maiden who turns half away from him and bends her eyes to the flower-dappled ground. Their bower is overhung with spring branches and bordered with columbine, and both are clothed in loose, belted, classical dresses which leave both pairs of arms and his right shoulder bare. From her thong sandals to the fashionable fair ringlets on her forehead, there is nothing Hebraic about her, and, except for his wings and halo, her lover seems merely mortal. In most respects, the illustration seems to show an elegant pastoral shepherd and his coy maiden. But in Moore's tale, the angel tells her the "mystic word" which lifts him to heaven; she repeats it, grows wings, and flies to a star, while he can fly no more and is left behind to mourn his folly.

The Second Angel, one of the Cherubim called Rubi,[33] falls in love with a girl called Lilis, whom he seduces by giving her dreams of an unattainably glorious figure (himself). She is so inflamed that she prays kneeling "at her altar" "Of purest marble" to the "idol of my dreams," be he "Demon or God" (pp. 56, 57, 59):

> "I do implore thee, o most bright
>   "And worshipp'd Spirit, shine but o'er
> "My waking, wondering eyes this night,
>   "This one blest night—I ask no more!"
>
>   . . .
>
> Sudden her brow again she rais'd,
>   And there, just lighted on the shrine,
> Beheld me—not as I had blaz'd

> Around her full of light divine,
> In her late dreams, but soften'd down
> Into more mortal grace...
> My wings shut up, like banners furl'd
>
> (p. 60)

Westall represents a radiant angel with wings half open stepping from a circle of clouds onto a marble altar of severely classical proportions, while on the pavement beneath kneels a dark-haired maiden looking up at him adoringly (Plate 123). Both angel and maiden are dressed as in the previous design, except that Lilis seems to have a dark mantle draped casually over her shoulder and calf. At least the context is divine, though the winged man indeed looks merely mortal.

She begs him:

> "Let me this once but feel the flame
> "Of those spread wings, the very pride
> "Will change my nature, and this frame
> "By the mere touch be deified!"
>
> (p. 83)

Her prayer is answered:

> [my] best pomp I now put on;
> And, proud that in her eyes I shone
> Thus glorious, glided to her arms
> Which still (though at a sight so splendid
> Her dazzled brow had instantly
> Sunk on her breast) were wide extended
> To clasp the form she durst not see!...
> Scarce had I touch'd her shrinking frame,
> When—oh most horrible!—I felt
> That every spark of that pure flame—
> Pure, while among the stars I dwelt—
> Was now, by my transgression turn'd
> Into gross, earthly fire, which burn'd
> Burn'd all it touch'd, as fast as eye
> Could follow the fierce ravening flashes
> Till there—oh God, I still ask why
> Such doom was hers?—I saw her lie
> Black'ning within my arms to ashes!...
> All, all, that seem'd, one minute since,

So full of love's own redolence,
Now, parch'd and black, before me lay
Withering in agony away;
And mine, o misery! mine the flame,
From which this desolation came—
And I the fiend, whose foul caress
Had blasted all that loveliness![34]

The scene seems beautifully adapted to that amatory poignancy at which Moore excelled.

The Third Story, of the love of the seraph Zaraph for the maiden Nama, is introduced when the three melancholy angels hear a woman singing "from a wood That crown'd that airy solitude" and then see her holding "a clear lamp, which . . . blaz'd Across the brow of one, who rais'd The flame aloft" (pp. 97, 101). Westall chose this scene for his title page (Plate 124). The first two angels with dim halos and drooping wings sit on the ground in a forest glade, while Zaraph, with bright halo and spread wings, gestures and moves upward toward Nama who stands at the top of the glade holding her lantern above her head. The angels are dressed as before, except that their costumes now cover their right shoulders. The undimmed radiance of Zaraph, echoed by the lamplight of Nama, indicates the difference of their story.

Zaraph is seduced by hearing Nama sing at twilight of her love for God:

He saw, upon the golden sand
Of the sea-shore a maiden stand,
Before whose feet the' expiring waves
    Flung their last tribute with a sigh . . .
And, while her lute hung by her, hush'd,
    As if unequal to the tide
Of song, that from her lips still gush'd
    She rais'd, like one beatified . . .
Such eyes, as may have look'd *from* heaven
    But ne'er were rais'd to it before!

(pp. 110–111)

Westall depicts the scene quite faithfully (Plate 125). Nama stands on rock (not sand) by a calm sea with a light cloak round her shoulders against the evening chill; she has a long, loosely-fitting, unbelted robe, thonged sandals (as in Plate 122), and a lute apparently slung behind her back, and her eyes are cast upward in a saintly gaze. The horizon has a faint sunset glow at the right, but the stars are already shining in the dark sky to the left, and on a cloud in the upper right Zaraph reclines with brilliant halo, clasped hands, and spread wings and gazes longingly downward at Nama. Zaraph is not described here by Moore, but Westall has introduced him plausibly, though the peaceful verticals of Nama are somewhat awkwardly distorted by the powerful diagonal formed by Zaraph and his cloud.

Considering the conclusions of the first two love tales, and for that matter of The Book of Enoch, it is distinctly disconcerting to discover that Zaraph and Nama get *married*. Moore has changed the ground rules, as it were, by making Nama angelic—at least she has angelic eyes—and the couple "trod Abash'd, but pure [*sic*] before their God" (p. 116). Apparently marriage makes all the difference, for "never did that God look down On error with a brow so mild" (p. 114), and "Their only punishment" is that "They both shall wander here" as long as the earth lasts (pp. 117-118). But their union is unique: "There is but *one* such pair below" (p. 122), and Moore says nothing of what will happen when mortality overtakes Nama and leaves Zaraph earthbound and forlorn.

In sum, Moore has described lovesick and lovelorn angels and maidens, three angels who fall from heaven and two women who seem to become divine, while Westall has depicted only the moments of their meeting, the beginnings of their stories, and has given distinctly classical local habitations to these airy spirits. The scores of Watchers in The Book of Enoch who swarm to earth to populate it with their giant offspring five hundred feet high have shrunk in Moore's poem to little more than winged, melancholy men, the Irish melodist singing Irish fairy stories with a Hebraic context and cover, a context which has been regularly altered to one of classical simplicity in Westall's designs. The first European illustrations of The Book of Enoch (at one remove, through Moore's *Loves of the Angels*) adapted the story so thoroughly to modern Georgian tastes that little remains of Enoch's moral ruthlessness and apocalyptic grandeur.

John Flaxman

John Flaxman's designs for The Book of Enoch must have been made between 1821, when Laurence's translation (to which they evidently refer) was published, and 1826, when Flaxman died.[35] None was published in his lifetime, they have never been reproduced as a group, and several have not been reproduced at all. They are apparently not referred to by Flaxman's contemporaries, and indeed I know only a few references to them in the last century. They deserve to be better known, for some of them are lovely.

There are thirteen Flaxman designs thus far associated with The Book of Enoch, illustrating nine different scenes; six of the designs are variants of only two scenes. Some designs are clearly associated with The Book of Enoch by their inscriptions (Plates 126, 129–32) or by their clear connection with inscribed drawings (Plates 127–28). These demonstrate that Flaxman *was* illustrating The Book of Enoch, but unfortunately these seven drawings represent only three scenes. The association of Flaxman's other "Enoch" drawings (Plates 133–38) with The Book of Enoch must be regarded as much more conjectural.[36] The scenes they represent, with struggling, naked athletes, are of a kind Flaxman represented repeatedly elsewhere, as in his published designs for *The Iliad* (1793), *The Odyssey* (1795), and Aeschylus (1795), and we must be careful to bear in mind, first, that these conjectural Enoch designs may be for some other work(s), and, second, that there are probably other Flaxman designs for Enoch which I have not yet identified.

Flaxman has represented the chief actions of the Watchers with the daughters of men except for their five-hundred-foot-high offspring. The two hundred Watchers, having become enamored of the "elegant and beautiful"[37] daughters of men, make a compact (Plate 126) binding themselves to each other "by mutual execrations" (7:1, 7). In Flaxman's design, a score of Watchers are in the sky, not on a mountain as in Enoch. It is noteworthy that Flaxman's Watchers are wingless and have merely human features, but that their actions uniformly mark them out as great spirits; in both respects they contrast strongly with Westall's. Flaxman's Watchers are always naked, though his women are mostly clothed.

The Watchers, having bound themselves to one another by their compact, descend toward the earth with their hands still clasped but already separating as they see the daughters of men below them (Plates 127–29). The effect of massed, harmonious flight just beginning to disperse is beautifully achieved, especially in Plate 128. The moment depicted is not described in The Book of Enoch, but it is clearly implied. Flaxman has skillfully focused our attention upon the Watchers, their original unity and subsequent fall, before he allows *us* to see the daughters of men. It is also striking, though perhaps not surprising, that these lusting, naked angels are almost genital-less.

In Plates 130-32, Flaxman depicts the moment when the Watchers said

> to each other, Come, let us select wives from the progeny of men, and let us beget children. . . . Then they took wives, each choosing for himself
>
> (7:2, 10)

Each Watcher is flying down to a different woman, there seems to be no dispute among them, and the women seem notably acquiescent. The effect of heavenly energies dispersed and dissipated is powerfully evoked, especially in the more airy Plates 128-29. The gestures of the central Watcher in particular are tender and passionate, eloquently combining gentleness and impulsiveness. Notice in these first designs the effect of figures materializing in bas-relief from a blank wall. Flaxman's profession of sculptor shows strongly here.

The Daughters of Men attacked by Angels (Plate 133) is only roughly sketched, and its subject is not described in The Book of Enoch, where the daughters of men accept the approach of the angels without protest. The lower woman in the design, however, seems much like those in Plates 130-32, and the somewhat ambiguous gestures may represent the pacific approach rather than the attack of the Watchers, making the design an obvious sequel to Plates 130-32.

After the Watchers had begotten giant sons and corrupted the earth, God sent Gabriel to "excite them [the offspring of the Watchers] one against another. Let them perish by *mutual* slaughter . . . for they have tyrannized over mankind" (10:13, 18). The magnificent contention of two men for a woman (Plate 134) may well be related to this passage in Enoch, but, if so, Flaxman has somewhat altered the literary details. These masculine warriors are about the same size as the woman and as the Watchers in Plates 127-32; therefore, if they illustrate Enoch, either they represent the Watchers in conflict (and such a conflict may be derived from the somewhat obscure grammar of Laurence's translation) or the five-hundred-foot stature of the offspring of the Watchers has been reduced to ordinary human dimensions. Whatever the interpretation intended by Flaxman, we must be grateful for the creation of such a splendid design—and remark on the similarity Flaxman evidently felt between The Book of Enoch and the works of Homer and Aeschylus which he also illustrated with similar heroic naked warriors.

In order to "vivify the earth," God sent Raphael to "Bind Azazyel hand and foot; cast him into darkness" (10:10, 6). This scene is apparently represented in Plate 135, in which a flying naked man lifts high above his head another naked man whose wrists and ankles seem to be bound. (Alternatively, the design may represent merely the contention of God's Angels with the fallen Watchers or with their offspring.) The aggressor at least must be a spirit, for he is clearly floating in air with his burden in a very Blakean way (compare Blake's *America* [1793] pl. 7 and *Europe* [1794] pl. 5), and the extraordinary elongation of limb is a common metaphor for spirituality, in Blake, El Greco, and elsewhere.

God sent Michael "to Samyaza, and to the others who are with him" to "bind them . . . underneath the earth, even to . . . the lowermost depths . . . shut up for ever" (10:15, 16). In Plate 136, three naked men are driven by a giant into a cavern in the earth which they seem to create by their struggles, and in Plate 137 two of the victims are firmly pressed into the same rocky cavern by a powerful bearded athlete in a gesture similar to that of Blake's "Ancient of Days" (*Europe* [1794] pl. 1). The inky blackness of that exitless rock-tomb indicates effectively the eternity of their punishment. Finally, Plate 138 seems to represent a Watcher brooding in his eternal rock-prison. The earth above him, according to the narrative in The Book of Enoch, has been flooded and cleansed, and peace and righteousness have been restored.

Flaxman has given the outline of the whole story of the Watchers of Heaven with the daughters of men, compressing powerfully the gigantic events into a few key actions. They gave him scope for depicting the struggles of heroic naked warriors and mighty spirits as he did in his engraved designs for Homer and Aeschylus (1793, 1795) and the feminine tenderness evoked so beautifully in his funerary monuments and in his unpublished designs for *Pilgrim's Progress*.[38] His death in 1826 cut short what might have been one of his finest series of engraved designs.

William Blake

Like Flaxman, Blake knew the Bible intimately, "And he warmly declared that all he knew was in the Bible."[39] He made a watercolor of "Satan and the Archangel Michael Contending for the

Body of Moses" from the Book of Jude,[40] and he doubtless knew the reference in Jude 9 to The Book of Enoch. Enoch appears among the biblical prophets in his *Milton* (1804–?8) pl. 37, l. 36, in *Jerusalem* (1808–?20) pl. 7, l. 25, and in his description of his drawing (?1807) for Hervey's *Meditations among the Tombs*. About the same time (1807), he drew his only lithograph, one of the earliest made in England, representing Enoch in prayer. His interest in Enoch and in prophetic literature, and the fact that he himself wrote prophecies, make his fascination with the new-found Book of Enoch very plausible. The interpretation which he imposed on The Book of Enoch is, however, less predictable.

Blake made at least six designs for The Book of Enoch sometime between 1821, when Laurence's translation was published, and 1827, when he died. All are powerful though unfinished, all have at least the word "Enoch" written on them (evidently in another hand), and all are on paper watermarked with a large crest or "W ELGAR/ 1796." Despite this early watermark date, we may be confident that the designs were made quite late, both because they derive from Laurence's 1821 translation (the fragments available previously in Greek and Latin do not account for some elements in Blake's designs) and because one of them (Plate 144) is on the verso of one of the series of designs Blake made for Dante about 1824–27—appropriately enough, "The Circle of Carnal Sinners." They may well have been commissioned by John Linnell,[41] for he certainly owned them in 1863 when W.M. Rossetti traced them to Linnell's collection in the catalogue of Blake's art he made for Alexander Gilchrist's *Life of William Blake, 'Pictor Ignotus'* (1863), II, 251, and they were sold posthumously with Linnell's collection at Christie's on 15 March 1918, lot 161. Later they were acquired by Allan R. Brown, who described and first reproduced them in his article in the *Burlington Magazine* (1940) and sold them to Mr Lessing J. Rosenwald, who gave them to the United States National Gallery of Art, retaining a life interest in them at Alverthorpe Gallery, Jenkintown, Pennsylvania. This history applies to only five of the designs; a sixth was discovered recently on the back of a Dante design (the whole series of which belonged to Linnell) and was reproduced for the first time in 1974.[42] This sixth design is now in the Fogg Art Museum of Harvard University, but its early history is probably the same as that of the other Enoch drawings.

In his drawings, Blake's emphasis is strongly upon the

superhuman erotic element in The Book of Enoch,[43] and in this he is much more faithful to the Hebrew prophet than was Thomas Moore, with his sentimental mortals dressed in wings, or John Flaxman, with his somewhat sexless gladiators floating in air or struggling in the rocky depths of earth. In some senses, Blake's daughters of men "who led astray the angels of heaven without resistance" (19:2) are carrying out the command of Enitharmon in his *Europe* (1794), pl. 5, l. 3, that "Woman, lovely Woman may have dominion." On a supernatural level, the relationship between the sexes has been reduced to mere sexuality, and the very stars of heaven have fallen to earth to enter the wombs of women. The monsters bred of this carnality are essential to Blake's interpretation, as they were to the author of Enoch, though they play no role in either Moore or Flaxman. Blake has characteristically drawn together disparate parts of The Book of Enoch, but the parts reinforce one another, and his interpretation is unique and justified.

His first Enoch design[44] represents an heroic naked man in a position like Blake's own Milton Doffing the Robe of Promise in *Milton* pl. 13 (Plate 100), encircled by four nude figures (Plate 139). The nobility of the central figure has led Brown, Keynes, and the authorities of The National Gallery to describe it as The Son of Man as Messiah[45] with Four Attendant Spirits, but a close examination makes this seem improbable: Those heavenly spirits are women with the breasts carefully emphasized, and the "Messiah" has an enormously enlarged penis extending most of the way across his hip. We have seen such phallic exaggeration in Blake before, for example in one colored copy (G) of *Europe* pl. 18[46] and in Apollyon Fighting with Christian in his *Pilgrim's Progress* designs of c. 1824,[47] but never in connection with the Messiah. This Enoch drawing represents one of the fallen Watchers, and his giant phallus is the reason for his attraction to the surrounding daughters of men. Note the plurality of women: Moore and Flaxman had presumed one woman per Watcher, but the text of Enoch is not explicit in this respect, and the orgiastic implications of this and Plate 141 are, it seems to me, perfectly consistent with the intentions of Enoch.

Blake's second design of A Watcher seducing a Daughter of Men, with two of their giant offspring (Plate 140), continues the same erotic motif. The naked Watcher,[48] plunging down from his natural place in the sun, seems to be whispering in the ear of the nude woman as he caresses her belly and she holds his arm gently.

On either side is one of their giant offspring, not three hundred cubits high, perhaps, but at least many times the bulk of their parents. They are not yet ravening and desolating the earth—perhaps they are not yet full grown—but are rather looking at their parents with expressions of pathos, explicable by the flames enveloping the one on the left and the vegetation perhaps enveloping that on the right.[49] In a sense, supernatural seduction, demonic propagation, and divine punishment are simultaneous, and the woman, looking not at the Watcher but at her monstrous offspring, sees the result of their transgression but yet does not resist it. Note that the Watcher seems as yet to have done little more than tell her the secrets of sin, of good and evil, but that the knowledge alone corrupts. In Enoch, the secrets of heaven are told after the seduction, but here they are not only coincidental with it, they are the same thing. In the eyes of God, there is no sin. Nothing is evil but thought makes it so.

Blake's third Enoch design, Two Watchers descending to a Daughter of Men (Plate 141), is one of the most finished, beautiful, and sexually explicit of the series. The focus of the design is the head of the nude woman poised between two enormous, light-giving phalli whose owners are in other respects far less distinct than their generative organs. The woman seems to have her left hand on one phallus while she gazes fixedly at the other; her vulva is carefully emphasized, and her right hand seems to be turning into claws or vegetation. The orgiastic implications of the first design (Plate 139) seem to be continued here; the woman appears to be tantalized by the difficulty of deciding which phallus to choose first.

The divinity of the Watchers is faintly implied by dim haloes but is concentrated on their starlike phalli. This feature is an addition to the story of the Watchers with the daughters of men as told in the section of Enoch called The Books of Watchers, the sections preserved in Latin and Greek. However, it is not Blake's invention, for it is clearly derived from a much later section of The Book of Enoch (87:5). There, in a story strikingly like the punishment of the Watchers, fallen angels are bound "hand and foot" and "cast . . . into the cavities of the earth" by God's four punishing angels. These fallen angels are seen by Enoch in a dream in the shape of "great stars, whose parts of shame resembled those of horses." Blake seems to have associated the two stories, quite plausibly, and his Watchers have starlike parts of shame like those of horses. Their divinity lies in their organs of generation. No wonder they were so attractive to the daughters of men—and no wonder their offspring were monsters.

The fourth of Blake's Enoch designs represents Two Daughters of Men with a prone figure (Plate 142). The horizontal figure stretched rigidly at the foot of the page may be dead, and its sex is obscure, but the tree or cross rising suggestively beyond its hips may help to confirm our inclination to call it a man. The woman on the left, ominously clad in scales from breast to thigh, seems to be rising exultingly from the body, while the nude woman at the right looks on with gestures of distress; notice that the vulva of each woman is carefully emphasized. Neither the scales nor the dead figure seem to derive from The Book of Enoch, so I can only guess at how to justify the inscription associating it with that work. Perhaps the scaly woman is one of the lascivious, already-corrupted daughters of men who has seduced, and perhaps killed, one of the merely mortal sons of men, whose mate looks on despairingly. Such a scene might at least be a plausible extension of the story told in Enoch.

The last of Blake's numbered Enoch drawings seems to show Enoch before the throne of One great in glory (Plate 143); this is the least distinct and one of the most impressive designs in the series. When Enoch was sent by the fallen Watchers to intercede for them with their angry God, he came to "One great in glory" sitting upon

> an exalted throne. . . . its circumference resembled the orb of the brilliant sun. . . . From underneath this mighty throne rivers of flaming fire issued. . . . the sanctified . . . were near him . . . And he raised me up. . . . My eye was directed to the ground.
>   (14:21, 17, 18, 19, 24, 25)

Blake suggests all this in his drawing, with a magnificent deity brooding on his throne, with vaguely indicated shapes of "the sanctified" beside him and two dim figures standing before him; there seems to be a canopy over his head, four or more steps lead up to his exalted throne, and rivers of flaming fire issue from it. Only two significant features remain to be accounted for. Is that an open book on his knees? And if Enoch is the figure on the right with bowed head and eye "directed to the ground," who is the figure at the left (on God's right)? The answer may be found in a later, and quite discrete, vision in which Enoch sees "the Ancient of days" on his throne accompanied by "the Son of man" (46:1, 2); further, the Ancient of Days has "the book of the living opened" before him

(47:3). Blake, like most early commentators, would have taken the Son of man to be the Messiah, Christ,[50] and it is appropriate that He should intercede for sinners with Enoch, standing at God's right hand.

But note the ominous implications of this design: God's forehead is furrowed in anger, and flames issue from his throne. There is to be no mercy for the Watchers from what Blake called "The Angry God of this World."[51] Their punishment for doing evil is what Blake would expect from a God of Good and Evil.

The newly discovered, unnumbered Enoch design of a Watcher punished (Plate 144) indicates the punishment meted out to the fallen angels. Despite the elaborate directions God gives in The Book of Enoch for burying them within the earth, this Watcher is free to fly from earth on a short tether. He is, like all mortals, chained to earth though with immortal aspirations for the stars; Blake had drawn similar soaring, tethered mortals elsewhere, for example in a design for Young's Night Thoughts (1797), pl. 16, and in his own Vala (?1796–1807), p. 2. The chief iconographic feature associating this design with The Book of Enoch is the great stars at the left. Previously we have seen such stars associated with the genitalia of the Watchers (Plate 141), but now they are separate from the Watcher, in the sky. Evidently the design represents one of the fallen Watchers confined with "seven great stars [which transgressed the commandment of God], like great blazing mountains" in a "desolate" spot which, "until the consummation of heaven and earth, will be the prison of the stars, and of the host of heaven" (18:14, 15, 16). Now we know why "the stars threw down their spears / And water'd heaven with their tears" (as Blake said in "The Tyger"): they were bound to earth by a jealous God.

Blake found in The Book of Enoch, as he did wherever he turned his outward eye, confirmation of his own visions. In his Marriage of Heaven and Hell (?1790–3) many years before, he had written of the giant antediluvians chained to earth who are our energies. In The Book of Enoch he found an ancient prophecy which expressed his own ideas in Hebraic form. No wonder he began to illustrate it with such enthusiasm; it was deep calling to deep, vision answering to vision. The graceful poignancy of Moore's Loves of the Angels, the sentimental invocations of Westall's designs for it, the classical warriors of Flaxman's illustrations to Enoch, all seem earthbound and immature compared to the erotic and spiritual intensity of Blake's great unfinished series.

The Book of Enoch had slept some nineteen hundred years in Ethiopian dress before it appeared in Europe in Laurence's translation of 1821. Then it created a brief flurry among theologians and provided inspiration for poets and painters like Byron and Moore and Westall and Flaxman and Blake, hanging for a moment

> upon the cheek of night
> Like a rich jewel in an Ethiop's ear;
> Beauty too rich for use, for earth too dear![52]

before it sank to artistic obscurity again. But the momentary inspiration it gave in the 1820s was indeed rich and dear. We must learn to value it once more.

NOTES

1. This essay concentrates on the illustrations of The Book of Enoch and therefore largely ignores Byron's *Heaven and Earth*.

2. I know no work at all on the Enoch designs of Westall or Flaxman. Blake's designs were described and reproduced in Allan R. Brown, "Blake's Drawings for *The Book of Enoch*," *Burlington Magazine*, 77 (1940), 80–85; rpt. *The Visionary Hand*, ed. Robert N. Essick (Los Angeles: Hennessey & Ingalls, 1977), pp. 104–15. They are reproduced in *Blake's Pencil Drawings*, ed. Geoffrey Keynes (London: Nonesuch Press, 1956), pls. 45–49; and again in Peter Alan Taylor, "Blake's Text for the *Enoch* Drawings," *Blake Newsletter*, 7 (1974), 82–86, which corrects Brown and Keynes by pointing out that their quotations had been misleadingly and silently taken from the Charles translation of 1912 rather than from that of 1821 which was the only one Blake could have read.

3. *The Interpreter's Dictionary of the Bible* (New York: Abingdon Press, 1962), I, 103–105.

4. Richard Laurence (translator, *The Book of Enoch* [Oxford: University Press, 1821], p. xxxvi) estimates 30 B.C.

5. Laurence, p. xxxviii. Today it is agreed that The Book of Enoch is a compilation from various sources at various places and times in the first century B.C. (*The Interpreter's Dictionary of the Bible*).

6. *The Book of Enoch*, trans. R. H. Charles (Oxford: Clarendon Press, 1912), p. xcv.

7. James Bruce, *Travels to Discover the Source of the Nile, In the Years 1768, 1769, 1770, 1771, 1772, and 1773* (Edinburgh and London, 1790), II, 498.

8. *The Interpreter's Dictionary of the Bible*.

9. Ibid.

10. This is the site of the novel by Blake's friend George Cumberland, *The Captive of the Castle of Sennaar*, [Part I] (London, 1798); Part 2 in MS of c. 1800.

11. Hiob Ludolph, *Commentarius ad Historiam Æthiopican*, p. 347 (cited in Laurence [1838], p. xii).

12. M. Macé defended the authenticity of the few fragments then known (Paris, 1713), according to *The Christian Observer*, 29 (1829), 422. *Enoch: A Poem* (London: Cadell, 1782), 4°, 1s.6d. is listed in R. Watt, *Bibliotheca Britannica* (Edinburgh, 1824), III, but I cannot trace it further in Britain or North America. Aristeas, *The History of the Seventy Two Interpreters . . .* To which is added The History of the Angels, and their Gallantry with the Daughters of Men, Written by Enoch the Patriarch, Published in Greek by Dr. [John Ernest] Grabe, made English by Mr. [Thomas] Lewis (Oxford, 1715), 175–96. William Whiston, *A Dissertation to Prove the Book of Enoch Equally Canonical* (1727) [I have not seen Whiston's book]. The Comte de Gabalis (trans. into English 1714) cites "le livre d'Enoch malentendu" (according to Moore's *Loves of the Angels,* The Fourth Edition, 1823, p. 142). Pope's *Rape of the Lock* (1712), which derives a good deal from the French edition of the Comte de Gabalis, may have in the background The Book of Enoch too.

13. Some of the factual stories, such as the one about the natives cutting steaks from the flanks of living, unprotesting cattle, seemed so improbable that they were flatly-disbelieved. Bruce's *Travels* became a synonym for a traveler's tall tales, and Baron Munchausen's *Travels* (1792 et seq.) [by R. E. Raspe et al] are partly modeled on Bruce's *Narrative*. Today it is agreed that the *Narrative* is factually accurate, if ill written.

14. Laurence (1821), p. ix. Murray also summarized it in his catalogue of Bruce's library (Laurence, p. x), and Bruce's Ethiopic copy of The Book of Enoch was offered at auction with his other Oriental MSS in May, 1827, but was not bought (*The Christian Observer*, p. 419).

15. This MS copy was in the hands of The Delegates of the Clarendon Press by 1821, according to Laurence (1821), p. vii.

16. The first edition, consisting of 250 copies (as the Printer's Archivist at the Oxford University Press tells me), was "entirely sold off" by 1827, according to *The Christian Observer* (1829), 419; there was a Second Edition in 1832; and a Third (including the Ethiopic text) in 1838. The Rev. E. Murray's *Enoch Restitutus, or An Attempt to Separate from the Books of Enoch, the*

Book quoted by St. Jude (1836) is reprinted in Laurence (1838), pp. 168–89. There was a new English translation by R. H. Charles in 1893, revised in 1912, and simplified in 1917.

17. *New Monthly Magazine,* 3 (Oct. 1, 1821), 525 says it is "highly satisfactory to the reader" and "well worthy of perusal."

18. *The Christian Observer* may have been alarmed in part by the merriment at the expense of Christian mysteries expressed in Byron's *Cain A Mystery* (1821) and in *The Book of Jasher, With Testimonies and Notes Explanatory of the Text, To which is prefixed various readings, Translated into English from the Hebrew of Alcuin, of Britain, who went a Pilgrimage into the Holy Land* (London, 1751; reissued with additions by the Rev. C. R. Bond, Bristol, 1829)—this is a crude fabrication by Jacob Ilive, deriving from the otherwise unknown Hebrew Book of Jasher mentioned in Joshua 10:13 and 2 Samuel 1:18; the 1829 *Book of Jasher* is referred to in *The Collected Letters of Samuel Taylor Coleridge,* ed. E. L. Griggs (Oxford: Clarendon Press, 1971), VI, 900.

19. There are seventeen other named Prefects. Nebuchadnezzar dreamt of a Watcher and a Holy One come down from heaven (Daniel 4:13, 17, 23). There is an obscure passage in Corinthians 11:10 implying that women ought to be veiled "because of the angels."

20. God reproaches the Watchers because they "have known a reprobated mystery. And this you have related to women in the hardness of your heart and by that mystery have women and mankind multiplied evils upon the earth" (16:3–4). Noah is *"free* from the reproach of *discovering* secrets" and will be saved, whereas the Watchers "have discovered secrets" and must be punished (64:10). "It is the opinion of some of the Fathers [e.g., *Clemens Alexandrinus, Stromat., lib. v., p. 48*], that the knowledge which the Heathens possessed of the Providence of God, a Future State, and other sublime doctrines of Christianity, was derived from the premature revelations of these fallen angels to the women of the earth" (Thomas Moore, *The Loves of the Angels,* The Fourth Edition, 1823, pp. 71, 144).

21. Elsewhere The Book of Enoch speaks of "the stars which . . . transgressed the commandment of God before their time arrived; for they came not in their proper season. Therefore was he offended with them, and bound them, until the period of the consummation of their crimes in the secret year" (18:16). One of the curious features of The Book of Enoch is that it reprobates astronomers at first but presents several elaborate chapters of astronomy (not astrology) at the end, in what Murray calls The Book of Astronomy (3–6:3; 72–83).

22. The fallen Watchers "made men profane, and caused them to err; so that they sacrificed to devils as to gods" (19:2).

23. The Book of Noah is included in The Book of Enoch.

24. "All the earth has been corrupted by the effects of the doctrine of Azazyel. To him therefore ascribe the whole crime" (10:12). Blake's character Zazel in *Tiriel* (?1789) is a distant relative of Azazyel.

25. Thomas Moore's Preface to his *Loves of the Angels,* The Fourth Edition (1823), p. vii.

26. Cf. Bishop Berkeley's *Alciphron, or the Minute Philosopher* (London, 1733).

27. Thomas Moore, *The Epicurean,* A Tale (London, 1827), p. 318.

28. Moore, *The Loves of the Angels,* The Fourth Edition (1823), p. vii. Byron's *Heaven and Earth* is also based on The Book of Enoch, for the text mentions "The scroll of Enoch" and a footnote cites "The book of Enoch, preserved by the Ethiopians" (*Poetical Works* [Oxford: Clarendon Press, 1957], pp. 552, 910). The story concerns the jealousy of two mortal men exhibited towards the angels Samiasa and Azaziel, whose mistresses the mortals love. Moore's *Loves of the Angels* and Byron's *Heaven and Earth* were reviewed together [by Francis Jeffrey] in *The Edinburgh Review,* 38 (Feb., 1823), 27-48.

29. *The Loves of the Angels,* The Fourth Edition (1823), pp. 125-27. Moore does not explain why the Jewish authors of The Book of Enoch living north of the Black Sea should have been misled by a *Greek* translation made for the Hellenized Jews of Alexandria.

30. Pp. 125-48, partly based on *The Edinburgh Review,* 24 (1814), 58-72.

31. I have found Westall's illustrations in my copy of the first edition (1823) and the Yale copy of the Second Edition (1823). The illustrated edition carries a duplicate, engraved title page: "ILLUSTRATIONS / OF / THE LOVES OF THE ANGELS. / A POEM / BY / THOMAS MOORE. / Engraved by Charles Heath, from drawings by / R. WESTALL, R.A. / [Vignette; see Plate 124] / . . . / PERKINS & HEATH. Patent Hardened Steel Plates." An advertisement in my copy of The Fourth Edition (1823) offers "ILLUSTRATIONS OF THE LOVES OF THE ANGELS . . . Engraved by Charles Heath from Paintings by R. Westall, R. A. [*price 5s.*] A few Proofs will be taken off." I presume the 5s. is the cost of the illustrated edition, though grammatically the price belongs only to the engravings. The plates are by Charles Heath (title page vignette and facing pp. 6, 104), and E. Portbury (facing p. 33), though Portbury is not mentioned on the engraved title page or the advertisement.

32. "Then felt I like some Watcher of the skies When a new maiden swims into his ken"?

33. Moore says that he has deliberately ignored the names of the Watchers given in The Book of Enoch (p. 134).

34. It seems odd that Westall did not choose to illustrate this scene, for an analogous scene in Thomson's *Seasons* of a maiden killed by lightning in her lover's arms was very popular with his illustrators.

35.   Flaxman had long been interested in Enoch, for a drawing in the British Museum Print Room is marked "And Enoch walked with God and he was not for God took him... Gen. ch. 5, ver. 24... J. Flaxman, May, 1792."

36.   They were first associated with The Book of Enoch in *The Drawings of Flaxman in the Gallery of University College London,* ed. Sidney Colvin (London: University College, 1876), where Plates 127, 129, 132–38 here are reproduced. Plate 131 here is reproduced in *Drawings by John Flaxman in the Huntington Collection,* ed. Robert R. Wark (San Marino: Huntington Library, 1970), p. 42, and Plate 126 was reproduced and offered for sale in the catalogue *John Flaxman* 10th March–9th April 1976 Presented by Christopher Powney and Heim Gallery (London) Ltd. (1976) as no. 27. No. 26 (18 x 20.7 cm.) in this catalogue is distantly related to the Enoch series, though puzzlingly inscribed "St. Paul"; it shows one man shouting and another in the group grasping his ankle. No. 39, a closely related drawing, shows a group of floating men, the first two pointing to the bottom right, inscribed "134 $X^n R^n$" (for paragraph 134 of Swedenborg's *The True Christian Religion). N.B.* No. 23 (15.8 x 15.8 cm.) represents a naked man forcing three others into a cavern, very like Enoch Plate 136; Powney identifies it as for Flaxman's Hesiod (1817), p. 33, The Brethren of Saturn Delivered. No. 82 (22 x 17.7 cm.) is inscribed "Destruction" and "casting into Dudael" and may therefore be for Enoch, and nos. 84–87 of falling men may be related to this fall also.

The association of Plates 130–38 here with The Book of Enoch is justified only by distant similarities with the inscribed Enoch drawings (including some in the same collection), and with similar scenes implied in The Book of Enoch.

37.   "Elegant" seems to have meant "classical" to Flaxman as it did to Westall. Perhaps it is needless to say that this is unlikely to have been its meaning in Ethiopic (from which it was translated by Laurence) or to the Jewish author living north of the Black Sea.

38.   Reproduced in *Woman in the 18th Century and Other Essays,* ed. Paul Fritz and Richard Morton (Toronto: A.M. Hakkert, 1976).

39.   According to Crabb Robinson in 1826 (*Blake Records* [Oxford: Clarendon Press, 1969], p. 322; see pp. 458, 467, 547).

40.   Allan R. Brown, "Blake's Drawings for the *Book of Enoch,*" points out that this event is recorded only in Jude. *Burlington Magazine,* 77 (1940), 80–85.

41.   Pace Brown, they were probably *not* among the works which Blake left at his death to his widow in 1827 and which she left at her death in 1831 to Frederick Tatham, for Tatham quarreled violently with Linnell about the ownership of Blake's surviving works and is unlikely to have sold Linnell anything. I do not know any Blake work which passed from Tatham to Linnell.

42. Taylor, "Blake's Text for the *Enoch* Drawings," pp. 82–86. No other *Enoch* drawing is known to Martin Butlin, whose catalogue raisonné of Blake's art is now in press.

43. In Blake's "I asked a Thief" (1796), an angel erotically "Enjoy'd the lady," and angels of evil and tyranny appear in his *Marriage* (?1790–93), *America* (1793), and *Europe* (1794).

44. The order is established by the numbers on five of the six designs; I have placed the unnumbered sixth design last. Brown and Keynes strangely give the design numbered "1" last.

45. Brown goes so far as to call it "by far the most successful of Blake's attempts at the portrayal of Christ."

46. Los fleeing from flames, repro. in *The Blake Collection of Mrs. Landon K. Thorne* (New York: Pierpont Morgan Library, 1971), pl. xvi.

47. Repro. in John Bunyan, *Pilgrim's Progress,* ed. G. B. Harrison, Introduction by Geoffrey Keynes (New York: Limited Editions Club, 1941), pl. xx.

48. I cannot find the "scaly covering" on the Watcher described by Brown.

49. There may be a tiny human on the arm, against the chest, of one or both giants, which I cannot account for. The features of the giant to the right are oddly lionlike, as if he were both vegetating and beastializing. Compare Blake's *Book of Los* (1795), pl. 3, lines 25–26: "And Wantonness on his own true love Begot a giant race" (E 90).

50. *The Christian Observer,* 29 (1829), 508, 500, concluded, partly on the basis of such references, that "the *Christian*" "forger of this prophecy was acquainted with the fact of the ascension of Christ, and that . . . it was not composed till after A.D. 135."

51. Annotation to his third Dante drawing, repro. in Albert S. Roe, *Blake's Illustrations to the Divine Comedy* (Princeton: Princeton Univ. Press, 1953), pl. 3.

52. *Romeo and Juliet,* I, v.

INDEX

Figures in italics are Plate numbers.